THE
FRENCH REVOLUTION
AS SEEN BY
MADAME TUSSAUD
WITNESS EXTRAORDINARY

THE
FRENCH REVOLUTION
AS SEEN BY
MADAME TUSSAUD
WITNESS EXTRAORDINARY

Pauline Chapman

QUILLER PRESS
London

First published 1989
by Quiller Press Ltd
46 Lillie Road
London SW6 1TN

Photosetting by Galleon Photosetting, Ipswich
Printed and bound in Great Britain by Camelot Press plc

Contents

List of Illustrations

Dust Jacket from a French Revolutionary print with a National Guardsman and a *sans-culottes*.

1. Marie Grosholtz (Madame Tussaud) aged 17, shortly before she went to Versailles.
2. Dr Philippe Guillaume Mathé Curtius wearing his National Guard uniform.
3. Tableau of 'The Royal Family at Dinner' in the *Salon de Cire*.
4. Outside the *Salon de Cire* in the Boulevard du Temple.
5. The Palais Royal Gardens.
6. 'Changing the Heads in the *Salon de Cire*'. A French cartoon of 1787.
7. Fashionable promenade on the ramparts of Paris.
8. Voltaire on his deathbed. Wax miniature by Curtius.
9. Wax miniatures by Curtius of Louis XVI and the Duc d'Orléans.
10. A Revolutionary orator harangues the crowd at the Palais Royal.
11. 12th July 1789. The wax heads of Necker and the Duc d'Orléans seized by the mob from the *Salon de Cire* for a protest march.
12. 12th July 1789. Rioting in the Place Louis XV after the protest march with the wax heads of Necker and the Duc d'Orleans taken from the *Salon de Cire*.
13. The opening of the newly convened States General at Versailles in May, 1789.
14. Louis XVI, Marie Antoinette, and the first Dauphin.
15. 10th August, 1792. The storming of the Tuileries by *sans-culottes* mobs.
16. 21st January, 1793. Louis XVI on the scaffold of the guillotine in the former Place Louis XV, now Place de la Révolution.
17. The assassination of Lepeletier, a Deputy who had voted for the King's execution. Curtius reproduced the scene as a tableau in the *Salon de Cire*.
18. Maximilien Robespierre who instituted the Terror of 1794.
19. Antoine Fouquier-Tinville. During his term as Public Prosecutor in 1794 Marie Grosholtz and her mother were arrested and imprisoned.
20. Guillotined death heads modelled by Marie Grosholtz, with her portrayal of the murdered Marat lying in his bath.
21. Full-size model of the guillotine constructed in 1854 by Joseph Tussaud, son of Madame Tussaud, from scale drawings he purchased from the grandson of executioner Charles-Henri Sanson.

Acknowledgements

MY most sincere thanks are due to the Management of Madame Tussaud's for permitting me free use of their archive material, also to Juliet Simkins, Head of Publicity, and Undine Concannon, my successor as Archivist, for their encouragement and help, especially with the picture selection.

I have been grateful over the years for the assistance given me by the staff of many public institutions such as the Bibliothèque Nationale, the Musée Carnavalet, the Archives de Paris, the Archives des Notaires, the British Library, and Rylands Library in my search for material relating to Dr Philippe Curtius's life and activities and his *Salon de Cire*.

Hundreds of books have been written about the French Revolution. I have read many, and have learned something from every author. It is impossible to list all those writers whose work has enlightened me in some way, but I thank them all for the information and interest they have given me.

Introduction

THERE can be no doubt that Madame Tussaud, born Marie Grosholtz, was, as a young woman, in an exceptional position as witness and participant during the troubled years that preceded the French Revolution of 1789, and then when she became personally caught up in the events of the bloody, political and social upheaval that smashed the *Ancien Régime* and gave birth to a new Republican France.

Of no aristocratic rank, bred in the showbusiness world of Paris, Marie's remarkable talent as a modeller in wax brought her the unexpected and almost bizarre opportunity of mingling closely over a period of years with members of the Royal Family of France and the glittering Court of Versailles.

At the same time she had equally unusual contact with many of those who were planning and working for a drastically reformed government and social system. When the cataclysm finally came it was inevitable that she should become actively involved, even if involuntarily.

'It required no supernatural power to see that a Revolution must take place in France,' Marie wrote in her Memoirs of that period of her long life, which were published in London in 1838 when she was seventy-seven years old. Few in Paris had been better placed to realise it was brewing and to be aware of the threat literally from childhood.

Dr Philippe Curtius, in whose house Marie Grosholtz had lived with her housekeeper mother since she was a baby, had been in contact with French liberal thought since the early 1760s when he set up in Paris as a sculptor in wax under the patronage of the Prince de Conti. This Prince, a member of the Royal Family, was in permanent disfavour with King Louis XV because he supported the new and growing concept of a constitutional instead of an absolute Monarchy. It was a disfavour shared by the Dauphin, later Louis XVI.

From the age of six the child Marie was trained by Dr Curtius in the skills of modelling in wax. A precocious little girl, she watched and listened to the visitors who came to her teacher and mentor's famous exhibition of life-size wax portrait figures, the *Salon de Cire*. She came to perceive that while most Royal and aristocratic personages clung rigidly to the feudal, social and political system that survived, the *Ancien Régime*, there were others of equally high rank who were more forward-looking and sought change and reform, as did many less exalted individuals.

As Marie grew up she met some of the men who would be architects of the Revolution. They were frequent dinner guests at Dr Curtius's table. She was regarded as his niece and always called him 'uncle' though there was no blood relationship. Though taught by Curtius to keep a discreetly silent tongue on matters political which she heard discussed, the training in observation necessary to her work as a modeller of portrait figures made her an exceptionally acute and intelligent witness of everything going on around her.

Thus when, at the age of nineteen, Marie Grosholtz was invited to become art tutor to Madame Elisabeth, King Louis XVI's sister, she was singularly capable of assessing all that she saw and participated in at the Court of Versailles. Her sharp eyes noted character as well as appearance, and while she appreciated the many good qualities of the King and Queen and members of the Royal Family, she never blinded herself to the Court scandals and political obtuseness that were under-mining the position of the King and his most influential advisers. Efficient, quiet, well mannered, Marie was sensitive to the under-currents as well as the splendours during the eight years she attended Court, nor was she cut off entirely from the very different trends discussed privately in her uncle's house.

It was no surprise to her when Dr Curtius thought it wise to get her away from royal service and back under his own roof in the spring of 1789. By then Curtius had become, outwardly at any rate, an enthusi-astic revolutionary supporter. He was convinced that some event catastrophic for the Monarchy could soon occur. It came with the fall of the Bastille on 14 July.

Marie now found herself closely involved in the tremendous and bloody changes that followed. Just as she had been in a unique position at Versailles during the crucial years that preceded the outbreak of Revolution, so she now was in the midst of the turmoil, terror, and total change that it brought in its wake. Not only did she have a ringside seat as witness, but she was forced to cope with horrifying experiences thrust on her.

Having already seen so much of Court life and politics, and now observing the destruction for ever of the *Ancien Régime*, Marie strove to keep her personal feelings neutral and detached, her private judgement unbiased and unemotional. She saw and memorised events as they happened, and she was no ordinary witness. She had learned from Curtius a journalistic flair that enabled her to register happenings and people vividly, even when she herself was in a state of terror and revulsion at what she was forced to do.

The French Revolution remained a part of Marie Grosholtz throughout her life of nearly ninety years. She only condemned the bloodshed and those responsible for it. She never lost a respect for the Royal Family of France with whom she had been able to mingle for such a long period. The Comtesse de Genlis, one-time mistress of the royal Duc d'Orléans and governess to his children, wrote, 'The Revolution was inevitable. Respect for the Monarchy died out.' It never died out for Madame Tussaud, though she had witnessed so much of its follies and weakness, and so much of what they brought about. Her opportunities had indeed been extraordinary.

Prologue:
The Guillotine Blade

IN Paris, in the summer of 1794, the French revolutionary Terror was at its height. Throughout France literally thousands of heads had parted from their shoulders under the guillotine blade.

Maximilien Robespierre, now in supreme political power, believed that the rule of fear, the organised Terror, and elimination of all dissident persons, even those who were merely lukewarm in their views, was the only way to establish the strong and orderly Republic of France which was the purpose of the preceding years of revolutionary upheaval.

One evening in the middle of July there was knocking at the door of Dr Philippe Curtius's famous wax exhibition, the *Salon de Cire* on the Boulevard du Temple, in the heart of the entertainment area of Paris. It was an unexpected disturbance, for Dr Curtius, an enthusiastic revolutionary and a friend—inasmuch as anyone was a friend—of Robespierre, was abroad, visiting the Rhineland on a mission for the Government that Robespierre controlled.

As always, Curtius had left his exhibition in the charge of Marie Grosholtz, a young woman of thirty-three whose mother had been his housekeeper since Marie was a baby, and to whom he had been mentor and teacher of the art of wax modelling since the little girl was six years old. She was highly skilled due to Curtius's training, and always called him 'Uncle'.

The knocking brought Marie to the door. She was astounded to see members of the police, from the Committee of Public Safety which had been created by the Government over a year earlier. And she was appalled to be told she was under arrest, and her mother as well.

It was true that she had spent eight years at the Court of Versailles in the service of the late King's sister, Madame Elisabeth, who, like her brother Louis XVI, had lost her head under the guillotine blade, but her Uncle Curtius, an active member of the revolutionary movement from its start and member of the Jacobin Club, had recalled her from that service before the fall of the Bastille five years ago.

[4]

Since then, Marie declared vehemently, she had had no contact at all with Royalist sympathisers, had not even spoken to any such people. Like any patriotic citizeness, she had participated in every possible revolutionary occasion of festivity.

She had danced on the ruins of the Bastille after the people had demolished it. She had modelled, without protest or visible horror, decapitated heads brought to her by the revolutionary mobs, and at the command of the Government had taken death masks and modelled death heads of the guillotined King and Queen. As for her mother, Madame Grosholtz, she had worked as cook and housekeeper to Dr Curtius for more than thirty years, and had never concerned herself with anything outside that rôle.

Marie knew that the protestations she was making were quite useless. Since the Law of Suspects had come into force the previous autumn, any person acceptable to the officers of the Committee as a patriot could denounce anyone he or she chose as a traitor to the Republic. It might be a neighbour with whom there had been some dispute, a colleague who had aroused jealousy, or just some man or woman who was personally disliked by the denouncer.

There would be no trial. Once arrested, unless someone powerful chose to intervene, or the victim could get a defence to the Committee which they might, miraculously, accept, then it was a matter of a few, a very few, days in prison. After that came the journey to the guillotine, standing in a tumbril, with hair cut short so that it would not impede the blade as it met the neck.

What defence could Marie find, and how could she convey it to an ear of power? In Curtius's absence she and her mother were so vulnerable. Their heads would be rolling into the basket long before he learned of their arrest.

Marie did not even know who had denounced them. She thought it might be a man called Jacques Dutruy, a *grimacier*, who amused audiences between acts in the theatres by pulling hideous faces. He and Marie had never found themselves congenial. If Jacques were the denouncer, Marie had little chance. He enjoyed the patronage of some prominent revolutionaries, and supplemented his earnings by working as one of the 'lads' who helped executioner Sanson.

Marie realised that her life had been an extraordinary mixture. Once Curtius had enjoyed much royal patronage in the *Salon de Cire*, which had led to her personal royal service during the years that preceded the outbreak of Revolution. Then she had been involved, often horribly, during the five dangerous years of turmoil that followed, with her uncle deeply committed, at least outwardly, to the new ideals and Government.

Now she and her mother were in the greatest danger. Prison was inevitable. From there she could try to get an appeal to someone with power who might take notice, otherwise she knew that only some unforeseeable stroke of fortune could spare their heads.

The Uneasy City

MARIE Grosholtz could not remember her first glimpse of a member of the royal family of France, for she was little more than a baby when the King's cousin, the Prince de Conti, in the early 1760s paid an unannounced visit to the house of Dr Philippe Curtius, who then resided in Berne, Switzerland. Marie's young mother worked as housekeeper to the Doctor.

Madame Grosholtz had given birth to her daughter in 1761, in her native town of Strasbourg in Alsace. The eighteen-year-old mother was already a widow. Her husband, a soldier from Frankfurt, had died of wounds shortly before the child was born. By taking up the post with Dr Curtius, a bachelor, she was able to keep her daughter with her and live comfortably in the prosperous Swiss town.

German-born Philippe Mathé Curtius was the son of a civil servant, but himself chose to qualify as a doctor, finally setting up his practice in Berne. Trained in medicine Philippe Curtius might be, but his hobby— indeed his passion—was the art of modelling in wax. He began with anatomical specimens, but soon found he could reproduce human features with accuracy, and he had a remarkable flair for catching the personality of his sitters.

Curtius set up a small museum or gallery of his work in his house, and became quite celebrated locally as a sculptor in wax. Visitors to Berne, as well as the local people, were attracted to it. Amongst those was the Prince de Conti, travelling incognito in Switzerland.

The Prince was in considerable disfavour with his royal relative, Louis XV. Firstly, the Prince de Conti had made clear his implacable dislike of the King's mistress, Madame de Pompadour, whose political ability and influence were considerable. The King never forgot or forgave this enmity, even after Madame de Pompadour died in 1764 and was replaced by the charming but totally unintellectual Madame du Barry who did not meddle in politics.

Secondly, Louis XV's dislike of his cousin was reinforced by his antipathy to the Prince de Conti's liberal views. Although an un-shakeable supporter of monarchy and aristocracy, the Prince also favoured the new idea of a constitutional monarch instead of an absolute one. He followed the advanced thinking of the intellectual group known as '*les Philosophes*'.

In particular the writer Jean Jacques Rousseau was treated with great kindness by the Prince de Conti, though his name was anathema in royal and aristocratic circles. Rousseau's writings publicised his theories that all civilisation was in a state of degradation, that perfection was only to be found in the life of a primitive savage, 'the noble savage'. He declared wealth and property were crimes, and all government a form of tyranny.

Rousseau's private life did not enhance his reputation. He had as mistress an illiterate and densely stupid servant girl from an inn. By her he had five children, each of whom he promptly consigned to the foundling hospital, making no attempt to support the girl, Thérèse Lavasseur, or the children he fathered.

When, in 1763, Rousseau's book *Émile* was published, giving his views on Kings, governments and education, it was the Prince de Conti who advised him and assisted him to flee the storm it aroused and take refuge in Switzerland. It was probably the exile of his protégé that brought about the Prince's private visit to that country, and thus his visit to the museum of Dr Curtius when he passed through Berne.

The Prince de Conti's visit was Dr Philippe Curtius's first contact with royalty. To be honoured thus by a member of the royal family of France, and one who was so well known for his liberal views, was something Curtius could not ever have anticipated. When the Prince showed great interest, and offered him patronage and work if he brought his artistry as a sculptor in wax to France and settled in Paris, the young doctor, still only in his late twenties, took a momentous decision. He would abandon medicine, and concentrate on building a career as an artist in wax, a profession that was to remain a passionate obsession as well as a livelihood until his death.

That such an invitation should come from the Prince de Conti was not surprising. In spite of the King's dislike of his cousin, the Prince lived in semi-royal state in the vast palace complex of the Temple in the centre of Paris. It included a fortress prison in which Louis XVI and Marie Antoinette would one day be incarcerated by a revolutionary government. At this time it was hardly used, and the Temple enclosure had fine buildings containing enormous, luxurious apartments in which the Prince and his very considerable retinue lived.

In a vast, high-windowed drawing-room large numbers of artists, musicians, writers, intellectuals and wits of both sexes from the high aristocracy frequently assembled. But the Prince disregarded rank in the society he kept around him, and in his palace one met people from varied walks of life who were talented and accomplished in the arts.

Dr Curtius left Berne for Paris, and Madame Grosholtz did not see her employer again until her daughter Marie was six years old. Prudent Curtius retained possession of his house in Berne as a safeguard until he felt confident of success in his new career as an artist. He left Madame Grosholtz to caretake his former home for him, until 1767 when he sent for her to come and take charge of his household in Paris, bringing her child with her.

He took up residence in the Hôtel d'Allègre, in which a number of artists lodged, worked and displayed the results of their labours in several small galleries. One of these galleries was used for the exhibition of paintings and sculpture which had failed to gain a place in the prestigious annual Salon, which resembled London's Royal Academy summer exhibition. This gallery was known as the Académie de St Luc.

Curtius had not yet been successful in the Salon, but some of his wax sculptures had been shown in the Académie de St Luc. He was still working on private commissions. Thanks to the excellent connections he made through the patronage of the Prince de Conti, he had plenty of commissions, and his sitters included many who had court associations.

The Paris to which Curtius had come was an uneasy city, as anyone with his acumen could not fail to be aware. The Crown's finances were in chaos, agriculture stagnant, and the parliament of France, the Estates General, had not been summoned for decades. These long-standing problems were highlighted by a group of writers, the 'Physiocrats', who were in fact the first economists. They suggested and pressed for reforms that were totally unacceptable to Louis XV.

The Physiocrats wanted a new and more equitable tax system, which would also bring in more revenue. As things stood nobles and clergy were exempt from taxation. The burden fell on the peasantry and other low-grade workers. Since harvests were poor, and production generally low, the Crown revenues were in a depressed state. But such arguments fell on deaf ears as far as the King and his ministers were concerned.

Paris was a crowded city, huddled within the walls erected to check the smuggling in of taxable produce and other commodities. The city walls were pierced by a large number of gates, known as *barrières*. Outside, the surrounding countryside was sparsely populated, but Paris was densely packed with buildings and humanity. Even the principal streets of the capital were narrow and extremely dirty. Rich people never walked on account of the filth. When cattle were brought in on the hoof and slaughtered, pools of blood and piles of stinking offal outside the butchers' shops were a common sight, attracting flies and hungry, homeless dogs. So narrow were most streets that those who had to walk ran the risk of being crushed by carriages and carts, as well as smothered in noisome mud thrown up by horses' hooves and the wheels. The more substantial houses had their walls protected from traffic by *bornes*, sturdy bollards erected to fend off damage. Sedan chairs jostled and sometimes knocked down passers-by.

The city authorities did nothing to improve this state of affairs which, like taxation, bore hardest against the poor. Eight years after Marie Grosholtz had arrived in Paris, the great Doctor Samuel Johnson, visiting the French capital for the first time, wrote that apart from the churches this was not the fine city one might expect. 'Nobody but mean people walk in Paris.'

Dr Johnson considered Paris shops mean too. He remarked that the meat sold by the butchers, whose activities so contaminated the streets and lanes, was of such poor quality that in England it would only be used to feed prisoners in gaol. However the water supply, conveyed to the public by means of fountains in the streets, was generally believed to be good. It was pumped from the Seine, and Seine water had a reputation for purity and wholesomeness.

The Rue St Honoré, where Curtius lived and worked in the Hôtel d'Allègre, was on the fringe of one of the poorest, most crowded, and insalubrious areas of the city. Six-year-old Marie, fresh from the cleanliness of Switzerland, was made aware from the first days of her arrival of the conditions under which hundreds of people around her were existing. On the other hand, there were a number of religious houses within the walls which still had fine gardens and orchards, and there were 'magnificent and splendid churches', as Dr Johnson noted.

The Court, with its literally thousands of courtiers, officials, and retainers, had resided outside Paris, at Versailles, since the time of Louis XIV. None the less, many aristocratic families maintained grand houses in the city, and from these Curtius drew many of his sitters. These noble personages were little concerned with the inhabitants of the fetid slums so near their luxurious residences. Huddled, dingy houses and hovels stretched from the Rue St Honoré right up to the Place du Carrousel in front of the now almost disused royal Tuileries palace. In some ways these slums were picturesque, as those who did venture into them discovered. A contemporary record describes how 'the hovels swarmed with bird-sellers, brokers, shabby wine-shops, and in the waste ground jugglers and dentists, quacks and dog-gelders. Everywhere a sprinkling of beggars.'

[10]

While he modelled the features of those who lived in the grandest style, Curtius also modelled, and listened to, lesser men whose views were more enlightened. Gossip said that the sculptor in wax also had a profitable sideline, artistic little groups of licentious figures which served to adorn aristocratic boudoirs.

Altogether, by the year 1770, Dr Philippe Curtius felt sufficient confidence in his new career to expand his field of work. He decided to open a public exhibition which would be populated by an always up-to-date assemblage of portrait figures representing a range of persons who attracted popular interest. His inborn showman's instinct convinced him that high and low would visit such an exhibition. There was nothing like it in Paris.

Curtius left his studio and lodging in the Rue St Honoré and took a suite of rooms in the *entresol*—between ground and first floors—of the Palais Royal, facing onto the gardens. These were open to the public, always crowded, and the lower floors of the Palais Royal, the palace of the royal Duc d'Orléans, already housed numerous shops and small galleries of many kinds. Henceforward his address would be '*Sieur Curtius, au Palais Royal, côté de l'Avenue de l'Opera, par la cour Desfontaines*'.

Little Marie was now nine years old. It was three years since Uncle Curtius had noted her aptitude for modelling, and had begun to train her rigorously in his skills. She was absorbed and happy as she learned how to oil a sitter's face and flatten any facial hair with pomade, before a mask of fine plaster of Paris was applied. The sitter breathed through quills or straws inserted in the nostrils.

She watched Curtius take a clay squeeze from the resulting life-mask, and skilfully refine the modelling of the features before a piece-mould was taken of the portrait head. Then hot wax was poured into the assembled mould. Accurate judgement was needed to assess the right moment for pouring off surplus cooling wax, so that when the piece-mould was finally taken apart, a hollow wax head emerged. This head was worked on with small tools to remove irregularities and perfect features before tinting, and the insertion, hair by hair, of real human hair. Glass eyes exactly matching those of the sitter were inserted in the sockets.

Marie learned that the greatest art lay in working the first clay squeeze from the life-mask, modelling it so that personality and character appeared. She had a talent for this, an observant eye, and the patience to ensure that the finished portrait bore the closest resemblance to life in every detail. Curtius's personal pride in his art as a sculptor in wax was immense, and he was determined that his only pupil should inherit the same pride.

[11]

When Curtius opened his new exhibition in the Palais Royal, the public from all walks of life flocked in as news of its impact spread. Marie was often at his side when he welcomed and talked with visitors, and she found that she now had a different lesson to learn.

These people who inspected and commented on the portrait figures as they walked or lingered round the exhibition were, like the sitters and those he liked to invite to dinner, of differing rank, and very different in their political outlook. When Marie was with her uncle she was expected to chat if required, and make herself agreeable. Her sharp ears would overhear talk of all kinds, some of which she would for some time be too young to comprehend entirely. While talking pleasantly to visitors, if they wished to pay her attention, there was no room, Curtius impressed on her, for childish *gaffes*, which might annoy either the great, or the not so great, and indicate to one or the other political views that were unacceptable to them. She must always think before she spoke, say nothing rash.

Marie learned this lesson well. Towards everyone she was pleasant, vivacious and entertaining in her conversation. But to the end of her long life of nearly ninety years, when political views or controversy were concerned her words were few and guarded. From her childhood Curtius trained her to observe not only features, but character and personality, and instilled in her the necessity for discretion. In the popular wax exhibition in the Palais Royal, with its visitors from many walks of life and from many foreign countries, neither of them could be too careful.

The New Dauphine

CURTIUS could not have obtained a better location for his new *Salon de Cire* than the Duc d'Orléans' great palace opposite the Louvre. The wing where the lower floors were let out as shops, galleries or cafés, gave on to extensive gardens which were open to the public.

The gardens were much bigger than they are today, for when the Duc reconstructed his palace, some ten years after Curtius installed himself there, the new building with its arcades encroached considerably on the gardens, much to public dissatisfaction.

In the mid-eighteenth century the most popular recreation of the inhabitants of Paris, apart from attending any spectacles such as parades, was promenading. Both the high and the low born promenaded in their leisure time, the working classes in the evenings and on Sundays, the rich and fashionable at all hours of the day. They strolled in the Champs Elysées, on the ramparts, and in royal palace gardens, all of which were freely open to the public. Even in the vast grounds of Versailles, courtiers and ordinary people rubbed shoulders as they walked round the parterres and shady alleys. In central Paris there were the Tuileries gardens, always very dusty according to contemporary comment, the Luxembourg, and the very popular Palais Royal gardens.

The Palais Royal gardens were always full of fashionables. In the 1770s they did not have the disreputable reputation that they acquired later, after the building of the arcades. Ladies were not expected to appear there in formal dress, except before and after Opéra performances. More comfortably dressed in less formal attire, they walked, or sat, under the shady chestnut trees, exchanging news and gossip. Under other groups of trees newspaper readers gathered and discussed the politics of the day, but there were none of the violent 'soap-box' orators who were to use the Palais Royal gardens as their platform in the months running up to the outbreak of the Revolution.

This was far in the future, but by 1780 the gardens had begun to

[13]

acquire a disreputable atmosphere. Even then, in spite of pickpockets, the soliciting of prostitutes, clandestine gaming-houses, and the sale of obscene books, people from all walks of life continued to jostle there. No foreigner visiting Paris failed to visit the Palais Royal gardens.

It was soon after Curtius was established in his new studio, living-rooms, and gallery, that Marie first heard of the new Dauphine, the Austrian Archduchess Maria Antonia (Marie Antoinette), who was married at Versailles early in May 1770 to Louis XV's grandson the Dauphin, another Louis. The Dauphin's parents had died while he was still a child, both smitten down with fatal illness.

At the end of April that year, a month or so before the wedding, the people of Paris were commanded to send wedding gifts for the youthful royal couple to the Palace of Versailles. The bride would not pass through Paris on the way to her wedding, so none but those who could make the journey to Versailles could hope to get a glimpse of her. None the less the Paris authorities hastened to despatch several cartloads of presents, for the King had ordered 'Do not fail in this, for it is my pleasure.'

Even at this early age Marie was well aware of what was happening outside the confines of her uncle's studio and gallery. Curtius was hospitable, and his dinner table soon became a popular rendezvous. This was not only because of the good German and Swiss-style food cooked by Madame Grosholtz, but also for the lively conversations and debate which took place round the table.

It was the custom of the house for Madame Grosholtz and Marie to join the company for a meal. The child was precocious, and understood a great deal of what was being discussed but, obedient to Curtius's training, she could be trusted not to chatter about anything she heard. To Curtius she could always talk freely and ask questions, but other-wise, among his guests, she must only display intelligence and pleasing manners.

The young Dauphine, the subject of much talk, was reported to be extremely charming, though she was not beautiful. She had, they said, the Hapsburg family's protruding lower lip and heavy jaw. But with her blue eyes, fair hair, vivacity, and a natural grace and dignity remark-able in a fifteen-year-old girl, she delighted her grandfather-in-law Louis XV. The Dauphin, in contrast, was a quiet, heavy and rather slow young man—kindly, but more interested in his hobby of lock-smithing and similar mechanical matters than in wit and vivacious conversation.

It was Marie Antoinette's great misfortune that she was ill-educated, and had received no training for the position she now filled. The pretty

Archduchess had never enjoyed lessons and was accustomed to do as she pleased, for her mother, the Empress Maria Theresa of Austria, had been too busy with her many cares of state to make sure her delightful little daughter was being made to learn, and to give thought to more serious matters that would affect her future.

There could have been no greater contrast than the upbringing of the royal 'little featherhead', as her brother called her, and that of the disciplined little Marie Grosholtz, who was destined one day to hold Marie Antoinette's guillotined head on her lap while she smoothed plaster over the dead features. Already, at the age of nine, Marie was conscious of political matters and the gulf between riches and poverty, and under Curtius's tuition was following a strict course of training for her future.

The people of Paris hoped, of course, that they would see the royal bride soon after the wedding, and on 30 May she was expected to attend a great festival of rejoicing to be held in the Place Louis XV (now the Place de la Concorde), where a splendid fireworks display was planned. At five o'clock on this great holiday the city's fountains began to flow with wine, and the trees in the Champs Elysées sparkled with lamps.

It was eight o'clock when the Dauphine entered her state coach in the courtyard of the palace of Versailles, and the royal procession set off for Paris. Marie Antoinette was to arrive in the Place Louis XV in time to watch the fireworks, but the timing was amiss, for by the time her coach arrived at the Cours de la Reine, a part of the Champs Elysées, the fireworks' set piece, the finale of the display, was already flaming in the sky. The royal coach was halted so that she could watch it. The coach remained halted where it was, for a terrible noise and clamour could be heard coming from the Place Louis XV, not cries of joy and amazement, but shouts and screams. A terrible disaster was happening.

An enormous crowd had flocked in from all directions to join in the festivities and watch the fireworks. Now that the set piece was burning itself out in the sky, people turned away and flowed into the Rue Royale and adjoining narrow streets. They were all making for the city's ramparts, where a large fair had been licensed for the occasion.

Everyone pushed at once in the same direction and the crush was appalling. People were jammed together, some falling underfoot and being trampled on. Some, who had been suffocated, were carried along upright in the crowd even though they were dead, as the panic-stricken mass of humanity strove to get away.

Later on the Paris authorities estimated that some 400,000 people had crammed into and around the Place Louis XV. When the area was

[15]

at last cleared one hundred and thirty-three corpses were laid out in the cemetery of the Madeleine nearby, the cemetery which would have such macabre associations for Marie during the revolutionary years to come.

Back in the Cours de la Reine, the Dauphine, bitterly disappointed and upset, turned her coach round and went back to Versailles with her retinue. Naturally people muttered that it was an evil omen for the royal pair that such a catastrophe should occur at a wedding festivity. Marie Antoinette did not visit Paris again for three years.

Those were not happy years for the royal bride for, owing to a slight genital deformity, the Dauphin was unable to consummate the marriage. Instead of expected motherhood and the hoped-for birth of an heir, the Dauphine had frustration night after night. Her reaction was to turn to frivolity and extravagance, thereby deeply offending older members of the Court, and in particular her aunts, the spinster sisters of Louis XV, with her mocking, biting, tongue.

The Court continually moved around, spending time at the palaces of Marly, Fontainebleau, and Compiègne (where Marie Antoinette shocked her aunts by leaving off her corset), while she gathered round her a sparkling, witty but irresponsible, circle of intimates, their days and nights devoted to pleasure.

Finally, after numerous requests from the people of Paris, who had sent costly wedding presents but had never had a chance to welcome their new Dauphine, a grand entry to the city was arranged for the royal couple on 8 June 1773.

This was the first opportunity for Marie Grosholtz to get a glimpse of Marie Antoinette. Neither she nor her uncle could have imagined, even in wildest fantasy, that Marie would ever have closer contact with the Dauphine and her husband than as a mere spectator in a crowd in the street, or at Versailles on some royal occasion.

On that day a splendid service was held in Nôtre Dame, followed by elaborate ceremonies, before the youthful pair and their retinue proceeded to the Tuileries. Here they appeared on the terrace of the palace, and even descended into the gardens and walked among the crowds of people gathered there. 'You could have touched her,' boasted the memoirs of one spectator.

Parisians were charmed with the Dauphine's radiance and gracious manner, while she herself was enchanted with Paris. She determined she would visit the capital as often as she could, even if incognito, and taste some of its pleasures away from the formalities of Court routine.

However, in spite of the city's warm reception, the place already buzzed with tales of the Dauphine's extravagance and flightiness. The

[16]

Dauphin's sexual problem was also common knowledge, as was the fact that he stubbornly refused to undergo the minor surgery that would put it right.

As for France's finances, they were in a desperate state. The Empress Maria Theresa, writing to her ambassador in Paris, described her daughter's new country as 'dilapidated'. In 1770 Louis XV had dismissed one of his ministers, Choiseul, one of Madame de Pompadour's choices, because of his efforts to make the King consider giving more power to the provincial and Paris *parlements*. After Choiseul's disgrace and dismissal the *parlements* refused to register one of the King's edicts, and were promptly dissolved by him. Harvests were poor due to inefficient agriculture, the price of bread high, and the poor hungry. Yet the concept of a less absolute form of monarchy was totally repugnant to Louis XV.

The Dauphine took no heed of any such matters. Bitterly frustrated by her husband's failure to consummate their marriage, she gave herself up to pleasure-seeking. It was rumoured everywhere that she often visited Paris incognito for entertainment, even attending masked balls of dubious repute. Some said that, with her young brother-in-law, the Comte d'Artois, already a libertine, she even visited *guingettes*. These small drinking and dancing places, though intended for working people, were often frequented by wealthy and fashionable ladies and gentlemen in search of new diversion, who whispered around that they had certainly recognised Marie Antoinette enjoying the dancing and gaiety. Marie Grosholtz heard all the gossip, and discussion, political or otherwise, round Curtius's dinner table, but she did not herself believe that all the accusations against the pretty young Dauphine were true.

A New Reign Begins

IN 1774 Louis XV died of smallpox. He was only sixty-four, but his constitution was undermined by years of sexual excesses. Though he had sat on the throne for nearly half a century, he died unwept. No mourning subjects lined the route as his funeral cortège, hastily put together, and without pomp, wended its way to St Denis where the kings of France were buried.

His mistress, Madame du Barry, had stepped into her waiting coach directly she heard that he had drawn his last breath. She rolled away to her estate at Louveçiennes. The royal gifts she had received during the five years that she had been *maîtresse en titre* and the country was sliding towards bankruptcy were generally believed to have amounted to 180 million *livres*. Yet her tenants found her a kind and generous lady.

Philippe Curtius had modelled Madame du Barry's portrait* soon after he was established in Paris. Then she was known as Jeanne Vaubernier, mistress of the disreputable Jean du Barry. When she attracted the King's notice she was hurriedly married off to his brother, Comte Guillaume du Barry, for only married ladies were received at Court.

Marie Grosholtz had always admired the recumbent likeness of Madame du Barry, which was never collected by the lady, and was still in the studio when as a child she had arrived in Paris with her mother. Curtius had caught perfectly the face with its slightly slanting eyes, delicate arched eyebrows, and a particular turn of the rather long neck.

As Marie grew up and learned her skills, she appreciated the artistry of this portrait, which Curtius put in his exhibition when it opened to the public in the Palais Royal. She retained this admiration all her life and when, as Madame Tussaud, she left for England in 1802, she took it with her. She always kept it in her own exhibition and when, in old age,

---

* As 'The Sleeping Beauty' this can still be seen in Madame Tussaud's exhibition in London today.

Marie Tussaud modelled her last self-portrait, she positioned the figure by the couch on which the graceful 'Sleeping Beauty' lay.

In the course of time Madame du Barry's head fell beneath the guillotine blade. Then Curtius again modelled the still attractive features, in very different surroundings from those when lovely Jeanne Vaubernier, aged twenty-two and at the beginning of her rise to fame, sat elegantly in his studio while he applied the plaster-of-Paris life-mask, the source of his admired portrait.

The new young King and Queen were crowned at Rheims Cathedral in 1775. Marie Antoinette was delighted at the number of people lining the route between Compiègne and Rheims, and at the enthusiastic welcome she received from the populace on arrival. She wrote to her mother, Empress Maria Theresa, 'It is at once amazing and gratifying to be so well received in spite of the dearness of bread.' She did not realise that, in the countryside, the peasant labourers who watched her on their knees, raising their arms first to heaven and then to their mouths, were pleading for bread, not gesticulating a welcome to their new Queen.

Back at Versailles, Marie Antoinette resumed her frivolous life of *distractions*, in spite of the admonitions of both her mother and the Austrian ambassador to the Court. In the actual year of her coronation she made a purchase, which was quickly noised abroad, of a costly pair of diamond earrings, and a bracelet of the same gems which she so loved. When Maria Theresa heard of this she wrote a severe letter of rebuke to her daughter, but Marie Antoinette brushed the matter aside, saying she did not understand the fuss over such *bagatelles* (trifles).

Then there was gossip and criticism over the new royal dressmaker, Rose Bertin, introduced to the Queen by one of the royal duchesses only a few months after Louis XV had died. Rose Bertin had a genius for creating novel colours in the expensive fabrics she used for her *toilettes*. When a new shade, such as puce, so-called because someone said it was the colour of a flea, pleased Marie Antoinette, then all the Court must follow her example and dress in puce.

Above all, Rose Bertin was famous for creating extravagant head-dresses. When the Queen sent her mother in Austria a portrait depicting herself elaborately dressed, with an excessively befeathered confection on her head, her mother returned, 'I do not see a picture of the Queen of France, but of an actress.'

Two years after the coronation Marie Antoinette's brother, Joseph II of Austria, came to Paris incognito (though everyone knew who he was) to reason with the King about his marital problem, and to try to instil some sense of responsibility into the giddy head of his sister, of whom he was very fond. The people of Paris adored Joseph for his simplicity of manner and conduct. In spite of his exalted rank he refused to live in the palace of Versailles, preferring to occupy two simple rooms in the town. Incognito, though actually nearly always recognised, he went about Paris alone, visiting places where ordinary people gathered, mingling with them, unobtrusively listening to their talk. Popular stanzas about him were sung in the streets and in taverns:

> Majesty without pomp our eyes have seen,
> But here how shameful has the contrast been,
> He has found only pomp, not majesty.

Having 'tested the water' of the people's mood through his own powers of observation, Joseph lectured his sister on the 'infallible and disastrous' consequences if she did not alter her behaviour and attitudes. He pressed his brother-in-law to undergo the minor surgery that would enable him to consummate his marriage, and thus hopefully provide a Dauphin for his subjects.

Among the places of interest that Joseph visited during his peregrinations about Paris was Dr Curtius's celebrated *Salon de Cire*. While walking round inspecting the portrait figures, like any private citizen, he smelt a savoury odour. 'Mein Gott! Sauerkraut!', he exclaimed. Yearning for some German-style cooking, he asked if he might join in the meal that was being prepared.

'Do let me partake!' he cried. Curtius, of course, spoke German, his native tongue, fluently still in spite of his years in Paris, and Joseph was delighted to be able to speak his own language throughout his visit to the *Salon*. Marie, too, still remembered the German that she had spoken in Curtius's Berne household during the first six years of her life. In fact, her French never lost a pronounced German accent.

After her years of training as a sculptor in wax, the sixteen-year-old Marie automatically noted the royal visitor's features—the protruding under-lip, the aquiline nose. He was dressed simply in a grey coat, as befitted his incognito, and Marie took particular note of the unusually long tail of hair which fell down his back.

During her growing-up years Marie Grosholtz was to observe at close quarters numerous royal personages, nobles, and aristocrats, as well as many men who were destined to become political leaders and revolutionaries. She always looked at them from a modeller's point of view, detached in her keen observation, not only of features and characteristic postures, but also of the clothes they wore. The clothing of the wax figures in the exhibition was a matter of great importance. Curtius insisted that every detail, down to buttons and shoebuckles, must be authentic, so that the finished portrait figure gave, as nearly as possible, a total representation of the living subject.

Not all the great persons who walked round the *Salon*, and often sat for their portraits, impressed Marie as favourably as did the Queen's brother, Joseph of Austria. There was, for example, Gustave III of Sweden, who had succeeded to his throne in 1771. He wanted his portrait modelled in wax, not an easy commission for one side of his face was smaller than the other. Marie thought he resembled a hare in looks. However, Curtius's skill produced a likeness that pleased the Swedish king, and he also purchased a couple of silver plates with wax portrait medallions mounted on them.

Nor was Paul of Russia, the son of Peter III and Catherine the Great, an impressive 'royal'. He was small and ugly, with rough, disagreeable manners. His silk attire was plain, and he wore an exceptionally high cravat, rising over his jawbone in order partially to conceal a scrofulous skin complaint from which he suffered.

Some of the nobles and aristocrats were eccentric in the extreme, such as one member of the great Polish family of Radziwill. He travelled accompanied by figures of the twelve Apostles cast in solid gold. The golden Apostles were heavy, and needed several vehicles to transport them. Curtius, always on the alert for anything that aroused popular curiosity, managed to get a glimpse of these figures, but could count only eleven. One had recently been melted down to provide the Prince with ready cash.

A flow of exalted visitors was essential for the reputation of Curtius's *Salon*. He made a point of receiving all important persons himself, and showing them round the exhibition. As she grew older, Marie assisted him with this, but she was far from overwhelmed by grandeur. She often found herself more interested in observing and listening to others among Curtius's visitors, whose ultimate role in the overthrow of the monarchy of France was, as yet, totally unforeseen.

[21]

Harbingers of Revolution

FROM early childhood Marie Grosholtz grew up with portents of revolution around her, with men who paved the way for the upheaval, and men who would become its leaders, all coming and going in her uncle's house.

Among the first she recollected meeting was Jean Jacques Rousseau, who shared a patron, the Prince de Conti, with Curtius. It was natural that he should frequent the household. Apart from other interests he liked the good Swiss food he found there.

Rousseau had been expelled from his exile in Switzerland by the government of Berne, which, tired of this stirrer-up of trouble in their midst, threatened him with arrest and prosecution. He fled to England, where he found protection in Staffordshire with the Scots-born philosopher David Hume whom he had previously met in Paris.

Unfortunately, Rousseau began imagining that the English government was seeking to kill him. Frightened, he rushed back across the Channel to the continuing patronage of the Prince de Conti and the 'anti-king', the Duc d'Orléans.

When Curtius opened his *Salon de Cire*, Rousseau was settled in Paris, pursuing his former, poorly paid, occupation as a copyist. The delusions that had led to his flight from England became stronger and stronger. Marie grew accustomed to his violent outbursts of rage against those— especially Voltaire—whom he believed had stolen his ideas for their own work. His mania cost him many friends, and Marie always remembered how 'he would exhaust all the abusive vocabulary of the French language in expressing his wrath'.

Finally, realising himself that his mind was becoming more and more unhinged, Rousseau fervently longed for the sanctuary of a hospital, but instead took refuge in a country cottage offered by a wealthy admirer. Here he died suddenly in July 1778. Some believed that he had committed suicide, others that he had been murdered, for his work had done much towards preparing for the cataclysm that would one day come, and had made him many enemies who feared for their future.

While Marie Grosholtz had been exposed to Rousseau's theories on man and government from the age when she could begin to comprehend such matters, she did not meet his hated arch-rival, Voltaire, until that sage left his Swiss residence at Ferney, which he had occupied for twenty years, and returned to Paris in February 1778. Ostensibly he came to supervise the performance of his last play. He was received with the wildest enthusiasm by all the liberal thinkers, and also by the people of Paris, but he found time to accept Curtius's invitation to visit the wax exhibition and dine at his table.

Voltaire was by then eighty years old, and a very ill man, but such a celebrity just had to be persuaded to sit for his portrait in wax. Marie, now seventeen, was entrusted by her uncle with this task, her first really important commission, though she had already modelled the portraits of many others who were in the public eye. After eleven years of training Curtius now considered her to be very highly skilled in the art that he had taught her.

She took a mask of the thin, shrivelled, sardonic face, and noted the sitter's habitually old-fashioned clothes, the flowing wig, the long-skirted coat, long lace jabot, striped silk stockings and large buckled shoes. The portrait she achieved did credit to her artistry. The following year Curtius's exhibition was visited by a young American, Elkanah Watson, who inspected the array of figures and wrote in his diary 'the most striking, however, was that of the celebrated Voltaire, who is closely engaged with a table full of books, papers, etc., before him. His countenance expressed the very sensation of being a philosopher.'

But by the time young Elkanah saw the portrait figure, its celebrated subject was dead. All the fuss and excitement proved too much for Voltaire's fragile health. He died in Paris in May 1778. Curtius himself modelled a miniature portrait of Voltaire as he lay dying in his bed. He called it 'The Dying Socrates'.*

'Curtius', Marie said, 'always knew the state of affairs, and was a man of acute penetration', but not even he could have envisaged his medical friend, Jean Paul Marat, as the rabid anti-royalist he would become, nor as founder of the scurrilous revolutionary newspaper, *L'Ami du Peuple*. Nor could he even have imagined that his friend would be stabbed in his bath by Charlotte Corday, a young woman from Normandy, and that Marie, acting on instructions from a revolutionary

---

* Madame Tussaud brought this miniature, with others created by Curtius, to London in 1802. It can still be seen in the exhibition today.

government then in power, would take a mask from his dead face as he lay there.

The later 'infamous' Marat, born in 1743, was the son of a Sardinian designer living in France. The young man studied medicine, as Curtius had done, but took his courses in Bordeaux and Paris, not in Germany. Marat then travelled to Holland and London, where he practised his profession with a good measure of success. He proceeded to Edinburgh where, at the age of thirty-one, he acquired the degree of Doctor of Medicine. He also published a couple of philosophical essays.

Then Marat returned to France and two years later the Comte d'Artois, the King's youngest brother, appointed him brevet-physician to his personal guard. This was a decided mark of royal favour, even if it did not carry any military pay, and Marat retained it for nine years.

It was not only their medical knowledge that formed a link between Philippe Curtius and Jean Paul Marat. Marat was deeply interested in the study of optics and light, subjects that were near to the heart of Curtius. In his *Salon de Cire* Curtius paid great attention to skilful lighting and special lighting effects. Marie absorbed her uncle's pioneering ideas in this field and throughout her life her own exhibition was always strikingly lit. Even during her years of travelling the length and breadth of the British Isles, when locations were often difficult to arrange to the best advantage, the striking *coup d'oeil*, the brilliantly illuminated vista that struck the visitor entering the exhibition, was of paramount importance in her showmanship. She managed to achieve it in assembly rooms, in theatres with the pit boarded over, in large upper rooms in high-class inns. This tradition of the importance of clever lighting, which she had learned in the Palais Royal, she passed on to her sons and their descendants.

Although Marie was interested in medicine from the anatomical point of view, and eagerly acquired a knowledge of the use of lighting effects, she did not like Jean Paul Marat, even during the years before he hurled himself into revolutionary politics. His face was unpleasantly sallow, and his piercing eyes had what she termed 'a fierceness' which made her wary.

Marat was always kindly to his friend's young pupil, calling her 'a good child', but his manners generally were abrupt, coarse, and rude. Above all she was repelled by his personal dirtiness and slovenliness. All the same, Marie could see why, with their common interests and sharp enquiring brains, Marat found such a good friend in Curtius, who also appreciated his extraordinary energy and wild enthusiasms.

There was another point in Marat's favour. He was but a moderate drinker, unlike some of Curtius's other dinner-table cronies, such as the Duc d'Orléans and the Comte de Mirabeau* who often became tiresomely drunk at the tolerant Curtius's mealtime gatherings.

The Comte de Mirabeau, future outstanding political leader, was at this time merely a wild young ex-cavalry officer, continually at logger-heads with his tyrannical father. Mirabeau was ugly, too, pitted with smallpox and with a shock of black hair on which he wore hardly any powder. However Marie observed a kind of power in his ill-favoured countenance which presaged a future, and she was impressed by his remarkable eloquence. He was not a flamboyant figure as regards his dress. Marie's sharp eye noted that his favourite garb seemed to be black corded velvet, which contrasted oddly with that of the Duc d'Orléans, who favoured a more sporting English style of dress, with top-boots.

There was never any shortage of material for debate and gossip among Curtius's guests during the years when he lived and built up his *Salon de Cire*. Unfortunately the new young king, Louis XVI, did not live up to the expectations of his subjects, who had been so delighted when the autocratic and oppressive rule of his grandfather came to an end.

Their hopes of a more constitutional monarchy, and a more equitable tax system to relieve the working-class people, and the peasants, of the burden that was crushing them, did not materialise. It was true that the new king had recalled the Paris and provincial *Parlements*, and restored their semi-political rights, but the reforms he introduced were inconsiderable.

Louis XVI had also reduced the enormous personal household, the King's Chamber, which had surrounded his grandfather. The Chamber included hundreds of trivial offices which were, none the less, extremely profitable to those who secured them. However, even with these economies, the cost of the Court with its hordes of officials and servants remained enormous.

As well as all the financial problems that were ruining the country, there was scandal and antagonism over the Queen's new female friend, the captivating Yolande, Comtesse de Polignac. When Marie Antoinette was still Dauphine the closeness of her friendship with a beautiful young widow, the Princesse de Lamballe, had given rise to jealousy, whispering, and scandalised mutterings among high and low alike. Now, in the year after her coronation, the Queen seemed to be infatuated, recklessly infatuated, with a different woman.

Madame de Polignac, Marie Antoinette's new intimate, had, according to her admirers, so lovely a face, such grace of bearing, that she would have inspired Raphael, that sixteenth-century Italian master-

---

*On 19 June 1790 a decree of the National Assembly formally abolished all hereditary titles.

painter of sweet-faced Madonnas, to pick up his brushes. She was twenty-six years old when she caught the Queen's eye as she sang at a Court concert. Marie Antoinette seemed instantly enchanted.

Neither Yolande de Polignac, nor her handsome husband, Comte Jules, had ever possessed adequate means to support the lifestyle that their rank and tastes demanded. Once she was firmly established as the Queen's favourite, and the former most intimate woman friend, the Princesse de Lamballe, had withdrawn into the wings, Madame de Polignac lost no time in obtaining lucrative appointments for her husband and many relatives, and introducing her friends into the close personal circle that the Queen entertained in the exquisite little building, the Petit Trianon, tucked away in a secluded corner of the royal park.

The Petit Trianon had been begun in 1762, as a toy for Madame de Pompadour, but the first users were Louis XV and Madame du Barry. Marie Antoinette had received it as a gift from her husband, and the little château was to be entirely hers. Even the King had to ask her permission to visit it. Elegantly decorated to the Queen's personal taste, it was the venue for gatherings and entertainments attended only by those who were specially invited. It was a completely private retreat.

The Queen's exclusive parties in this jewel-box of a miniature palace give rise to envious stories of extravagance and excesses, and her friendship with Madame de Polignac did nothing to lessen the rumours. Soon scurrilous cartoons were appearing in Paris news-sheets hinting in no uncertain terms that there was something more than normal friendship between the Queen and her lovely Yolande. Marie heard these scandals discussed at length in her uncle's dining-room.

But other matters were soon to dominate the conversation. France became embroiled with her old enemy, England. On 4 July 1776, England's American colony declared its independence, after a long dispute over the English parliament's desire to levy taxes on the Crown's American possessions.

The rebellious Americans sent an envoy, Benjamin Franklin, to Paris to raise support in their struggle. He was well received at court as well as by the Parisian people. The King's Foreign Minister Vergennes, who had been closely watching the revolt, favoured possible French participation, but his opponents argued loudly that the disastrous state of France's finances made any question of going to war totally impossible.

Although it would be several years before Benjamin Franklin sat for Marie to model his portrait in wax, she, like so many of her fellow Parisians who caught glimpses of the American envoy, was favourably impressed by his appearance and personality. His cool, philosophic countenance, now and then enlivened by a faint smile, his tall, stout and imposing figure, dressed in plain Quaker-like black, supported by a stick, and his long grey hair, made him seem the very symbol of the liberty his people were claiming.

Benjamin Franklin disdained wearing a wig, and though this was *de rigueur* in the King's presence, none could be found to fit his large head with its noble forehead. So even at Court he was outstanding, with his hair combed over his shoulders. His only concession to grandeur was a brown velvet suit. He was applauded everywhere.

It was not surprising that a year after this 'Ambassador of the Thirteen United Provinces' of America had arrived in France a young French officer, well known to Marie as a visitor to Curtius's house, should decide to sail from his native land to join the American army, where he was given a command. This officer was the twenty-year-old Marquis de Lafayette. Marie described him as 'full of fire, with features expressive of his temperament'. Young Lafayette was an ardent supporter of liberty, but in those early days, before he was matured by his fighting service, level-headed Marie felt that his enthusiasm was more romantic than practical.

For the mass of the French people, the exciting news was not the American struggle for independence, of which they knew or cared little, but the pregnancy of their Queen. Louis XVI had yielded to his brother-in-law Joseph's advice, and submitted to the necessary minor operation with satisfactory results. At last Marie Antoinette was able to enjoy a normal marriage.

The prospect of an heir to the throne diminished the unpopularity she had earned by her irresponsible behaviour, in spite of talk that she had taken to meddling in politics at the instigation of her mother and the Austrian ambassador to France.

On 19 December 1778 the Queen gave birth to a princess, Marie Thérèse Charlotte, Madame Royale. Of course a boy had been hoped for, but the fact that the royal marriage was at last fruitful was sufficient cause for general rejoicing and celebration, especially when the news spread abroad that rigid court etiquette had nearly caused the Queen's death in childbirth.

A royal birth had to take place in public. The crowds that crammed into Marie Antoinette's chamber were such that, in the words of one of her waiting-women, 'It might have been a public square!' All the windows were closed and sealed with strips of paper. In this stifling atmosphere the Queen showed signs of acute distress immediately after the birth.

'Air! Air!', shouted the *accoucheur*. The King himself struggled forward, reached a window, and broke it open. Marie Antoinette was bled from the foot and revived. Great alarm gave way to great joy, though the Princesse de Lamballe, once the closest of the Queen's women friends, had to be carried out fainting and unconscious.

Processions and bonfires were quickly organised, but the Parisians' new enthusiasm for their Queen did not last very long. When in February 1779, less than two months after the royal birth, Louis XVI and Marie Antoinette paid a formal visit to Paris their reception was cold and silent. Once the first excitement had passed people remembered again the Queen's extravagance, her frivolous diversions and amusements, and her apparent lack of interest in the sufferings of the poor. Gossip and rumour again abounded.

The greatest danger to Marie Antoinette's already tarnished reputation came from her association with a young officer of the Swedish Light Dragoons, Axel Fersen, who had arrived at Versailles in the summer of 1778. An aristocrat and a favourite of the Swedish court, his good looks and good manners also ensured him a flattering welcome at Versailles, but at first he remained reserved and unobtrusive. Soon, however, no one could fail to notice that this newcomer pleased the Queen. It was observed that he had become a frequent guest at her Sunday card parties.

By the summer of 1779 the handsome young Count Fersen was included in the Queen's personal circle, and was invited to her Petit Trianon retreat. In spite of his reserved and rather melancholy disposition, it was perhaps inevitable that the young man should fall in love with his royal patroness. As for Marie Antoinette her affection for Axel Fersen was made clear to all when he bade her farewell, having signed on for one of the expeditionary forces being sent to fight in the American War. The Queen's eyes were seen to be brimming with tears.

But the expedition was postponed, and Axel Fersen returned to Versailles. He reappeared at the Queen's intimate receptions at the Petit Trianon, but seemed determined not to compromise her reputation, in spite of Marie Antoinette's obvious inclination for him. When another opportunity for him to join an expeditionary force occurred, he took it, and sailed off to America.

Marie Antoinette's sadness at losing a friend who she knew loved her without self-interest, together with the experience of motherhood and the continued admonitions of her mother and the Austrian ambassador, combined at last to abate her giddiness and the irresponsibility of her perpetual quest for amusement and pleasure. Her extravagance, however, she found difficult to curb.

During the year 1779 the Queen ordered ninety-three dresses, with a

[28]

further forty-three for formal occasions, and fifty-six *manteaux*. They were extremely expensive, even though many were in the newly fashionable simple style, made in thin muslins, silks and gauzes, and worn with straw 'shepherdess' hats. Marie Antoinette no longer favoured the elaborate plumed head-dresses that had aroused her mother's indignant disapproval.

At last America's envoy, Benjamin Franklin, had obtained what he sought, a Treaty of Alliance between France and America, which was signed on 6 February 1778. A new Controller-General, the Swiss banker Necker, appointed by the King, judged that France could take the enormous financial risk of possible participation in a war.

Necker's portrait in wax was modelled by Curtius, and consequently Marie met both the Swiss financier himself and his daughter. This young woman was destined to become the famous authoress, Madame de Staël, celebrated for her love affairs as well as her books. Marie did not care for the already self-important girl, whose rather heavy features were not appealing, she thought. Indeed she never became an admirer of Madame de Staël or her works, in spite of the acclaim she received after her marriage.

It was Marie who was accorded the privilege of visiting Benjamin Franklin in his residence at Passy, then a quiet suburb of Paris, in order to model him for the *Salon*.* It was to be one of her best portraits. She had always admired his countenance and bearing, while Franklin himself was interested in portraiture in wax, and was forming a collection of miniatures which he displayed in his house when he returned to America, having achieved his objective, which was to bring war to Europe.

The English government was furious when the Franco-American treaty became publicly known. England promptly declared war on her old enemy. There was a battle in the Channel, off Ushant, and Louis XVI sent a fleet to aid the American rebels. It was the start of a long conflict, its outcome not finally resolved till the autumn of 1783. America gained independence, and France a moral success but no material advantages. Her long-tottering finances collapsed as a result of her ill-advised involvement, and the vast expenditure it entailed.

In the meantime, however, the fighting on the other side of the world did not change life for the French people, in Paris or in the country. It certainly had no adverse effects on Dr Philippe Curtius's *Salon de Cire* in the Palais Royal. Indeed the flow of visitors was increased by portrait figures of political, naval, and military personalities such as Lafayette,

---

* Marie Grosholtz's portrait of Franklin can be seen in Madame Tussaud's exhibition today.

Admiral D'Estaing who commanded the expeditionary fleet, and Conrad-Alexandre Gérard, the first French ambassador to America.

Marie, working hard in studio and exhibition, hearing news, rumours, and gossip as her uncle entertained in his private rooms, could have had no suspicion that an extraordinary change in her life was imminent. For the next eight years she would have little contact with Curtius's liberal-minded guests, nor the political discussions and debates to which she had for so long listened intently, if unobtrusively: she was to go and live amongst royalty and the aristocracy at Versailles.

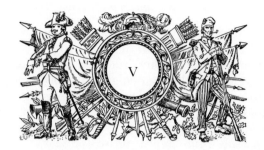

The King's Sister

THE figure behind this complete *bouleversement* in Marie Grosholtz's life was, of all unlikely persons, the King's sister, Madame Elisabeth.

The Princess was three years younger than Marie, who would reach her nineteenth birthday at the end of 1780. Madame Elisabeth's three older brothers were Louis XVI, the Comte de Provence (later Louis XVIII), and the Comte d'Artois (later Charles X). She also had an older sister, Madame Clotilde. These five royal children had been orphaned by the premature deaths of King Louis XV's son, the Dauphin, and his daughter-in-law, Maria Josepha, who both succumbed to a severe illness, possibly measles, when Elisabeth was still a small child.

When the children's grandmother, Queen Marie Leczinska, died in 1768, the two little girls were put under the care of the Comtesse de Marsan, Governess to the Children of France. Clotilde had a happy, equable nature, but Elisabeth was a proud, passionate and obstinate child.

It was the governess's assistant, Madame Mackau, who helped the younger princess to conquer these faults. Madame Mackau herself had been educated at St Cyr. This famous girls' school owed its foundation to Madame de Maintenon, Louis XIV's last mistress (and possibly morganatic wife). She was pious and high-minded in spite of her rôle as mistress, which she reluctantly undertook under pressure from her religious mentors, who felt she could save the King from possible further debauches.

Under Madame Mackau's kind, but extremely firm, guidance according to the strict rules learnt at St Cyr, Madame Elisabeth gradually became pious and high-principled too. She was always devoted to her brothers, and inseparable from her sister Clotilde.

It was, therefore, a terrible blow to Elisabeth when, in 1775, the sister to whom she was so close was betrothed to the King of Sardinia, and had to prepare to leave for her new country soon after the coronation of Louis XVI and Marie Antoinette.

The new Queen was fond of her little sister-in-law, and described in a letter to her mother how the poor child had turned faint and suffered a severe nervous attack when the moment of parting came. Madame Clotilde's equable temperament, on the other hand, enabled her to accept calmly the inevitable fate of princesses, marriage to a foreign royal and departure from family and native land.

Three years later, in 1778, the year in which Marie Grosholtz modelled her portrait of Voltaire, Madame Elisabeth 'came out'. Her education was considered complete and she must take her place as a grown-up member of the royal family of France.

A quiet girl, Madame Elisabeth did not enjoy the ceremonies and gaieties of the Court, in which she now had to participate. She continued to study seriously, and her artistic gifts found expression in needlework and embroidery, which she executed with an almost professional skill. It was time for such a princess to marry, but when negotiations for three possible prospective husbands broke down, for a variety of political reasons, Elisabeth showed no regret, although, submissive, she had not raised objections to any of the suitors.

The Court atmosphere of constant rivalry, deception, intrigue, envy, and search for pleasure and profit, was obviously distasteful to Madame Elisabeth, who was sensible and prudent in her behaviour. It was probably these factors, together with a decision that some of her ladies would transfer to the household of the royal baby the Queen was now expecting, that led Louis XVI to grant his sister, who was fifteen, her own separate establishment with her own suite of apartments at Versailles. Madame Elisabeth was happy with her new independence.

About 1780 the Princess decided she wished to expand her artistic talents, and chose to learn how to model in wax. It was a fashionable art form, which included the modelling of fruit and flowers, and, for the pious who had afflicted friends, the opportunity to fashion miniature limbs, votive offerings to help cure pain and disablement. She needed an accomplished tutor to teach her this art.

Madame Elisabeth, like many young members of the royal family, had been taken to see the celebrated *Salon de Cire* in the Palais Royal. She had been ceremoniously received by Dr Curtius himself, and introduced to the niece, little older than herself, who was so skilled in the craft.

There happened to be a curious resemblance between the features of the two girls, although Marie was tiny and dark and Princess Elisabeth was plump, fair-haired and blue-eyed. Marie possessed a long nose,

closely resembling the characteristic Bourbon nose that Princess
Elisabeth had inherited. It gave them a kind of 'family likeness' when
they were together. Perhaps because of this, Madame Elisabeth
specially remembered Marie Grosholtz, whose talent she had admired
and whose quiet but assured and intelligent good manners had pleased
her.

It came as a total surprise when Marie was invited to come and live
at Versailles and work as art tutor to the Princess. Of course, such an
invitation could not be refused, though Marie's departure would be a
considerable loss to Curtius. Not only was she doing a good share of the
modelling, but she was competent in the running of the exhibition and
the keeping of accounts.

However she was promised enough free time, and permission, to
come home fairly regularly, and even to undertake some portrait
modelling for her uncle's *Salon*. Marie herself was not greatly awed by
the prospect of serving in a royal household. She had been in contact
with royal persons since her early years, and had heard a great deal of
discussion and argument about them, not always flattering. So, even if
not greatly excited or enthusiastic about the change in her way of life,
Marie took the road to Versailles with few qualms. Unlike the narrow,
twisted thoroughfares of central Paris, it was a fine, wide road,
thronged with carriages and foot passengers travelling to and from the
small town and vast palace of Versailles. This road, which she would
travel many times in the next eight years, was well paved and tree-
lined. At night it was lit by oil lamps with double reflectors slung across
it.

Marie was allotted a room of her own in Madame Elisabeth's suite at
Versailles, and also in the country house that Louis XVI gave to his
sister in 1781. This was the small estate of Montreuil on the outskirts of
Versailles. The house, with a white peristyle, and surrounded by trees
and flowers, was set in a park, and there was a small farm attached. The
Princess was delighted to have such a peaceful home of her own,
although the King insisted that, until she reached the age of twenty-
four, she and her ladies must return to their apartments at the palace to
sleep.

In this comparatively simple household Marie became, as far as their
differing status would allow, a friend of Madame Elisabeth. As well as
being talented and efficient, Marie was naturally agreeable and
amusing. She was also well mannered and discreet. Perhaps the
Princess found in this slightly older girl, though far beneath her in rank,
some substitute for her beloved older sister Clotilde, whose equable
temperament Marie shared.

[33]

There were no heated political or social discussions and debates at Montreuil. Nothing could have been farther removed than the crowded rooms of the *Salon de Cire*, Curtius's argumentative guests, and the noisy bustle of the Palais Royal gardens. Days at Montreuil were spent walking and riding, with hours set aside for reading and study. It was informal. Madame Elisabeth and her ladies dined at the same table when she was at Montreuil. Prayers were said each evening before the Princess and her immediate household left each night for her apartments in the palace.

In spite of the contrast with her former life Marie did not grow bored. Madame Elisabeth's family and friends visited her at Montreuill, though the entertainment was never elaborate, and there Marie was able to observe the King and Queen far more closely than she could have done at the palace. They frequently spoke to her—the King kindly and serious, the Queen affable, with a grace that Marie could not resist, though she was well aware of the stories about Madame de Polignac and the frivolities that went on at the Petit Trianon.

She tried to put gossip out of her mind, endeavouring to judge the royal family as she saw them, though she did once lose her usual discretion, and slap the Comte de Provence in the face when he took what she regarded as a 'liberty' as they met on a little-used staircase. The Comte de Provence accepted the rebuff amiably, knowing full well that his sister would approve Marie's refusal to be drawn into any sort of familiarity with members of the Court, let alone the royal family. Marie had lived too long in the Palais Royal to be flustered by any such situations.

Soon Marie's duties with Madame Elisabeth grew beyond teaching her how to model in wax. It was quickly apparent to Marie that the pious Princess distributed charity in an over-generous and totally indiscriminate way. Madame Elisabeth had had no contact whatsoever with life beyond the confines of the Court. She was completely incapable of assessing the merits of an appeal. Her heart was moved to pity by any tale of misery, however blatantly false, and her well-known charity and generosity brought plenty of these. Madame Elisabeth's personal purse was often emptied as she showered alms on all who claimed them. Living under Curtius's roof, Marie had never known poverty herself, but she had lived since childhood on the fringe of the worst slums in central Paris and had watched the pickpockets, sharpers, prostitutes, charlatans and quacks who haunted the gardens of the Palais Royal. She was not easily taken in, though all too familiar with the desperate deprivation of the poor. She had been trained in business and accounts by Curtius, and gradually she managed to establish some control over the Princess's haphazard and unbridled charity.

Not all the time could be spent at quiet Montreuil. Madame Elisabeth was the King's sister and as such she was obliged to attend Court, and take her place at ceremonies and festivities. Then, she and her ladies remained in their apartments in the palace, and, as one of her household, Marie had unique opportunities for contact with courtiers and politicians, many of whom wanted their portraits modelled in wax. She was thus able to follow political trends which she had so often heard argued at Curtius's table. She heard, and made her own judgements on, the scandals that spread so rapidly outside the palace gates and further undermined the reputation and popularity of Marie Antoinette, even though the Queen was now showing a growing preference for mock-country pastimes and fêtes in the secluded grounds of the Petit Trianon which she personally supervised with so much enthusiasm and romantic taste.

Marie had not been long in Madame Elisabeth's service before she realised how virulent was the gossip and antagonism that surrounded the Queen, who was always so gracious and affable when she visited her sister-in-law at Montreuil. Though Marie Antoinette had abandoned her incognito forays to Paris in search of diversion, she still wanted a continuous round of pleasure and entertainment, preferably at the Petit Trianon. Here she gathered round her a small circle of intimates to whom she allowed many favours and great freedom of behaviour. Naturally this aroused envy and malice in those courtiers who were excluded from the circle.

The Queen's dignity was diminished when talk circulated that at Trianon nobody even stood up when the Queen entered a salon. The ladies, dressed in muslin with gauze fichus, continued chatting, embroidering or playing cards and trivial games, attended by gentlemen in informal attire.

The scandalous stories that hitherto Marie had heard only at secondhand, around her uncle's dinner table, now buzzed directly in her ears. Madame Elisabeth was completely deaf to gossip, and Marie found it hard to believe that the Queen's morality was so frail and could be questioned so openly.

Certainly Marie Antoinette sometimes acted in a way that seemed to Marie incredibly foolish. In May 1780 her closest friend, her 'dear heart' the Comtesse de Polignac, married off her daughter in great style, and then herself gave birth to a son.

Even though her husband, Comte Jules, had been out of the country for about a year, this event might not have aroused a great deal of comment. The Comtesse was commonly reputed to have a lover, M. Vaudreuil, who was also a member of the Queen's circle.

However, the Queen had taken the extraordinary action of moving her small personal court to the Château de la Muette, just outside Paris, where Madame de Polignac was to lie-in. There Marie Antoinette closeted herself in her friend's bedchamber.

When the birth was safely over, she took the even more indiscreet step of raising Madame de Polignac to the rank of duchess. Not only did the Queen give her a large present of money to accompany the new title, but she also favoured M. Vaudreuil with a substantial cash gift.

To Marie it was small wonder that slanderous tongues began asking whether it was not the Queen herself who had been delivered of the child at la Muette, sired by one of the numerous lovers she was whispered to entertain at the Petit Trianon. Was the new Duchesse de Polignac being rewarded for shielding her royal mistress, and M. Vaudreuil for keeping silent; or was the gentleman himself perhaps one of Marie Antoinette's lovers, as well as being the lover of Madame de Polignac?

The following year all entertainment at Court stopped and everyone, including Marie, had to go into deep mourning, for the Queen's mother died. Marie Antoinette was plunged in grief. It was reported that the Empress, on her deathbed, had blessed each one of her children by name. When she pronounced 'Marie Antoinette, Queen of France', the dying woman burst into terrible sobs.

Altogether it was an unhappy year. The Court was perpetually shadowed by the country's ever-worsening financial state. Though Louis XVI had declared 'I want to bring economy to every part of my household', nobody listened, and the King was too lethargic and ineffectual to put his words into action. Marie Antoinette intensely disliked the Controller-General, Necker, because of his insistence that retrenchments must be made, now that France's contribution to the American war was draining the Treasury even further.

Then Necker created a mighty uproar by publishing his *Compte Rendu*, a document setting out a stark, detailed analysis of France's financial plight. Everyone read it, or knew about it, not only government ministers, politicians and aristocrats, but the people on the streets as well. All Necker got for his efforts was disgrace and dismissal by the King, but among the people he was regarded as a hero, a man who understood their burdens and their miseries and wished to relieve them, though he could do no more than try to introduce the necessary reforms. Told by the King to leave the country, Necker went to his native Switzerland to continue his successful banking career. In due course he would be called back, but too late.

Working in a Royal Household

MARIE's prolonged absences at Versailles caused Curtius a great deal of inconvenience and extra work in the *Salon de Cire*. She was his invaluable and highly trained aide, impossible to replace, yet at the same time he was well aware of the advantages her new position brought him.

Curtius was passionately concerned with the accuracy of the likenesses he created, a concern he had taught Marie to share. In her present situation she was able to make a really close observation of personages at Court, royal or otherwise, whose portraits in wax were likely to attract visitors to the exhibition in the Palais Royal. There the curious could now inspect uncannily lifelike figures of the great and important whose names were being bandied about but who could seldom be looked at in person.

Marie had a room of her own, both at Versailles and Montreuil, where she could make her sketches and record her notes in privacy. Her sharp eyes and photographic memory were put to good use when making drawings from all angles of those she wanted to portray, but who were unwilling to sit for a plaster life-mask to be applied. Every detail of features, hair and stance was reproduced by her pencil. Curtius no longer had to rely on what limited sightings he could get of those who did not pay a visit to his studio. As ministers were appointed in turn by the King, and in turn dismissed as they failed to rectify the country's financial difficulties, so Marie, accepted as Madame Elisabeth's skilled young protégée, was able either to model their portraits from a sitting, or supply Curtius with the information he needed by means of her scrutiny and her pencil. Even the great Dr Benjamin Franklin, America's first envoy to the Court, willingly gave her a sitting before he retired to his native land in 1785. It was an honour to be invited to his quiet Passy residence for the purpose.

It was Marie's connection with the Court, and her opportunities for close observation, that made it possible for Curtius to create, in 1783, his most resoundingly successful tableau, 'The Royal Family at dinner'. By custom the royal family dined in public when at Versailles, where the populace was freely admitted. Any person who was decently dressed, and if male wore a sword (which could be hired) was able to go to Versailles, enter the royal apartments, and watch the King and Queen and members of the royal family as they sat at table and ate.

It was always an occasion that Marie Antoinette detested. She merely picked at the food. Madame Elisabeth also disliked dining in public. However the Princess had a hearty Bourbon appetite, and usually took the precaution of having a meal beforehand, so that she too only toyed with the vast sequence of dishes. The King and his brothers did not seem to mind eating before a staring throng, which pushed and jostled for a better view.

Marie carefully noted all the details of the table and its appointments. She sketched the attitude in which each member of the royal family habitually sat during meals, and any individual mannerisms in eating. It was not surprising that Curtius's new tableau was highly praised in contemporary almanacks, and proved an outstanding attraction for visitors to Paris who could not find time to make a trip to Versailles when the King was in residence and watch the actual spectacle. In the *Salon de Cire* they found a most realistic alternative. The wax Queen was even wearing a dress made by her own dressmaker, Rose Bertin. Where else could ordinary folk view at close hand a *toilette* designed and made by the famous seamstress? It cost Curtius a considerable sum of money, but it was an elegant and flattering tableau which gave no offence at Court.

An opportunity to gaze so closely at this portrait figure of Marie Antoinette did not diminish the people's dislike of their Queen. The few glimpses they got of her in person displeased them. The reaction of a young man, Camille Desmoulins, who a decade later voted in the National Convention for the King's execution, was the one she seemed usually to evoke. He watched the Queen riding in her coach through the streets of Paris, and was struck only by her 'arrogant air and haughty look'.

Marie Antoinette's reputation remained tainted, though it was said that since the birth of Madame Royale she had put a curb on ribald stories being told in her presence. Circulating among the people of Paris were whispers that her brother Joseph, who had paid her a second visit in 1781, and again won popular approbation for his simplicity, voiced disapproval of the 'prevailing licentious tone' of Marie Antoinette's close personal circle of friends.

Marie herself saw a different side of the Queen's nature, gracious and

[38]

affable as she was to Madame Elisabeth's little wax modeller when she happened to notice her in the salons of Montreuil. She knew too that on many occasions Marie Antoinette extended this kindness and graciousness to subjects who were far humbler than she. For example, when the Court was at Versailles and a royal birthday occurred, it was the custom of the fishwives of Paris to march all the way to the palace with offerings of flowers.

Some twenty of these women would be admitted to the Queen's presence, and she thanked them in the most simple and charming manner. The fishwives' leader, Madame Beaupré, could not actually be described as 'humble' in spite of her lowly status. She was reputed to be the richest vendor of fish in the market, and came to Court gaily dressed and adorned with jewellery. Madame Beaupré was much admired by her less prosperous sisters.

But it was not always easy for Marie, spending most of her time in Madame Elisabeth's household. She needed all the discretion she had learned in order to retain her position when Curtius embarked on a new venture in 1783. It was fortunate that no talk of the entertainment world ever reached the Princess's ears, and that Marie fitted so unobtrusively into her niche in the household that her close link with Curtius and the *Salon de Cire* in the Palais Royal was scarcely realised.

Curtius's inexhaustible energy, his passion for something new, and his wish to increase the takings of his wax exhibition, led him to consider a new field of activity. What was it, he asked himself, that always drew the biggest crowds in Paris? What attracted people from all walks of life to gather and stare? It was the public punishment of criminals, carried out not in secluded places, but in city squares, and even on street corners.

There were all kinds of minor punishments, of course, but over a hundred offences carried the death penalty. When this was meted out criminals could expect to meet their end in circumstances of great cruelty. While beheading had been out of use for some time, there was much hanging, often in batches and blunderingly performed, and, worst of all, quartering, and breaking on the wheel. The former sentence meant that the prisoner's limbs were attached to four horses which, under the executioner's surveillance, were whipped by specially hired men in different directions. For the latter punishment the felon was spread-eagled on a flat wheel, while the executioner, manipulating the wheel, broke his bones with blows from an iron bar. The comparatively humane guillotine, which at least gave instant death, would not come into use for another decade.

These horrible spectacles drew enormous crowds. The rich came in

[39]

carriages and hired places in windows and on rooftops overlooking the place of execution. Poor people crammed the area, pushing and fighting to get the best possible view.

Curtius decided that if he created a second exhibition, separate from the *Salon de Cire*, containing only portraits in wax of condemned criminals who had met their fate, hundreds of curious visitors would come flocking to its doors. Here, as in the *Salon*, they could gaze at and examine the portraits in detail, and it would not be expensive for Curtius intended to hire a barker, who would shout an invitation to enter for the price of only two *sous*.

This new venture was located away from the Palais Royal. Curtius had already acquired premises at No. 20 Boulevard du Temple, where the new exhibition was launched. This was in the heart of the entertainment area on the ramparts which was growing increasingly popular with upper- and lower-class people alike. The shows on the Boulevard catered for a wide variety of tastes, with theatres, jugglers and acrobats and, later, the famous Astley's Circus which was patronised by the Queen herself.

Curtius's judgement did not fail him. When the new exhibition opened, people fought to get in, while the *Salon de Cire* remained celebrated and popular. Curtius did not wish to move this, in spite of the rebuilding of the Palais Royal which had begun in 1781 and continued for several years. Although the gardens were starting to take on a somewhat disreputable tone, everyone still came there, especially foreign visitors to Paris. As late as 1786 the *Almanack des Voyageurs à Paris* recommended both exhibitions as worth a visit, the famous *Salon* and the abode of wax criminals, named the *Caverne des Grands Voleurs*.

The continuing success of the *Salon de Cire* with its portraits of the meritorious great and famous, made it much easier for Marie not to be associated with the *Caverne des Grands Voleurs* and its felons on the Boulevard du Temple. Indeed, fortunately, no one seemed to connect her with it in any way. It would have been unthinkable for any member, however minor, of Madame Elisabeth's entourage to be involved in taking the likenesses of criminals and murderers, a process which necessitated 'arrangements' with gaolers and executioners, according to whether the plaster mask was applied to the appropriate face before or after death.

The Palais Royal exhibition always had a dignified atmosphere, though, as well as royalty and politicians, generals and admirals, there were portrait figures of much less important persons who caught the public attention, such as 'Le Géant', the huge figure of a man much talked about because of his exceptional height and girth.

Marie could visit the *Salon de Cire* and the family apartment with impunity when she was not required by Madame Elisabeth. Here she still heard news of her uncle's liberal-minded friends and connections. And here, in central Paris, she was also made aware of a changing attitude among the deprived working classes. Through street-corner orators, dissemination of pamphlets, broadsheets, street songs, and common talk, these people, living in poverty, often hungry and miserable, were gaining a new sense of their identity. With it went an increasing hostility towards the absolute monarchy, which brought them only squalor, high bread prices, food shortages and tax burdens, from which the nobility, aristocracy and the clergy were entirely free.

The Great Scandal

NO contemporary Queen in Europe except Marie Antoinette of
France could have found herself embroiled in such a bizarre and
damaging affair as the scandal of the diamond necklace, for no other
Queen had earned herself such a widespread reputation for light
conduct, extravagance, imprudence and an excessive love of diamonds.

Marie Grosholtz could scarcely credit the story when it became
public. Apart from her contacts with the Queen, she was acquainted
with two of the other people concerned. She had scant respect for either,
and could never force herself to believe that Marie Antoinette was
guilty of such an intrigue.

The whole business began in 1784, when Böhmer, the Court jeweller,
approached the Queen in the confident hope that she would buy a
magnificent diamond necklace he had created. He had spent years, and
a fortune, in collecting the gems for this *chef d'oeuvre*. It was an extremely
showy ornament, with festoons, drops and tassels of diamonds depend-
ing from a collar of exceptionally large stones. The necklace contained
more than six hundred and forty fine diamonds, and its value was
estimated at 1,600,000 gold *livres*.

To Böhmer's dismay, Marie Antoinette refused to purchase this
glittering array of her favourite stones. However tempted, she did not
have enough money in her personal purse, and dared not approach
the King. On several previous occasions she had incurred his anger
when he had to find the money to purchase jewellery she could not
pay for.

The jeweller had to take his necklace away, acutely distressed and
embarrassed. He himself was heavily in debt, largely through his
investment in these stones, and his creditors were pressing. He had
been certain the Queen would be unable to resist such a splendid
addition to her collection, but her refusal was adamant.

Böhmer knew it would be almost impossible to find another client
who would purchase this costly ornament. As for the Queen, she did

not even mention the matter to the King. There were other things to occupy her attention.

In March 1785 she gave birth to a second son, the long-awaited Dauphin being nearly three years old. What celebrations there had been on that happy occasion, what popular acclaim! This time there had, of course, been rejoicings too, but when, two months later, Marie Antoinette made a state visit to Paris, she was indignant and outraged by the frigid reception she got from the people.

This ceremonial visit so ill-received even aroused international comment. The Queen's Swedish admirer, Axel Fersen, now returned from his service in the American War of Independence, was a witness. Sadly he wrote to his monarch, King Gustave, that Marie Antoinette had been greeted by 'complete silence' on the part of her Parisian subjects.

When she got back to Versailles, the Queen retired to her apartments and wept, possibly realising for the first time the immense gulf between herself and the people, though she was still unable to comprehend the reasons for their hostility.

Her concern, however, was short-lived, as she busied herself with plans and rehearsals for a production of *The Barber of Seville* to be acted in the Trianon theatre by her troupe of relatives and friends. She herself would perform the leading part of Rosina. She admired the witty play, though she knew the King detested its author Beaumarchais who, he said, was only interested in undermining, through his writings, the authority and dignity of the nobility.

Meanwhile the jeweller Böhmer was frantically trying to find some way of getting the Queen to buy his necklace. He consulted an attorney friend, who put him in touch with a Comtesse de la Motte Valois. This lady claimed descent from the former Valois kings of France and was the recipient of a small royal pension. She was not, however, received at Court and was not known there.

This did not prevent Madame de la Motte Valois convincing the jeweller that she was always in attendance at Versailles and was one of the Queen's confidantes. She told Böhmer that she knew that Marie Antoinette coveted the necklace, and suggested that she might purchase it through an intermediary. The intermediary might be none other than the great Cardinal Rohan.

How could a cardinal be suggested for such a rôle? In view of Rohan's history and reputation it was not so far-fetched a notion as might first appear. The cardinal concerned had been born Prince Louis de Rohan, scion of a large and powerful feudal family, whose members held a variety of influential positions at Court. Prince Louis, however, embraced the clerical life in spite of his reputation as a dissolute and womanising young man. He was appointed to assist his uncle, the Bishop of Strasbourg, a provincial position that was not pleasing to an ambitious young priest of excellent family and many parts.

He was delighted when, in 1772, Louis XV sent him as Ambassador to Vienna. Here Louis de Rohan and his staff proved effective at gathering political information useful to France, but his lifestyle, and in particular his conquests of women, both high- and low-born, incurred the severe displeasure of the Empress Maria Theresa. She was outraged at his disregard of his priestly calling. When it came to her ears that he was spreading slanderous stories about her daughter Marie Antoinette, she was furious, and repeatedly expressed her wish that Louis de Rohan should be removed from Vienna.

Louis XV took no notice of these accusations against his Ambassador, who was supported by both his numerous family at Court, and his own diplomatic ability and usefulness. But when Louis XV died and Marie Antoinette became Queen, one of her first actions was to persuade her husband to recall the Ambassador so hated by her mother, and so disparaging to herself.

She got her way. When Louis de Rohan came back to France for the coronation in 1774, he was coldly told by Louis XVI that he would not be returning to Vienna. Later on an appointment might be found for him, but for the moment he would return to his clerical duties in the bishopric of Strasbourg. The Queen refused to see—let alone speak to—him before his departure to his uncle's provincial see.

This virtual disgrace angered the powerful de Rohan family. One of them had obtained a promise in writing from Louis XV, before he became ill and died, that Louis de Rohan should be appointed Grand Almoner of France when the present ageing incumbent died.

When this happened, and the office became vacant, Madame de Marsan, former Governess of the Children of France, and an aunt of Louis de Rohan, presented this document to Louis XVI, and insisted that he should uphold his grandfather's written promise.

The office of Grand Almoner carried with it power and rich emoluments. Marie Antoinette raged in vain against an appointment that would bring the hated cleric back to Versailles, and equally in vain when he received a cardinal's hat on the death of an aged French prelate. All she could do was obstinately to refuse to receive, speak to, or even set eyes on, if she could avoid it, the new Cardinal Rohan, Grand Almoner of France.

Cardinal Rohan's ambitions were not yet satisfied, and he realised that the Queen's antagonism was blocking his path. Somehow he must overcome it. As time passed the desire to reinstate himself in Marie Antoinette's favour became an undisguised obsession. Of course he denied that he had ever spoken disparagingly about her in Vienna, and he was received by other members of the royal family.

Urbane and witty, Cardinal Rohan was a frequent visitor to Madame Elisabeth's retreat at Montreuil. Marie often encountered him there and though she acknowledged his charm and courtesy, she had too much experience of the world not to recognise an ambitious man when she saw one. But even her gentle sister-in-law's friendship with the Cardinal could not soften the Queen's hostility.

All this being common knowledge, it did not seem ridiculous to jeweller Böhmer that the Queen might consider using Cardinal Rohan as an intermediary to effect a purchase of jewellery that she could not afford and the King would not approve. The Cardinal was wealthy, and would do anything to get back into Marie Antoinette's favour. Madame de la Motte, intimate of the Queen as Böhmer thought, could approach the Cardinal on her royal mistress's behalf.

It did not prove difficult for Madame de la Motte to involve Cardinal Rohan. He was completely isolated from Marie Antoinette's personal circle and knew only a few of the ladies who enjoyed her confidence. When Madame de la Motte brought him the first of a series of notes in what he believed was the Queen's own hand, and signed 'Marie Antoinette' he was delighted and wrote passionately grateful replies.

Only once during the drawn-out negotiations did the Cardinal's confidence waver. He could not understand, he told Madame de la Motte, why the Queen, when she wrote to him so graciously, gave not the slightest sign of recognising him in public. Madame de la Motte promised to tell the Queen of his great wish for some sign from her. In due course the lady informed him that Marie Antoinette felt it might arouse some inconvenient comment about their new relationship if she acknowledged him publicly, but she would meet him after dark in one of the groves of Versailles' park for a brief rendezvous. Then she would give him a token of her friendship and gratitude.

The Cardinal, whose common sense had clearly deserted him in his joy at apparently becoming on good terms with the Queen, was only too eager to comply. It was easy for Madame de la Motte and her equally unscrupulous husband to arrange such a rendezvous. The palace gardens were open to all, and the Queen's pleasure in taking late-night strolls in the fresh air well known. All the conspiring couple had to do was to find a suitable young woman to impersonate Marie Antoinette, and they already knew of one.

As Curtius and Marie realised, the Palais Royal gardens were becoming increasingly disreputable, and frequented by many prostitutes. There was one such girl they both knew by sight and remarked on because, in profile in particular, she had a remarkable likeness to the Queen, and there was a similarity of height and figure. If not seeking a client immediately, this girl often strolled or sat in the gardens accompanied by her landlady's little boy.

Madame de la Motte, who often promenaded in the gardens herself, had also noticed this girl, and knew her name—Leguay d'Oliva. She was a simple soul, and easily persuaded by the richly dressed lady who approached her to play a part in a charade—for good payment, of course.

On the night arranged with the Cardinal, Mademoiselle d'Oliva, cloaked and with her head swathed in a lace shawl, was stationed in a dark grove not too far from the palace at Versailles. A rose was placed in her hand, and she was told to hand it to the gentleman who would approach her.

It was too dark to see any features. When the Cardinal, dressed in ordinary attire, and taken to the rendezvous by Madame de la Motte, came towards Mademoiselle d'Oliva, and bowed deeply, she handed over the flower as instructed, a gift that seemed to be received with great emotion. Then she quickly turned away into the trees as she had been bidden. Cardinal Rohan was convinced that he had, indeed, had a brief encounter with the Queen for, though he could not recognise the features in the dark, the figure of the cloaked lady resembled that of Marie Antoinette.

The negotiations about the diamond necklace could now be completed. The relieved Böhmer drew up a contract. Payment for the jewels would be made by instalments. After Cardinal Rohan had read the document, Madame de la Motte took it, saying that it must be approved by the Queen before the necklace was handed over.

She brought it back to Cardinal Rohan with each clause signed 'Marie Antoinette de France'. All was now in order for the delivery of the necklace, which, said Madame de la Motte, would be effected in a house she owned in Versailles. There the Cardinal himself could hand it over to a special messenger sent by the Queen.

The Cardinal, incognito and again dressed in non-clerical garb, drove to the house in Versailles indicated by Madame de la Motte, carrying the necklace in its great velvet-lined case. Not letting it out of his hands, he was received by Madame de la Motte. They waited a short time in the luxuriously furnished salon. The door opened, and a man dressed in black stood there silently. 'This is the Queen's personal messenger', said Madame de la Motte. 'Hand him the case.' The Cardinal obeyed and the man departed, still silent.

Cardinal Rohan drove back to Paris, content that Marie Antoinette had achieved her desire and that the brilliant ornament was safely lodged in her personal jewellery collection. In fact, Böhmer's *chef d'oeuvre* was never seen again. Madame de la Motte's husband took it straight to England, where it was broken up and the stones sold.

Marie Antoinette herself, fully occupied with her theatricals and pleasures, had no inkling of what was brewing up. She had not given a thought to the diamond necklace, nor to Böhmer's distress when she did not buy it. It was only recalled to her on the baptism of her second son in the early summer.

Indulgent as ever to his wife's tastes, Louis XVI had ordered from Böhmer a buckle and a shoulder ornament in diamonds as a gift to mark the occasion. The court jeweller arrived in person to hand the jewels to the Queen and, as he left, he gave her a folded piece of paper, a note. Marie Antoinette was surprised, but when he had left the room she read the letter. She could make no sense of the rigmarole it contained—something about the jeweller's great joy over 'arrangements proposed' by which the Queen would obtain the diamond necklace he had offered her.

Marie Antoinette showed the letter to Madame Campan, one of her ladies in whom she had great confidence, and asked her if she could make out what the jeweller was talking about. Madame Campan said it made no sense to her either. The Queen asked Madame Campan to see if Böhmer was still in the palace and, if so, to bring him back to her. He could not be found.

Marie Antoinette, with her usual heedless lack of thought, simply held the letter in a candle-flame and burned it. She was not interested. Had she taken the letter to the King, or asked the advice of a responsible person, she would have been saved dire trouble. But she forgot it and turned back to the rehearsals for *The Barber of Seville*.

Cardinal Rohan retained the contract that Madame de la Motte had brought back to him with its clauses supposedly signed by the Queen. When the money for the first instalment was sent him, he would pass it on to the jeweller. However, shortly before the date on which the first payment was due Madame de la Motte, on the point of leaving Paris for the country, brought the Cardinal another letter signed 'Marie Antoinette', asking for a short postponement of the first instalment due.

When Cardinal Rohan took this note to Böhmer, the jeweller was much disturbed, for he was in urgent need of the money. The Cardinal made him a small payment as interest on the sum due, but could do no more. He himself was severely financially embarrassed. In spite of his valuable appointments, he had been forced to sell some of his estates to raise cash and keep his creditors quiet.

Time passed and there was still no sign of payment. Madame de la Motte had left Paris. In despair, Böhmer decided to talk to Madame Campan, with whom he was quite well acquainted, and ask her to put his plight to the Queen. When Madame Campan expressed bafflement at this peculiar request, the jeweller broke down and poured into her thunderstruck ears the whole story, including Cardinal Rohan's secret rendezvous with, as he believed, Marie Antoinette, in the dark grove at Versailles.

There was nothing Madame Campan could do but repeat this extraordinary tale she had heard from Böhmer to her royal mistress. Marie Antoinette denied any knowledge of such a business. She was particularly outraged that Cardinal Rohan, who she detested and would not even glance at, claimed he had met her at night in the gardens. Urged by Madame Campan, she realised that the King must be called in to investigate the affair.

Louis XVI's immediate action was to send for Cardinal Rohan, who arrived in his scarlet silk clerical garb. The King accused him of using the Queen's name in order to steal the diamond necklace from Böhmer, so that he could sell the gems and relieve his financial difficulties. Cardinal Rohan insisted vehemently that he had acted solely to meet the Queen's wishes and instructions, and give her the pleasure of obtaining the necklace she coveted.

To support his claim he produced the contract drawn up by Böhmer, and with each clause approved by the signature 'Marie Antoinette de France'. The Queen was astounded. 'That is not my signature,' she cried, 'I have never signed myself "Marie Antoinette de France".'

The King would have been well advised to go no further, to settle Böhmer's account in spite of the appalling state of the Treasury, and cover up the whole affair while issuing a *lettre de cachet*, which required no reason to be given, for the arrest and imprisonment of Madame de la Motte.

Instead, he accused Cardinal Rohan of forging Marie Antoinette's signature, and ordered his immediate arrest. This order was issued in public before all those assembled at Court. It was a bombshell. The Grand Almoner of France, Cardinal and member of the powerful de Rohan family, charged with forgery and the theft of a diamond necklace—it was unbelievable.

Cardinal Rohan, though bewildered at the turn of events, realised only too clearly that he had been duped, hideously duped, blinded by his obsessional desire for Marie Antoinette's good graces. Before he was led away he managed to get a note to his confidential secretary, telling him to burn immediately papers he would find in the 'red portfolio'. These were the little notes signed 'Marie Antoinette' that had landed him in this terrible predicament.

Madame de la Motte was arrested at her luxurious country house. She already knew what had happened, and she too had done some burning—the passionately grateful letters Cardinal Rohan had written to the Queen in reply to the forged letters she had carried to him throughout the affair. Madame de la Motte was clapped into the Bastille, like the Cardinal, and complicated matters by accusing as the instigator of the plot a so-called alchemist, a charlatan known as Cagliostro.

This extraordinary man was celebrated in Paris for his wild and widely spread claims that he was two thousand years old and had the elixir of life. He was no reclusive sage, but lived in fine style with a beautiful and striking young wife, and mingled in high society.

There were lengthy interrogations and preparation of written defences, Madame de la Motte sticking to her story that she had acted as go-between on the Queen's personal instructions, indeed commands. It was not until May 1786 that the case was brought to judgement before the *parlement* of Paris, sitting without princes of the blood or peers.

Cardinal Rohan had spent the intervening period in the Bastille, a prisoner but living in a considerable degree of comfort in the lodging allotted to him, always wearing his cardinal's robes, his only physical ordeal being an attack of food poisoning from food cooked in verdigrised pots. This left him pale, weak and trembling, so that when he appeared before his judges he was permitted to sit.

By twenty-six votes to twenty-two Cardinal Rohan was finally acquitted, 'discharged from every species of allegation'. A crowd of ten thousand people were waiting to cheer him after the verdict, which was regarded by the people of Paris as a humiliation for their hated Queen.

Gossip averred that Marie Antoinette had been involved from the start, that the Cardinal was one of her secret lovers, and that even her brother, Joseph of Austria, and her brothers-in-law, the Comte de Provence and the Comte d'Artois, were openly far from certain of her innocence.

Madame de la Motte was convicted, branded and imprisoned, but not subdued. Ten months later she escaped and fled to join her husband, Comte de la Motte, in London. People said that the Queen had arranged her escape because the Comte was threatening to publish letters that proved his wife's intimacy with Marie Antoinette, and proved moreover that, as with the Duchesse de Polignac, the friendship of the two ladies exceeded the bounds of normality.

Madame Elisabeth naturally found the whole affair shocking, upsetting and distasteful. As a member of her household, hearing Court gossip and talk at her uncle's table at the Palais Royal, Marie found silence her best policy. But, although she did not find much to admire in the Queen, beyond her charm, and deplored—though only to herself—Marie Antoinette's apparently reckless lack of sense and discretion, she always maintained in later life that she could never believe the Queen guilty of involvement in the sordid tangle.

No one gave further thought to the wretched jeweller, Böhmer, who was ruined, his *chef d'oeuvre* stolen, broken up and dispersed, his debts unpaid.

Marie Leaves Royal Service

MARIE Antoinette was much distressed and angered at Cardinal Rohan's acquittal. 'Come weep with me and console your friend . . . come to me, dear heart!,' she wrote to the woman closest to her, the Duchesse de Polignac.

At the same time the Queen was glad that the affair of the diamond necklace was, as she believed, over and done with. She could now get on with putting the finishing touches to her new diversion, her *Hameau* ('Hamlet'), which was located in the park at Versailles not far from the Petit Trianon and on which work was now virtually completed.

The *Hameau* was a miniature farm, with rustic buildings including a cow-shed, a dairy, and a little house where Marie Antoinette, now advanced in her fourth pregnancy, could repose and drink milk freshly drawn from her own cows.

For sojourns at the *Hameau* the Queen and her ladies dressed in expensively simple cotton and muslin 'milkmaid' dresses. They escaped to a fantasy rural life, learning to milk scrubbed and docile cows into porcelain buckets embossed with flowers and the Queen's cipher. They herded spotless, combed and ribboned sheep, and collected eggs laid by pretty hens. A farmer and his wife, helped by a considerable staff, took care of this establishment, where Marie Antoinette delighted to picnic in rustic simplicity.

Marie Grosholtz sometimes had to visit the *Hameau* with Madame Elisabeth. The Princess was charmed with the place, but Marie had little use for this 'folly'. City-bred, and trained to work hard, she felt no enthusiasm for bucolic frolics. Moreover, the miniature farm was expensive to maintain, and Marie was well aware of public talk that the Queen had overspent her dress budget by more than 150,000 *livres*. In spite of their simplicity, the 'milkmaid' outfits cost a considerable sum of money, and even more costly were the enormous bonnets, designed and made by Rose Bertin, that topped them. People scoffed that this headgear was more suitable for hanging outside milliner's

[51]

shops than decorating the heads of Queen and Court ladies.

Marie Antoinette deluded herself when she believed that the acquittal of Cardinal Rohan was the end of the diamond necklace affair and the ensuing scandal. The *parlement* may have found him not guilty, and given him back his full liberty, but the King punished him. Louis, deeply upset over the business, vented his anger by dismissing Cardinal Rohan from his post as Grand Almoner of France and ordering him to retire and lead a reclusive life at the Abbey of Chaise Dieu.

This unprecedented disgrace aroused a storm. The powerful de Rohan family was furious. The Comtesse de Marsan, former Governess to the Children of France, even went so far as to prostrate herself in public at the Queen's feet to plead for her nephew. She received a cold, negative rejoinder. The people of Paris, who had hailed the Cardinal's release, were also angered at his dismissal and banishment to a remote Abbey. A vulgar pun circulated in the streets:

> Le Parlement l'a purgé
> Le Roi a l'envoyé à la Chaise.

> (The *Parlement* has purged him
> The King has sent him to the close-stool.)

The King also took action against the charlatan alchemist, Cagliostro, who had been accused by Madame de la Motte of instigating the theft of the necklace. He too had been cleared and released. He was a well-known and popular figure, even if a probable rogue. Cagliostro was ordered by the King to quit France immediately—bag, baggage, and wife.

There was not much popular goodwill when Marie Antoinette gave birth to her fourth child, Princess Sophie, in spite of the usual free distribution of wine from the fountains of Paris. Then a crisis broke. Colonne, the latest Minister appointed by the King to try to put some order into the country's finances, suddenly gave up the useless struggle. He threw open his accounts to the princes of the blood, the nobility, the aristocracy, and the magistrates of the Paris and provincial *parlements*.

Now all France knew what the royal family, the Court, and the fifteen thousand or so retainers serving them at Versailles, were costing those who toiled and staggered under the burden of taxation.

The deficit was enormous, the Treasury bankrupt and, as Marie was to recall in her *Memoirs*, 'The peasantry were in the last stages of deprivation and misery, due to taxes and poor harvests.'

The fury of the people concentrated on the Queen. They dismissed other factors, such as the huge cost to France of the American War in which she had participated regardless of the depleted Treasury. Marie Antoinette was blamed for it all. A magistrate called Turelle voiced the hatred that boiled up against 'the Austrian woman' who had 'squandered the finances of France, provided by the toil of the people, on her irregular pleasures'.

Someone coined the nickname 'Madame Déficit', a nickname that stuck and was bandied about the streets all over France. An effigy of the Duchesse de Polignac was rolled in the gutters of Paris. Henceforward the Queen would be, in the eyes of her subjects, the main, if not the sole, source of France's evils.

In this atmosphere of disaster Curtius took the decision to move the *Salon de Cire* out of the Palais Royal, and instal it in the spacious premises he already owned, No. 20 Boulevard du Temple. The chamber of criminals, the *Caverne des Grands Voleurs*, had been in this location for three years, and was bringing in excellent takings. There were plenty of other rooms to accommodate the prestigious *Salon* as a separate exhibition.

He was influenced by the fact that the character of the Palais Royal gardens had gradually changed. Now, as well as being increasingly the haunt of prostitutes and con-men, they had become a 'Speaker's Corner'. Where once quiet groups of men had sat beneath the trees discussing the news, and fashionable ladies had promenaded and chatted, now frenzied orators climbed on boxes and tables and harangued audiences on Liberty and the appalling state of the poor.

Curtius himself had prospered, with his collection of wax portrait figures attracting plenty of interested visitors, but he was all too well aware of the current political atmosphere. His old medical friend Marat, for example, had abandoned his appointment as physician to the Comte d'Artois' personal guard, and was devoting his furious energies to pamphlet writing and the launching of his anti-royalist newspaper, *L'Ami du Peuple (the People's Friend)*. Marat frequently had to go into hiding to escape arrest, several times concealing himself in Curtius's apartment, and even on occasion taking refuge in the sewers. Marie always knew, uneasily, when he was hiding with her uncle.

Pleasure-seekers from all walks of life were turning their backs on the Palais Royal and making their way to the entertainments offered along the tree-lined Boulevard du Temple. Curtius's large house there was easily accessible to his dinner-table cronies, who still included the 'anti-royal' Duc d'Orléans, and General Lafayette whose experience in the American War had both stimulated and made more practical his ideals of freedom. Curtius now owned a second house in the vicinity. In 1785 he had acquired a plot of land in the Rue des Fossés du Temple, for which he was paying by instalments. He had built a house on it, not for his own use but to rent as an additional source of income. It was already let and bringing in a good return.

Curtius's move proved a success. The prevailing climate of crisis did not prevent large numbers of people seeking amusement, and his always up-to-date collection of wax figures, whether depicting the great or the criminal, was more popular than ever. There were always enough people with money to spend on diversion in the Boulevard du Temple, even if the nation's finances were in disastrous disarray.

The new address of the *Salon de Cire* made little difference to Marie. Madame Elisabeth showed no signs of wishing to dispense with her services. In spite of the disquiet which invaded even the peaceful household at Montreuil, Madame Elisabeth did not alter the routine of her life. She continued to pursue her artistic hobbies which Marie supervised and guided. From time to time she was called on to fulfil a special commission, either for some notable at Court who desired to sit for a wax portrait, or occasionally actually by royal command. One such important piece of work came her way in 1787, when an embassy sent by Tippoo Sahib, the Sultan of Mysore in India, arrived at Versailles seeking audience with the King.

Three years earlier Tippoo had signed a peace treaty with the English, whose sphere of control in India was steadily increasing. That did not prevent him hoping to stir up more trouble in India between the English East India Company and the French, whose rival trading company always presented a dangerous threat. There had been open hostilities between the two during the recent American War. Since then they had been more or less at peace.

Before the Mysore embassy went to Versailles their sightseeing included a visit to Curtius's *Salon de Cire*, where they were greatly intrigued by the portrait figures. This came to the ears of the King and Queen, who decided it would be diverting to play a trick on their Eastern visitors.

When the Mysore ambassadors were finally received at Versailles, they entered a salon with what they took to be a number of richly dressed, full-size, wax models, standing motionless in glass cases. Louis and Marie Antoinette were highly amused at the astonishment of their visitors when the supposed wax figures suddenly came to life and stepped out of their cases to be introduced as members of the Court.

Marie did not find this kind of practical joke particularly entertaining, but she was pleased and flattered at being commanded to make life-size portraits in wax of the ministers in the embassy and their attendants. She was requested to dress them in exact copies of their exotic and colourful Eastern garb. When she had completed the group, she set it up under a striped tent in the Petit Trianon gardens to divert courtiers and invited friends.

It was being a difficult year, and Curtius, ever more engrossed in political matters, watched events closely. After the Controller-General Calonne's revelations about the terrible state of France's finances, the King was pressed to take some action. On Calonne's advice he convoked what was called the Assembly of Notables. This proved to be a useless body, composed entirely of members of the nobility and opposed to tax reforms or any relaxation of the present autocratic form of government. The Notables dismissed Calonne and refused to take any action to remedy the situation.

Heavy rains and floods increased the misery of the peasantry, and damaged the harvest. The Court went into mourning for the baby Princess Sophie, who died at eleven months old from lung disease. This cut down the customary round of festivities and balls at Versailles, and the King did introduce some economies in the royal household which greatly annoyed Marie Antoinette. Several of the Queen's favourites thereby lost lucrative appointments, since some functions in the household were abolished or merged. For example, the hitherto separate functions of the Master of the Great Stables and the Master of the Little Stables were combined. Courtiers who were deprived of such profitable positions, which involved little work, complained bitterly. 'One is not sure of possessing on one day what one had the day before', they moaned.

No one at Versailles appeared really to appreciate the peril of their situation, it seemed to Marie, as she pursued her duties with Madame Elisabeth. Outside Versailles there were increasingly hostile mutterings that the Queen was interfering more and more in political matters, and influencing the King against remedial action and reforms. The *parlement* of Paris, shocked by what it had learned from Calonne's account-books, demanded that the States General should be convened. The King refused, and was so angry that he exiled the *parlement*, saying that in future it must sit at provincial Troyes, not in Paris.

The States General, which the *parlement* of Paris demanded, had its origins in the fourteenth century when the then King of France, Philip the Fair, called for consultation over his country's troubled affairs. Representatives were drawn from the nobility, the clergy, and provincial citizens. These three Estates remained throughout the centuries as separate bodies. Their function was purely a passive one, to listen and to give approval to measures proposed by the monarch.

Even with this limited purpose, the States General did not sit permanently, or at regular intervals. It was only called together at the King's will. When the *parlement* of Paris decided it was time the States General should be convened, it had not sat for more than a hundred and fifty years. New deputies would have to be elected from all over France to represent the three Estates.

Louis XVI vacillated. Axel Fersen, the Swedish officer who was still reputed to be the Queen's lover, and to have secret *rendezvous* with her in the park at Versailles, wrote to his King, Gustave, on the subject of Marie Antoinette's alleged continual meddling in matters of State of which she had no understanding. He described Louis as 'weak and suspicious'.

All over France throughout the year 1788 the cry for the States General swelled, with a demand that the Swiss banker Necker, still regarded by the people as their champion, should be recalled to take over the management of the country's finances. Calonne had been followed by a succession of ineffectual Controllers-General appointed by the King. Sporadic rioting in Paris and the provinces expressed popular dissatisfaction.

It was not until August 1788 that Louis XVI finally reached a decision. He recalled Necker from Switzerland, and promised the States General would be called the following year. When the people of Paris learned, on New Year's Day 1789, that in the new States General the number of citizen deputies in the Third Estate would equal the number of those in the other two Estates put together, there was rejoicing, and people illumined their houses as a sign of their joy.

In spite of the troubled year that had passed, the festivities at Court at the end of 1788 were considered as brilliant as they ever had been. The municipality of Versailles presented the King with the customary gift of silver coins. There were entertainments and balls which some said must challenge the celebrated festivities that had taken place at the Court of the Sun King, Louis XIV. But it was bitterly cold, and the poor suffered.

After a poor harvest, the winter was the worst for many years. Marie Grosholtz's journeys between Versailles and the Boulevard du Temple were freezing. In Versailles, at the turn of the year, the windows were covered with thick ice, and the rooms were filled with smoke because there were no dry logs to burn, and the wet ones smouldered.

In the Chapel Royal, mass was shortened as it was so cold. The King and Queen's public dinners were almost unbearable for the ladies who still had to appear in low-cut Court dresses, without wraps. Marie Antoinette did not even pretend to eat at these now. She sat silent through the long succession of dishes.

That bitter winter, with its brilliant Court functions, and the frozen hunger of the poor, was to be the last one that Marie Grosholtz would spend in Madame Elisabeth's household at Versailles and Montreuil.

The Threshold of Revolution

CURTIUS had been for some time increasingly anxious to detach Marie from her service with Madame Elisabeth. He was convinced that a radical change in the government of France was round the corner, and possibly a violent change.

Everyone who watched the political scene knew that the recalled Swiss financier Necker did not believe it possible to reform and re-establish France's finances without some form of constitutional government.

If there was no relaxing of Louis XVI's obtuseness and obstinacy on this matter, with a change of attitude in the advice of those he mistakenly heeded, including Marie Antoinette, the meeting of the newly convened States General in May 1789 would inevitably bring some serious clash.

A number of Curtius's friends, including Marat and Mirabeau, were putting themselves forward as candidates for the Third Estate. Curtius himself, while not aspiring to prominence, was determined, if opportunity came, to play a part in whatever reorganisation came about in his own local district.

Any such activity would mean considerable absences from the *Salon de Cire*. Marie's full-time presence there was absolutely essential. She was twenty-seven years old and fully competent to take charge, if necessary, of the studio and the running of the exhibition. She must be brought home.

It was impossible just to resign from royal service except perhaps on grounds of acute ill-health. Marie, though small and thin, was obviously robust. The only means of securing her release was a petition from Curtius. He could put forward good grounds for making the plea without any hint of being influenced by the difficult times the country was going through.

The premises at No. 20 Boulevard du Temple were much larger than those Curtius's exhibition had occupied at the Palais Royal. More and more people were flocking to the *Salon* (to say nothing of that forerunner of the Chamber of Horrors, the *Caverne des Grands Voleurs*, with its population of executed felons). Madame Elisabeth was too well aware of Marie's abilities and competence to think that he could easily find someone else to assist him. It was reasonable to plead that he was finding his business too much to manage with only irregular, part-time help from his highly skilled pupil.

Marie herself was ready to leave Versailles and Montreuil. She had been attached to the household for eight years and had long ago taught Madame Elisabeth all she was likely to learn about her hobby of wax modelling. The Princess had retained Marie's services for so long because she was useful, discreet, loyal and generally a help, particularly with the distribution of charity.

There was a kind of affection between the two young women, but, apart from the difference in their rank, the contrasts in character and experience of life made a really close bond impossible. Marie admired, as everyone did, Madame Elisabeth's genuine goodness, kindness, and piety, but her unworldliness, resulting from a totally sheltered life from birth, could at times be irritating—even exasperating—for a girl with Marie's background and upbringing.

Madame Elisabeth acceded graciously and without demur to the petition that Marie presented. However much she tried to keep away from the political scene, the Princess could not avoid being apprehensive as well as disquieted. She could not keep Marie by her, and she let her go with gentleness and understanding. She even told her departing art tutor to take with her any furniture she wanted from the rooms she had occupied at Versailles and Montreuil.

Marie was never a collector of personal possessions, but she appreciated Madame Elisabeth's kind generosity and chose a few pieces, including two chairs bearing the signature of the Queen's cabinet maker, Jacob.*

By the turn of the year Marie Grosholtz was back in Curtius's house, never to see Madame Elisabeth again after their affectionate farewell. 'States General fever' now gripped the nation. The once all-important 'deficit' was forgotten. The talk now was all of the Third Estate and the election of deputies to serve from it. Every male householder over twenty-five, who paid taxes, had a vote. Everyone declared that the much-enlarged body of the people's representatives would wield real power, not merely sit subservient to the 'upper houses' of the nobility and clergy.

---

* These two chairs survive in Madame Tussaud's exhibition today.

Political clubs sprang up. Already, in 1788, Danton, the Paris advocate with the huge head and thunderous voice, had founded the Cordeliers Club, where the more violent and revolutionary spirits gathered to discuss their plans. Mirabeau, too, founded a club, the Jacobin Club, so-called because it met in a disused Dominican monastery, whose brothers had been known as Jacobins.

Later the Jacobin Club would become the most notorious of revolutionary clubs, but at the outset its members did not want to eliminate the monarchy, but urged for a Constitution so that the people's representatives would have a say in the nation's affairs, and the tax burden could be more equitably distributed. The feeling that radical change was at last imminent spread through France.

These were busy times in Curtius's *Salon de Cire*. So many new persons in the public eye had to be modelled. Necker's portrait was updated, and Danton's portrait figure went on show. Its massive head was a great contrast to that of the thin, meagre Abbé Sieyès.

The Abbé Sieyès, a canon of Chartres, had been a visitor at Curtius's house for some time. In February 1789 he published a pamphlet entitled *What is the Third Estate?*, which created a great stir. In it he concluded that the Third Estate, the people's representative body, was, in fact, the Nation, and that the nobility should be excluded from the Nation, having alienated itself by idleness.

As well as talk and pamphlets there were sporadic riots. On 13 April 1789, the workpeople of the Faubourg St Antoine, a district neighbouring that of the Temple where Curtius had his *Salon*, unexpectedly gathered into a crowd, their numbers augmented by vagabonds and people from other parts of Paris. They invaded and sacked the house of a wealthy and well-known manufacturer who specialised in the production of painted and marbled papers, currently much in fashion as wall-coverings for grand rooms.

No civilian police force existed at that time, so a detachment of the *Garde Française* was despatched to deal with the trouble. This regiment formed part of the King's Household, and units of its soldiers were dispersed in various barracks around Paris. These troops had always got on well with the local people, and to begin with they tried to disperse the rioters without using force. However, they were met with screamed insults and volleys of bricks, tiles and any other missiles which were to hand.

When the soldiers finally received orders to use arms they reacted with ferocious fury. A newspaper, *Le Moniteur*, vividly reported what happened:

The vengeance was terrible. Those who tried to flee over the rooftops were shot down, and those who were trapped in the cellars and pillaged rooms were bayonetted.

Such incidents alarmed all property-owning citizens, however liberal their political views. A group of these citizens from the Temple district, Curtius among them, approached the Paris Municipality, a weak and ineffectual body, to suggest the formation of some sort of volunteer civilian militia, which could protect buildings and dwellings, and try to prevent any gathering of disgruntled workpeople turning into a riotous mob. Their suggestion was turned down.

Marie hoped that with the advent of the States General the situation, which was only what she had feared, might settle down. When she said goodbye to Madame Elisabeth she had completely severed her connection with Versailles, and had no idea what people there were now thinking and saying. She had been worried to hear that the young Dauphin had been in poor health for some time. It was said that he was feverish and listless all the time, and that some of his vertebrae were protruding. The child was now living in the palace of Meudon where the air, doctors thought, was better than that of Versailles.

Marie had modelled the attractive little boy during her stay in Madame Elisabeth's household. She still had the portrait figure, and that of Madame Royale, a laughing little girl with beautiful long fair hair. Marie heard that the King and Queen were visiting Meudon daily, such was their anxiety over the heir to the throne. It was fortunate the second royal boy, the Duc d'Angoulême, seemed healthy like his sister.

Finally, after months of excitement and canvassing, the deputies of the Third Estate had been chosen by the people of France. Among Curtius's close acquaintances who had been elected were Marat and Danton, both to Paris seats. Mirabeau, who by virtue of his title belonged to the nobility of Provence in southern France, had been turned down by his peers as an unsuitable candidate on account of his liberal views. Banned from sitting in as a deputy of the nobility, Mirabeau got himself elected to the Third Estate, representing Marseilles and Aix. General Lafayette had fared better in spite of his liberal views, and was elected for the nobility.

There was a newcomer on the scene, who was noticed particularly by the astute Curtius as one whose star should be carefully watched. This was Maximilien Robespierre, a lawyer, who had been elected to represent Artois in north-east France. Arrived in Paris as a deputy, he

[61]

attached himself to the extreme Left, and joined the Jacobin Club, where his influence seemed likely to grow.

Each deputy of the Third Estate drew up a list of the particular grievances of the people he represented. These *cahiers de doléances*, as they were called, not only set out complaints but a number of them also suggested a sort of idealised Constitution to take the place of the present absolute monarchy, with the King and the people's representatives working harmoniously together to govern the country. Most Parisians were in favour of some such constitutional monarchy for, in spite of their detestation of Marie Antoinette, they did not want to get rid of their King.

On 5 May the three houses of the States General, the nobility, the clergy and the enlarged Third Estate, assembled for their first session. They met in the town of Versailles, in the great hall of the Hôtel des Menus Plaisirs, situated on the Avenue de Paris. The King presided, and Necker delivered a speech on the country's financial situation.

Matters did not proceed smoothly. The King demanded that the credentials of each representative should be examined and verified before any decisions could be voted on. The nobility and the clergy agreed to this, but the Third Estate refused. The entire assembly was paralysed.

By early June nothing had been accomplished. Deputies of the Third Estate occupied the time by sorting themselves into different groups according to their views. The news of the death of the Dauphin was received with indifference, while the King and Queen went into mourning at their palace at Marly. Each day the public swarmed into the galleries surrounding the hall in which the States General gathered, and tension grew as inactivity continued.

At last the deputies of the Third Estate suggested a sitting of all three houses, or Estates, at which a roll-call would be taken. Any deputy who failed to be present would cease to be considered as a representative. In accordance with this suggestion the Third Estate's deputies gathered, but the nobility stayed away, and only a handful of clergy turned up.

On 17 June, after two days of debate, the angry Third Estate took a historic decision. It refused to continue as one of three Estates. Henceforward the Third Estate would consider itself an independent body, and its name would be changed to the National Assembly of France.

By this decision the whole existing structure of government was overturned. For the first time the people of France had a representative authority totally independent of the King. If Louis XVI had acted wisely and with liberality at this point, the French Revolution would have begun and ended there.

During these happenings at Versailles the day-to-day life of Paris, and of Curtius's *Salon de Cire* in the Boulevard du Temple, went on as usual. Curtius had absented himself a good deal from his studio and exhibition, as he had anticipated would happen when he brought Marie home from Versailles. He frequently joined the crowd in the public galleries of the assembly hall, and talked with those deputies who were already his friends, and made himself known to others, such as Maximilien Robespierre, who were clearly going to be influential. He was already quite well acquainted with the deputy Bailly, an astronomer by calling, who had been elected as President of the Third Estate, and his appetite for mingling with politicians grew.

The King, indecisive, wavering between advisers who recommended him to accept the new National Assembly and compromise, and those, including Marie Antoinette and his two brothers, who urged him to reverse the situation by force, took neither of these courses. Instead he announced that a royal session of all three Estates would be held at the end of June. Meanwhile he ordered the doors of the Hôtel des Menus Plaisirs to be locked, on the pretext that the great hall needed to be got ready for this occasion.

The deputies of the new National Assembly, faced with these locked doors, moved into the indoor tennis court, the *Jeu de Paume*, which was nearby and large enough to hold them all. There they took the famous Tennis Court Oath that the National Assembly would never disperse until a Constitution of France had been established on a firm basis.

In spite of that oath the royal session earlier announced took place on 23 June, with all three houses present. Opening the session, the King put forward certain reforms, but also made it clear that, while the monarchy was prepared to cede some liberal measures, it totally repudiated the principle of equal rights for all classes of society. The structure of the nobility, aristocracy and clergy, privileged and in authority, would not be altered. The King then most unwisely concluded his address with a veiled threat that the new National Assembly would be dissolved.

The deputies of the National Assembly, formerly the Third Estate, were understandably enraged. When the King had left the hall two historic statements were made. President Bailly announced 'The Nation in assembly cannot receive orders!', while Mirabeau sprang to his feet and cried out 'We will not move from our seats unless forced by bayonets!' The King was quickly informed of these statements, but took no notice.

Gradually the resistance of the other two Estates began to crumble. First the clergy decided to join the National Assembly, with the

Archbishop of Vienne and the astronomer Bailly presiding jointly. Then the nobility gave way. The Duc d'Orléans, with three noblemen at his side, led the representatives of the nobility to join the clergy in the hall and thus recognise the National Assembly.

Louis XVI now accepted the facts and invited all three bodies to assemble as one in the future. That night the joyous citizens of Paris illuminated their houses. When, on 7 July, it became known that a Constitutional Committee had been appointed everyone thought that France's problems would soon be resolved.

More and more people flocked to Curtius's *Salon de Cire* to see the portrait figures of new notabilities who were representing the ordinary people of France. Many of these were already longtime friends of Curtius. While her uncle had been busy mingling in the political scenes at Versailles, Marie had been active in modelling new portraits, and rearranging groups in the exhibition to reflect the new day that had dawned for France.

The People's Conquest: The Bastille Falls

MARIE Grosholtz had acquired Curtius's flair for judging what would hold public attention and interest, but she was not interested in politics beyond the awareness that was essential for her work in the exhibition. She had no wish to discuss, argue, or take sides, and any opinions she might form while listening to the eloquence of others, she preferred to keep to herself.

Marie assumed that her personal rôle during this period of disturbance would be limited to keeping the *Salon de Cire* topical, working under Curtius's guidance and direction at modelling new portraits, and rearranging the groupings. It was for Curtius to buzz from one political venue to another like an energetic bee, sharply observing the veers and gusts of the political wind, meeting old friends and making new ones, and often bringing them back to the Boulevard du Temple to sample Madame Grosholtz's excellent cooking.

Marie met Maximilien Robespierre several times. He had visited the *Salon*, dined, and Curtius was modelling his portrait as an up-and-coming deputy. She found this cold, detached man somewhat repellent, even sinister, though his manners were courteous, and he had earned a reputation for single-minded devotion to his beliefs and total incorruptibility. Robespierre dressed with scrupulous refinement. When the Third Estate had gathered for the first time, and processed into the assembly hall, Robespierre had stood out in the throng—a tall, slight figure, clad entirely in black, with a black silk cloak, only his cravat and ruffles snowy-white.

That June, 1789, while the Third Estate, having renamed itself the National Assembly, was asserting its rights at Versailles, the atmosphere in Paris was tense and agitated. Foreign visitors were astonished at the popular political fervour. It bewildered one Englishman, Arthur Young, a gentleman farmer from Suffolk, who arrived in Paris early in the month. He was preparing a treatise on agriculture, and had been touring round France for some time observing the systems, or rather the lack of them, under which France's farming areas were being cultivated.

When Arthur Young reached Paris on 9 June he found pamphleteers doing a roaring trade. 'Nineteen-twentieths of their pamphlets were in favour of Liberty,' he noted in his diary, 'In the streets one was struck by the number of hawkers selling seditious pamphlets.'

Like most visitors, Mr Young went to the gardens of the Palais Royal, and was again astounded at the scene. He saw crowds 'agape' listening to the orators, 'each haranguing his audience from chair or table in terms of more than common violence against the present government. The thunder of applause cannot easily be imagined.'

After the appointment of the Constitutional Committee this general excitement might have been expected to cool off, but on 11 July the King exploded a bombshell. He suddenly dismissed and exiled Necker, the people's hero, and sent packing the other ministers who shared a liberal outlook.

Necker himself was taken by surprise. Somehow the Court party, headed by Marie Antoinette, the King's brothers and a number of the Queen's favourites such as the Polignacs, had managed to goad the usually hesitant and lethargic Louis XVI into this disastrous action. When this news reached Paris, together with a rumour that the other popular hero, the Duc d'Orléans, the people's friend, was also being exiled, the city was thunderstruck. Gone were the hopes raised by the King's recognition of the National Assembly at the end of June. From now on Curtius and Marie—the one eager, the other reluctant but helpless—became participants, not just onlookers, as the French Revolution broke out and gathered momentum.

Curtius recorded the events a year later in a brochure he entitled *Les Services du Sieur Curtius*, which he published for all to read. 'On July 12th', he wrote, 'after a resolution taken (by the people) in the Palais Royal Gardens on the news of the exile of Mr Necker which had recently become known, a crowd of citizens surged to my *Salon* on the Boulevard du Temple.'

Curtius related how he saw this crowd approaching, closed his gates, but quickly decided to reopen them. The leaders of the mob peremptorily demanded the wax heads of Necker and the Duc d'Orléans, which they proposed to parade triumphantly through the city. 'I quickly handed them over, begging them (the mob) not to damage them in any way,' Curtius recalled. He did, however, manage to dissuade some of the men who wanted to seize also the full-length portrait-figure of the King, by pointing out that it would be heavy, cumbersome, and awkward to handle.

The mob then departed, bearing on high the wax busts of 'the Prince and Minister who were regarded as citizens'. Someone had produced some pieces of crêpe which draped the busts. In spite of his normal desire always to be in the thick of things, Curtius did not follow them. A section of the crowd had begun shouting that places of entertainment should be closed down on this day of the people's sorrow.

There were cries of 'Burn them down!' The threat passed but Curtius, mindful of the fate of the paper-merchant's house a couple of months earlier, shuttered and locked the *Salon de Cire* and hurried along the boulevard warning his fellow showmen of the danger. Marie remained in the exhibition with her mother and the staff while Curtius was contacting and helping his neighbours, urging the prudence of a temporary shut-down, so neither of them personally saw the events recorded by a college professor, Beffroi de Regny.

De Regny had intended using some tickets he had been given for a theatre on the Boulevard du Temple, but soon realised he must abandon his plans. 'All the spectacles were closed,' he wrote in his account of the day, 'No actor dared play his rôle in the general fright which inspired all Parisians, a sure expectation of the misfortunes that were about to befall them.'

Some hours later, as all appeared to be quiet in the closed-down Boulevard du Temple, Curtius went out to try to discover what had happened to his two wax busts. The news he learned was horrifying.

On the King's orders, extra troops had been assembled at points around Paris, in case of uproar in the city over Necker's dismissal. They were on the alert and when the procession, augmented by people who had joined in as it passed through the streets, reached the Place Louis XV (now Place de la Concorde) it clashed with some cavalry of the Royal German Regiment. The Garde Française arrived to help in dispersing the mob. There were scuffles, shots were fired, and several demonstrators were killed or wounded before the Place Louis XV was cleared.

It is difficult to know exactly what happened in the mêlée, but it was the first bloodshed of the Revolution. Curtius wrote: 'I can only say that the man who carried the bust of M. le Duc d'Orléans was wounded by a bayonet thrust in the pit of the stomach, and the one who carried M. Necker was killed by a Dragoon in the Place Vendôme.'

It was a surprise to Curtius when one of the men who had taken part in the demonstration turned up at the *Salon de Cire* to return the bust of the Duc d'Orléans. Incredibly, it had suffered little damage. Six days later the bust of Necker was brought back. It had been retrieved by a guard in the Palais Royal gardens. The hair was burned and the face slashed with several sabre cuts. After this frightening day Paris was in a

[67]

ferment. Even the lethargic Municipality was aroused to some action. A committee of citizens representing the sixty districts of Paris was set up to form a civil militia, as Curtius and his friends and neighbours had previously suggested.

This new force was named The National Guard, and was sanctioned by the National Assembly at Versailles on 13 July. Curtius was gratified at being elected Captain for his locality. While Marie concentrated on the work of the exhibition, Curtius collected all the arms he could lay hands on, and hired four men, paying them out of his own pocket, to keep constant surveillance over the neighbourhood, watching for any threat of trouble.

That night National Guardsmen patrolled all the streets of Paris. Householders were ordered to place lights in their windows to give some illumination in the dark, narrow network. Curtius felt his own vigilance was well justified when, just after midnight, his men managed peacefully to disperse a small mob of people who were marching, torches in hand, with the intention of setting fire to the Opéra and theatres. 'How could one have checked the spread of flames', he wrote, 'in conditions of such trouble and confusion?'

Captain Curtius had forty National Guardsmen under his command. It was next day, the fateful 14 July, that he heard, news spreading quickly by word of mouth, that citizens living in the vicinity of the grim fortress-prison of the Bastille, which stood not far from the Boulevard du Temple, were planning to attack it. The huge ancient edifice had become a symbol of oppression. Into it, for centuries, had been thrown the victims of the French Kings' *lettres de cachet*, the dreaded arrest-warrants that gave no reason.

In more recent times the Bastille had in fact been used for short-stay prisoners, or as a staging-point for those condemned to long years of confinement in other fortress-prisons scattered throughout France. Cardinal Rohan had been put there to await trial in the scandalous Queen's diamond necklace affair. On 14 July 1789 there were only a handful of prisoners incarcerated.

The Governor, de Launay, was a mild man. He had already promised the Municipality that he would not open fire on any crowd unless actually under attack. The garrison of the enormous fortress was ludicrously small. It had been reduced to some thirty men from the King's Swiss Guards and eighty or so *invalides*, pensioned-off soldiers who were elderly or disabled to some degree.

Since the formation of the National Guard on the previous day citizens had been besieging the Hôtel de Ville, the headquarters of the Municipality, clamouring for an issue of arms. No arms were available for distribution. The motivation behind the idea of an attack on the Bastille was probably as much the seizure of the armoury as any desire to storm a symbol of oppression.

When Curtius, at the *Salon de Cire*, learned that the 'rampart of despotism' was to be assaulted, he hastened to round up his squad of National Guardsmen, handing out all the arms he had managed to collect. He hoped to arrive on the scene in time to take part in the storming, the capture of the Governor and garrison, and the release of prisoners.

Marie was left in charge at No. 20 Boulevard du Temple, with instructions to close the exhibition if necessary—there were not likely to be many visitors anyway, with the city in such a state of tension. Curtius told her to keep her mother, and any staff who stayed around, at the back of the premises. If any incident did occur, she must deal with it herself, using her discretion and judgement. The essential was to safeguard the exhibition which represented the life-work of them both.

When Curtius and his men got within sight of the Bastille and the people swarming round it, he halted his squad, telling most of them to wait while he went ahead with a few comrades. The fury of the crowd was obviously mounting. The Governor had evacuated the outer courtyards and taken his stand beyond the moat. The great drawbridge was still down, but the heavy doors at the entrance shut.

When the menacing mob suddenly surged forward into the big outer courtyard the garrison opened fire, and some of the invaders were killed or wounded. The hostility rose to fever-pitch. An assault on the great drawbridge was about to begin when some of the defenders lowered another small drawbridge to the left of the massive entrance. Those who had been about to attack saw this, turned aside, and swarmed across this secondary bridge, securing bolts so that it could not be raised again.

The rest of the infuriated mob followed, surging across into the inner precincts of the fortress. Curtius was among them. He and his comrades had been out of range of the fire and, always one to make the most of his rôle, however minor, he rejoiced, as he later recorded, at being on the spot 'to share the final dangers and the glory of a conquest that put the seal on our liberty!'

The Governor, de Launay, and the garrison were taken prisoner. Curtius had pushed his way forward, and he and his small band were allotted the task of escorting a group of decrepit *invalides* to the Hôtel de Ville. When he arrived there, having met with some hostility en route, he spent some time arguing and pleading with the guards to let his elderly and exhausted prisoners go free.

These poor old men were obviously no menace in any situation.

[69]

Everything was in confusion, and finally the guards agreed, glad to be rid of one responsibility. Curtius quickly removed his charges before anyone could reverse the decision. He took them to a hostelry called *La Nouvelle France* where he arranged for them to be given some food.

Having left the Hôtel de Ville, Curtius did not witness what followed. The citizen, a man named Élie, who had actually taken the Governor prisoner, promised him safe conduct for, apart from the one volley of fire, there had been virtually no resistance to the invaders, no more bloodshed. But when the Governor and his escort safely reached the Hôtel de Ville they were faced with a mob avid to avenge those who had been killed or wounded in the assault. Beyond control, they set upon Governor de Launay and murdered him. They also seized and killed the official representative of the Paris Guilds, the Provost of the Merchants, Flesselles, who had gone to the Hôtel de Ville on hearing that the Bastille was being attacked.

With frenzied hatred men in the crowd decapitated both bodies. It was five o'clock in the evening when, in the centre of the milling mob, the two severed heads were stuck on poles and hoisted on high. Where to take them? 'To Curtius!' a voice shouted. 'Let them join the criminals in his *Caverne!*' The clamouring procession set off to the Boulevard du Temple.

Marie had spent an anxious day. She did not know whether Curtius had reached the Bastille with his National Guardsmen, whether there had been bloodshed or when he would arrive home. Her mother, as instructed, had kept to the back of the house all day. Late in the afternoon Marie was standing at the door of the house, debating whether to close the exhibition and lock the gate. She looked down the Boulevard du Temple and saw, and heard, what appeared to be a mob of people approaching, just as they had come when they carried off the busts of Necker and the Duc d'Orléans. She saw two pikes were being held aloft with something on the spikes.

Alarmed, she realised that this crowd was making for the *Salon de Cire*. Horrorstruck, she realised that the objects stuck on the pikes were human heads, but whose heads they might be she had no idea. When the mob was within shouting distance she heard voices yelling 'Heads of criminals! For Curtius's *Caverne!*'

Marie could have fainted, could have shrieked a refusal and fled, but she controlled herself. If she collapsed, or refused whatever they wanted, the whole gang would charge in and destroy the exhibition as they had destroyed the paper-merchant's house. Everything would be smashed, pillaged, and then the house set alight with herself and her mother in it.

She heard the familiar names of de Launay and Flesselles being bandied about. Nothing would induce her to let the mob into the house. She realised what they wanted. 'Stay where you are!' she told them 'I will bring my materials here, you can watch!'

She fetched a chair and planted it outside the door. From the studio she collected plaster, oil, pomade, tools and a cloth and basin of water. One after the other she took the decapitated heads on her lap. She sponged the bloodstains from the faces and smoothed the distorted features, oiled the skin and applied the plaster mask. No need for quills in the nostrils with these 'subjects'.

Marie managed to keep her hands steady as the men watched her. Her work did not take long. With the living one often had to soothe, to reassure, as the mask went on. At least the dead could not get alarmed, but these grisly objects were the first she had handled. Curtius had always done the modelling for criminals' chamber, the *Caverne des Grands Voleurs*.

Marie thought that no-one saw her apart from the crowd pressing round. Concentrating on her work, she did not notice that Philip Astley, the English proprietor of the famous circus just along the Boulevard du Temple, passed by, paused for a few seconds and watched what she was doing. Prudently, he did not linger. Everyone knew that Marie Antoinette admired his trick-riding, and he did not want his premises attacked. When he got home he noted in his diary how he had seen Marie Grosholtz, seated at her door, making the death masks of the murdered de Launay and Flesselles.

A few days later he went back to No. 20, visited Curtius, and secretly ordered copies of the wax heads that had been completed. These he smuggled across the Channel and put on show, and advertised them as a horrifying attraction, at his London circus. He did not say who modelled or supplied them.

Marie might have kept an air of calm, but she had been shaking when she handed back the heads to the mob. They were hoisted on the pikes again and borne off to the Palais Royal gardens. It would be several days before the wax portraits would appear in the *Caverne*, for Curtius and his niece never hurried or botched work. Marie gathered up the chair and materials. She locked the gates, and shuttered the house.

It was after seven o'clock when Curtius finally arrived home, well pleased at having taken an active part in the storming of the Bastille. He received a considerable shock when he found Marie white-faced and unnerved, for he had no inkling of what had happened during the evening. She took heart from Curtius's praise of her self-control and

[71]

handling alone of a very dangerous situation. 'The mobs are out of control, and will kill and burn in their present mood,' he warned her. 'It is not enough to be passive if something flares up. One must be prepared to go along with whatever is demanded, if the exhibition and the household are to be saved. Nothing is safe at the moment.'

Marie realised the truth of what her uncle was saying. Everyone *must* appear committed to the new Liberty, and convincingly so. Marie had remained impartial during her years at Versailles, but nothing she had seen there made her ready to risk all their lives and their work for the sake of the King and Queen and the absolute monarchy which had brought so much misery and starvation. She steeled herself to meet possible trouble on her own, while Curtius went about his various activities. She had managed to deal with one horror. She would face, and deal with, others if they came.

15 July was sightseeing day at the Bastille. Streams of people converged to explore the labyrinth of passages, cells, and dungeons within the hitherto unbreached walls of the fortress. Curtius took Marie along, her nerves now steadied again after the previous day's stress.

When they arrived they encountered a number of Curtius's deputy friends and learned that Bailly, the astronomer President of the National Assembly, had been elected Mayor of Paris.

Robespierre joined them on their tour. When Marie slipped on one of the narrow, worn stairs, he put out an arm and caught her. 'It would be a pity', he said, 'for such a pretty patriot to break her neck.' 'Patriot?', Marie laughed, and thanked him, but she was alert and wary. Had there been a hint of sarcasm in his voice when he called her 'patriot'?

One could not be too careful. Marie determined to guard not only her tongue, as she had always done, but her expression as well. She pretended not to hear someone rashly saying that Governor de Launay had always moved his prisoners out of the dungeons when the waters of the Seine rose and flooded them. She blotted from her mind the picture of his severed head.

They looked into many of the cells, damp and evil-smelling. Most were furnished with a bedstead, straw mattress, table, chair, and pitcher. Their tour took much longer than necessary because Robespierre insisted on stopping at intervals to harangue the other sightseers. Marie noticed that his high-flown eloquence seemed to grip his audiences. Again Curtius had been right. Robespierre was a man to watch.

As far as Marie was concerned, this one visit to the Bastille was enough, but Curtius could not keep away. Next day he went there again, and succeeded in collaring a few barrels of gunpowder for the use of his National Guardsmen, should it be required. The Bastille was being cleared of everything movable.

While Curtius was away on this foray, Marie received with apprehension a group of men who were half carrying along an ancient man. He was a prisoner, one of the handful found and released. This unfortunate old man had, it seemed, been incarcerated for thirty years, under a *lettre de cachet*, and completely forgotten. The reason for his arrest was not known—*lettres de cachet* issued by the king gave none, and any relatives or friends had long given up pleas for his release.

The men who dragged the poor creature to Curtius's exhibition wanted a wax portrait of this victim of oppression and tyranny to take its place in the *Salon de Cire*. The *Salon* was indeed being updated, thought Marie as she complied. The old man was emaciated, had hardly any teeth, and his long hair and beard, white with age, were wild and unkempt.

In spite of her efforts at detachment, Marie found it tragically pathetic that this poor old man kept begging to be taken back to his cell. After so long hidden from the world, he could not face it. His cell, no doubt one of those Marie had peered into, had become his home. He craved its shelter and the provision of food, poor as it may have been.

This ancient man was given a haven in a citizen's house, but continued to plead to go back to the Bastille. He died a few days later. People thought he might have been a Comte de Lorge, and so his portrait was labelled when it was put in the *Salon*, but no-one was ever certain who he really was.

Marie could only hope that, after the fall of the Bastille, mob fury would evaporate. She wrote in her recollections of the period, 'A fearful excitement pervaded all Paris, but the mob, as if astonished by its own prowess, and expecting that next day armed forces would bear down on them, forbore any demonstration of their strength. But it was the awful calm that precedes the storm.'

XI

'It is a Revolution!'

THE crowds gathered and drifted, uneasy and sullen. No military force appeared to disperse them. At Versailles the King had seemed indifferent to the riot and subsequent bloodshed of 12 July, after the dismissal of Necker. As for the storming of the Bastille two days later, Louis XVI knew nothing about it until it was all over and done with.

Louis had left the palace early that morning for a day's hunting. He returned late, and tired from his long day in the saddle. He went straight to bed and slept till aroused in the night by the Duc de Liancourt, who told him how the fortress had fallen to the mob and the fate of its Governor and the Provost of the Merchants.

'Is it a rebellion?' asked the King drowsily. 'No, Sire,' replied the Duc de Liancourt, 'it is a Revolution!' The King did not appear agitated by the news, and gave no instructions. When it was morning, Louis's ceremonial *levée* took place as usual.

When the King was dressed, and the valets gone, Marie Antoinette, the Comte d'Artois and others of the Court party tried to persuade him that he ought to leave Paris and go to Metz, near the safety of the eastern frontier of France. There were still plenty of loyal troops who would see the royal party through the disturbed countryside, and flight would be easy if danger threatened. Louis would not agree, and was supported in this by his elder brother, the Comte de Provence, but he did not forbid flight for anyone who wanted to leave.

With this permission, the first of the royal and noble *emigrés* at once began their preparations to leave the country, the Comte d'Artois and the Queen's favourites, the Polignacs, being among the first to depart.

The Duchesse de Polignac, Marie Antoinette's 'dear heart', was all too well aware that the people of Paris were as hostile to her as they were to her royal mistress. Had they not rolled her effigy in the gutters? She removed herself, her son, valuables and money as quickly as possible. Madame de Polignac never saw Marie Antoinette again. She died in Vienna in 1793, while her husband, recipient of so many lucrative royal favours, ended up in Russia, in St Petersburg, and outlived his wife by fourteen years.

Many, however, did not abandon the Court. Among those who stayed at their posts, in her case as Superintendent of the Queen's Household, was the Princess de Lamballe who had been ousted as Marie Antoinette's most intimate woman friend by the Duchesse de Polignac. She had taken her 'demotion' with good grace, her kind and amiable nature unembittered. She was to pay for her loyalty to the royal family with a terrible and degrading death.

On 15 July, the day after the fall of the Bastille, while the first *emigrés* were hastily getting ready to leave, Louis XVI attended a session of the National Assembly. There he announced that he was withdrawing all the royal troops that had been drafted into Paris earlier in the month.

At this unexpected concession the deputies broke into applause. Most of them were moderate men, and they hoped sincerely that the King would now co-operate with the Assembly to form a constitutional government, especially as they knew that Necker and the other liberal ministers who had been sent packing, had been recalled and restored to office.

The King next decided to pay a visit to Paris, where Bailly was now Mayor, and Lafayette commanded the new civilian militia, the National Guard. Large crowds were expected to gather as soon as this news spread, but the Municipality and Commander Lafayette believed the National Guard could control them without the support of troops, whose presence might inflame some sections of the people.

Curtius was ordered to take his detachment, men from the district named *Pères de Nazareth* after a religious order established in it, and post them at the entrance to the Place de Grève not far away. It was here that the King would be officially received by the Mayor on 17 July.

The Place de Grève was a familiar spot to Curtius for it was here that many public executions took place. Portraits of the more notorious felons who had met their fate there, could be viewed in his *Caverne des Grands Voleurs*. The crowd in the Place de Grève was dense, but Curtius deployed his men strategically, and congratulated himself that the King's reception passed off without any incidents, or even murmurings, from the people.

The King had but a cold reception from the citizens as he made his way to the Hôtel de Ville. They were silent, but the atmosphere suddenly changed when Louis XVI emerged from the Hôtel de Ville wearing a tricolour cockade, symbol of Liberty. All the onlookers applauded enthusiastically, and the royal departure from the capital back to Versailles was marked by a heartening warmth engendered by his gesture of conciliation.

The palace of Versailles, to which the King was returning up that wide Avenue which Marie Grosholtz had traversed so often during her years with Madame Elisabeth, had already become a desolate place, its glory a fading memory. Many of its occupants had removed themselves, not only those who had emigrated, but many who had deemed it prudent to leave Court and retire to their country estates.

Some of these, like the Comte de Rochechouart, who held a commission in one of the royal regiments, stayed quietly in the country and rode out the Revolution protected by loyal tenants. Among those who chose emigration was the Prince de Condé, who, with his household and retainers, had occupied a whole wing of the palace. His former apartments were already shuttered and deserted. So, too, were the great rooms of the south wing, where the Comte d'Artois and the Polignacs had had their lodgings, once the scene of splendid festivities. A miasma of melancholy pervaded the once-thronged palace and its gardens.

Throughout France the news of the storming of the Bastille had sparked off similar reactions against the absolute monarchy and the royal bureaucracy that oppressed the people. Buildings were seized and new local councils set up and National Guards formed, with weapons looted from depots and armouries.

There was little resistance. In Bordeaux, for example, the new citizen militia took over the arms of the local garrison, while its commander made no attempt to interfere. But everywhere, as in Paris, there were not enough arms to supply the hordes of citizen volunteers who demanded them.

In Paris hatred and blood-lust simmered beneath the surface in extremist mobs, always ready to erupt if opportunity occurred. It was only a matter of weeks after the decapitated heads of Governor de Launay, and the Provost of Merchants, Flesselles, had been put on exhibition in the *Caverne*, among the portraits of condemned criminals, that another grisly wax head came to join them.

Foulon, a finance official in the King's ministry, had been heard to remark during a period of bread shortage that if the peasants had no grain they could always eat their hay. This callous sentence had been picked up and widely circulated among the people of Paris. Curtius and Marie heard it. They were acquainted with Foulon, whose house was not far from the *Salon de Cire*.

When the rioting after Necker's dismissal began, Foulon and his son-in-law thought it prudent to disappear from Paris. Foulon had it put about that he had died suddenly in some country retreat. The people of Paris did not believe this. After the fall of the Bastille, Foulon was tracked down in his hiding-place, and, with his son-in-law, carried back to Paris, to face the fury of a mob.

Both of them were murdered. Foulon was hanged from a lamp-post near his residence, his mouth stuffed with hay. When the body was cut down it was decapitated. Marie happened to be out walking in the neighbourhood and saw the head being carried on a pike in the direction of Curtius's house. This time Marie was spared the nauseating task. Curtius was at home and carried out the job, and the crowd departed, rehoisting the severed head, jubilant that another enemy of the people would shortly be represented in the chamber of criminals.

Curtius was apprehensive, however, that the violent elements might not be satisfied with a mere display of the heads of those they had summarily executed. He introduced Foulon's head in a macabre setting with the effect of blood streaming from it on the ground. This brought people flocking in, and it remained an attraction long after Foulon's actual 'crime' had been forgotten.

It remained so popular that when, early in 1794, Curtius and Marie were packing up a selection of their work, to be taken to India by an Italian showman, Dominic Laurency, they included this 'shocker'. The presentation of Foulon's head was graphically described in Calcutta and Madras newspapers, when they reviewed this new wax exhibition imported from France. The gentlemen of the East India Company and their ladies willingly paid out gold pagodas to see for themselves some of the horrors of the French Revolution, details of which had only reached them late and at long intervals.

It was spontaneous mob executions as well as the cruelty of the official death penalties which spurred on Dr Guillotin, a physician and a deputy in the National Assembly, to put forward in October his plea for a single method of capital punishment to be used for all crimes that demanded the death sentence. A humane man, he had long been disturbed by the barbarity of the public executions attended by such enormous crowds.

He put forward a design for an instrument with a heavy, falling knife, which would remove the victim's head comparatively humanely, with a single blow. His concern was not heeded at the time, and it was not until April 1792 that the doctor succeeded in getting his device adopted as the only means of execution to be used. The instrument was nicknamed 'Madame Guillotine' after its sponsor.

The first head that rolled under the guillotine blade in the Place de Grève was that of a common pickpocket of no importance to anyone, though the populace gathered to see this first demonstration of the new machine. Though Dr Guillotin would be distressed and horrified at the number of heads that rolled as the Revolution progressed, it did not prevent mob massacres as fury grew.

In Paris work went on clearing out the Bastille, and preparing for its demolition and razing to the ground, while at Versailles the deputies of the National Assembly strove to consolidate the gains it had wrung from the King. After much debate, the deputies produced a decree which unequivocally abolished everything the *ancien régime* stood for. In future there would be no more privileges for any section of society, public office would be open to all, and there would be equality in justice. Personal servitude, the basis of the old feudal system, would disappear. The clergy would lose their right to tithes which they had enjoyed for centuries. This was followed by a Declaration of Rights inspired by the American example, which set out man's 'natural and imprescriptible' rights, rights which cannot legally be taken away. The decree and the Declaration of Rights embodied the concept of liberty and equality for the people, which would be made possible under a constitutional monarchy, if Louis XVI could be persuaded to accept such a monarchy.

The optimism which had followed the King's visit to Paris and adoption of the tricolour cockade proved ill-founded. The deputies' radical proposals met with no favour from Louis or his supporters. Marie Antoinette was the most adamant antagonist. The King absolutely refused to consider any diminution of the old privileges of class, and clung to his own ancient right of veto on any measures of which he disapproved, no matter if the representative parliamentary body did now assert it was the State.

In Paris the King and Queen were jeeringly christened 'Monsieur et Madame Veto', and Madame Veto was the one most vilified. More moderate members of the National Assembly, such as Mirabeau, realised that some compromise would have to be found, if another serious and bloody clash were to be avoided. Others, Curtius's old friend Marat among them, were increasingly violent in their hostility to the monarchy.

It was put to the King that he might be permitted to retain his right of veto for a period of four years, in return for his sanction of the two measures, the decree and the Declaration, virtually abolishing the old feudal system. Louis XVI quibbled. No one could be certain what he intended, but he ordered the Royal Flanders Regiment, which was stationed at Douai, to be brought to Versailles and arrive there at the end of September.

By September, the social and economic situation in both town and country was extremely bad. The harvest of 1789 was a good one, but with all the agitation and forming of local councils and bodies of National Guards throughout country areas, it had not been gathered in or threshed properly. The peasants had neglected good husbandry for politics and a grain shortage was inevitable.

In provincial towns, as well as in Paris, unemployment increased. The emigration of so many of the nobility and aristocracy, and the reluctance of people who had money to spend it on any form of display, caused the luxury trades, which gave employment to many, to collapse. There was no alternative employment for those who had catered for the wealthy and their households.

Even people with lesser establishments spent as little as possible, and many complained, as Curtius did, that their new civic duties with the National Guard and district councils seriously affected their incomes by cutting into their working hours. Curtius wrote, 'I have proved my zeal by the sacrifice of time normally dedicated to my work. It is a loss for an artist. To this I should add considerable and exceptional expenses.' He had in fact paid out of his own pocket for the men he posted on surveillance after the events of 12 July. There was no way of reclaiming any such patriotic expenditure.

In Paris efforts were made by Bailly, the Mayor, and Lafayette, Commander of the National Guard, to set up a proper municipal control. An elected Commune was formed, with representatives from all the city's districts. This was not an entire success, for each district, especially those where the more violent elements of society lived, seemed more intent on setting itself up as an autonomous authority. Curtius, however, was well pleased with the growing strength of the National Guard. Volunteers flowed in. He also approved of the District Committees, which were elected by citizens like himself who paid direct personal taxes.

By 1 October 1789, these local committees had been given police powers, and powers to issue orders and decrees. Curtius, as Captain of the National Guard for his own *Pères de Nazareth* district, enjoyed his new authority in spite of his moans about the amount of time it consumed. He was now committed to involvement in the new order, while Marie confined herself to maintaining the standards of the *Salon de Cire* in these new and difficult circumstances.

Retreat From Versailles

THE arrival of the Royal Flanders Regiment to join the King's Guard at Versailles aroused intense public unease and suspicion. The regiment was a thousand strong. Why did the King want it at the palace? Did he lack confidence in the new civilian National Guard as an instrument of law and order? Bailly, as President of the National Assembly and Mayor of Paris, tried to get some satisfactory answers out of the King's ministers. They were evasive.

Anxiety increased. The newssheet *Révolutions de Paris*, a widely circulated publication, asked, 'What dire plot is being hatched? We must be on our guard . . . we need a second Revolution.' In such an atmosphere of tension Marie Antoinette made another of her calamitous errors of judgement: she persuaded the King to accompany her to a banquet staged in honour of the Royal Flanders Regiment in the opera house of the palace.

It was quite a splendid occasion. The King and Queen appeared in the royal box with their second son, the new Dauphin since his brother's death in early summer. They stood there to receive a tremendous ovation, while the tricolour cockade, symbol of the new order, was trampled underfoot. It was a private occasion, but no such royal festivities could ever be kept private.

News of the banquet, and what happened there, appeared in Paris in the *Courier* on 3 October. The hungry people reacted as they had done to the news of Necker's dismissal in July. This time they wanted not only protestation, but revenge for the insult to the symbol of the Nation. The Commune demanded the instant removal of the Royal Flanders Regiment, and the King's immediate sanction for the National Assembly's decree and Declaration of Rights.

On the following day, Sunday 4 October, crowds gathered again in the Palais Royal gardens. There the decision was taken to march on Versailles and bring the King back to the poverty-stricken and starving capital. The idea took on a vast political significance.

The following day a throng of more than six thousand people gathered at the Hôtel de Ville. A large proportion were women from poor quarters like the Faubourg St Antoine, and fishwives and market women from the great market-place of Les Halles. It was the women who bore the brunt of the struggle to feed their children. Some said there were men dressed as women among them.

They were led by Maillard, one of those who had been in the van at the storming of the Bastille. Marie Grosholtz knew this man, and had no use for him. She said that while serving as a common soldier he had been branded for robbing his comrades. He had stolen from a respectable father too, and was suspected of being a police informer. Now all such opinions must be forgotten. His actions on 14 July had erased past misdemeanours. This rough, ferocious man was now held in public esteem and accepted as a leader.

Their Commander, Lafayette, and a large contingent of National Guardsmen, were to follow at the rear of the long procession of citizens. Curtius, who could never bear to be away from any centre of action, was extremely annoyed that he was not allowed to lead his squad of National Guardsmen in the procession. Instead his superior officer, Hulin, who was himself going to head a detachment drawn from various districts, ordered Curtius to pick eight men and go to the Bastille to take charge of the fortress. Its normal garrison, which guarded the now empty and denuded former prison, was being withdrawn to join Hulin on the march to Versailles.

Curtius was told to remain with his men at the Bastille until further notice. Usually one to avoid any kind of unpleasant confrontation, Curtius's disappointment and chagrin was such that when he got to the Bastille he became involved in an altercation with some people he found there. He restored order, he recorded later, by dint of 'patience and firmness'.

It was to Curtius's lasting regret that he was thus denied the opportunity to participate in the dramatic events that took place at Versailles on 5 and 6 October 1789. The King had to be called back from a hunting excursion when news of the citizens' march reached the palace. He was back by the time the van of the enormous procession arrived at about four o'clock in the afternoon.

Louis XVI received a deputation with soothing words, promising he would have supplies of food sent to Paris to relieve the acute shortage of bread and other commodities. Later in the evening he made it known that he was now ready to accept the provisions of the decree and the Declaration of Rights drawn up by the National Assembly.

[81]

The hostility of the crowd seemed to be appeased by this announcement, but tension rose again when Lafayette and his National Guardsmen, who had followed behind the tail of the procession, arrived on the scene. Lafayette, once a general in the royal army, and emissaries from the Paris municipality, demanded an audience. When they reached the royal presence they requested the King to accompany them to Paris.

Louis XVI was understandably staggered. No such demand had ever been made before of a king of France! As usual, when faced with a crisis, Louis equivocated. He would give his answer the following night.

Lafayette had already posted men from the National Guard round the palace, having come to an agreement with the Royal Guards on duty inside. These soldiers remained at their customary posts, and the royal family retired to bed, reassured in the knowledge that they were protected by loyal troops.

Outside the palace the vast horde of people settled down for the night to await the King's reply. They lit huge bonfires, sitting around singing the revolutionary songs that had circulated in the streets of Paris, drinking, eating what they could get, and never wavering in their determination to carry their King back to Paris with them.

All seemed under control, but early in the morning some groups of men broke away and penetrated the palace courtyard. One of them was confronted and killed by a palace guard. Fighting broke out, and several of the royal soldiers were left lying dead or wounded. The anger of the invaders rose to fever-pitch. They dashed up the great staircase that led to the Queen's apartments. Marie Antoinette, terrified at the tumult, escaped by a private passage to the King's rooms.

Outside the gates Lafayette, roused from sleep, gathered his men and quickly took charge. With the help of the Royal Guard his National Guardsmen cleared the disorderly mob from the staircase and gained control of the palace. But it was not possible to disperse the hundreds who now packed the marble courtyard, screaming 'To Paris! To Paris!'

Then Lafayette came out on to the balcony overlooking the courtyard. The King, the Queen and the little Dauphin were with him. Louis XVI addressed the sea of faces below him. 'My friends,' he said, 'I will come to Paris with my wife and family.' The mood of the crowd changed suddenly from fury to enthusiasm. The King was popular again, as he had been briefly when he emerged from the Hôtel de Ville wearing the tricolour cockade, arousing a hope that had proved false.

The cortège that left Versailles that afternoon, never to return, numbered some thirty-thousand people, including the people of Paris marching back, escorting the King they had vowed to bring with them, home to the capital.

There was no trouble, no violence. When the coaches containing the King and his family, and his immediate household, arrived after a slow journey down the wide avenue he would never see again, they were directed to the Tuileries.

In the Tuileries confusion reigned. This palace, which had been practically unused by the royal family for decades, was mostly let out in 'grace and favour' apartments to elderly Court pensioners. These had to be evicted to make room for courtiers and servants, before the royal family were finally installed in a hastily prepared and uncomfortable lodging in the neglected state rooms.

During this exciting time Curtius, fretting and frustrated, had been obliged to remain with his handful of men for a day and a night in the deserted Bastille, picking up what bits of news he could. When it came to his ears on 6 October that the royal family, escorted by the huge crowd that had left the Hôtel de Ville the previous day, were actually en route for Paris, he could bear it no longer.

He handed over his command to one of his comrades, a veteran of the storming of the Bastille, whose 'prudence and activity' he felt he could trust. He hurried to the Hôtel de Ville, where he offered his services to an official, reminding him of how effectively he, Curtius, had handled the crowd with his squad of men of the National Guard when the King had arrived at the Place de Grève on 17 June.

The harassed official accepted his offer. The crowd was much larger than it had been on 17 June, as Curtius recalled later, writing that 'the immense procession that accompanied the royal family was preceded by a great convoy of flour wagons, a train of artillery, and a multitude of carriages'.

Delighted to be again in the thick of events, Curtius bustled about with his usual vigour, helping to make a way through the crowd for the flour wagons and guns, and forcing another passage for some cavalry. 'There was no disorder', he recollected.

Later on he had to give an account of his actions to his superior officer, Hulin, who had so inconsiderately posted him to the Bastille while history was in the making at Versailles. Curtius was slightly mollified when Hulin, who had himself witnessed everything, embraced his disgruntled comrade, crying 'My dear comrade! You have rendered us just as good a service as if you had come to Versailles with us!'

When the King agreed to leave Versailles, the deputies of the National Assembly, who had been sitting in the same location since the States General had first gathered there, hastily collected their belongings, and also took the road to Paris. After a brief stay in the Archbishop's palace, the deputies established themselves in the former

Manège, or riding-school, of the Tuileries, where tiers of seats were hurriedly erected.

It seemed incredible to everyone that only five months had elapsed between the first meeting of the States General and the arrival of the King in Paris, virtually a prisoner of the people. Tension eased, and some private entertaining even started again. Madame Necker and Madame Bailly gave parties. Some ladies attended such occasions wearing a type of hat they called 'a Liberty hat', and sporting ribbons of a particular shade of red, which they called, with lamentably bad taste, 'Foulon's blood'.

In the former Tuileries riding-school the proceedings of the National Assembly were interrupted irritatingly often by applause or hostile shouts from people in the public gallery. All the deputies were aware that they had played no part in the spontaneous revolutionary outbreaks that had taken place in Paris. These had erupted with no reference to the Assembly that represented the nation. The deputies were also uncomfortably aware that popular feeling throughout the country had become exceedingly difficult to control.

They had to contend not only with an obstinate monarch who still believed his will should be absolute, and with an aristocracy and clergy fundamentally opposed to reform, but also with popular elements which did not refer their unpredictable actions to the deputies they had elected to represent them.

The extreme left-wing deputies in the National Assembly, who called themselves the Patriots, hoped to woo the people to support their often violent anti-monarchist views. In opposition the moderates still aimed at achieving a constitutional government by peaceful means. They wished to retain the King on his throne, but with his powers severely limited.

In the currently more relaxed atmosphere, crowds were to be seen daily at the Tuileries, waiting hopefully to get a glimpse of members of the royal family. Marie Grosholtz did not join them. She dared not be seen lingering there. Too many people knew of her long connection with Madame Elisabeth at Versailles, even though she had never flaunted it in any way. The mood of the people was too volatile. If someone who thought her tainted by her previous relations with the royal family and court were to recognise her there and shout out some provocative remark, she could find herself in a dangerous situation. In any case she was too busy with the exhibition and studio to stand gaping in crowds.

Curtius himself was uneasy and nervous. His political perceptions had always been acute. He could see all too clearly that the National Assembly was not welding itself into a united body representing citizens from every province of France. It was rapidly developing into a body rent by factions, whose differing views must inevitably lead to clashes in which some would rise to greater power and some would fall.

Curtius himself had friends and acquaintances in all camps. If his waxworks were to continue to flourish, he had to tread a difficult path. In such fraught times the vast majority of ordinary people tried to keep quiet, to pursue their work if they were lucky enough to have it still, to undertake civic duties if they had to, but to remain as far as possible neutral and disinterested.

Curtius, however, was not an ordinary person. He had spent nineteen years making himself and his *Salon de Cire* a feature of the Paris scene, recognised and visited by people from all walks of life. How well he had succeeded had been resoundingly demonstrated on 12 July when the mob spontaneously surged to the Boulevard du Temple to seize his wax busts of Necker and the Duc d'Orléans.

The exhibition had always reflected events and personalities of current public interest. Now it seemed to be turning into what was essentially a political focus, and what political party would finally wield power? No-one could foresee. Curtius had no wish to link himself too closely with any particular group, or star figure, that could fall as well as rise.

For the moment he decided that the best course was to make sure his patriotism could not be questioned. He had already, on 23 July, resigned his command as Captain of the National Guard of the Pères de Nazareth district. The superior status, though gratifying at the time, involved more time than he could spare.

Curtius remained, of course, in the National Guard, and took the precaution of obtaining from the Hôtel de Ville a paper accepting his resignation from the captaincy with regret and recognising the valuable service he had given in the position. Although he disliked parting with hard-earned money, the following day he made a voluntary contribution of forty-eight *livres* to the District Committee's funds.

Still nervous of the tightrope it seemed he would have to walk in the foreseeable future, Curtius sought further proofs, as he called them, of the 'zeal and activity' he had displayed. Between July and December 1789 he obtained no less than ten certificates testifying to his patriotic services and that he had been one of those who participated actively in the storming of the Bastille. No detail of his service was overlooked. He even managed to get a written statement that a short spell of duty in the Montmartre district, to which he had been posted as a National Guardsman between 29 August and 4 September, 'must be considered as having done a service to the Commune'.

[85]

To consolidate his status as a true patriot Curtius joined the Jacobin Club towards the end of 1789. Here again he had been faced with a dilemma. His old friend Marat was a co-founder with Danton of the violently left-wing Cordeliers Club. Another who belonged to the Cordeliers was Hébert, a former servant, convicted several times of embezzling from his employers, but now becoming influential through his virulently anti-royalist newspaper *Le Père Duchesne*.

Even though he felt it would be unwise to offend such men in case they finally gained the aims they sought, Curtius decided in the end to join the Jacobins, still moderate and favouring constitutional monarchy. He already knew a number of members, including Mirabeau, on whom the hopes of many for peace and justice in equality were centred; also among them was Robespierre, the unknown quantity, privately considered by Curtius to be a rising star.

The first year of the Revolution drew to its close. There had been no further bloodshed, and the King, albeit involuntarily, was with his subjects in the capital instead of isolated from them in the Court at now deserted Versailles. 1789 ended with the nationalisation of the Church's lands, though religious orders were allowed to function still for teaching and charitable purposes only. And paper money was introduced with the *assignat*, a note whose purchasing power would quickly and steadily decline.

For Dr Philippe Curtius and Marie Grosholtz the year 1789 was the most crucial in their lives. They were plunged, willy-nilly, into the revolutionary tide, to sink or swim. For both of them the survival of the *Salon de Cire* was the most important necessity.

The Great Anniversary

THE demolition of the Bastille was placed under the supervision of a Paris master-mason named Palloy. It was a tremendous task to reduce to rubble a fortress of such size and solidarity. Yet it was accomplished in a remarkably short time with the aid of explosives and an army of willing and eager labourers, glad of employment paid by the State and imbued with a sense of patriotic endeavour.

The stone and rubble was carted away from the city, but in the New Year master-mason Palloy was making a little profit for himself by selling suitably sized stones as mementos, each accompanied by a certificate of authenticity signed by Palloy.

On 18 January 1790 Curtius purchased a stone said to have come from near the entrance to one of the dungeons. He had it engraved with an inscription in Latin. This couplet, of no great poetic merit, was supplied by one M. Deduit, who described himself as 'Patriotic Author'. Since few of those likely to view the stone would be Latin scholars, a French translation was provided:

> Le Temps et les Tyrans ont construit la Bastille
> Les Français dans un jour l'ont detruit en famille.
>
> (Time and Tyrants built the Bastille
> The French people as a family destroyed it in a day.)

Curtius unfortunately mislaid his certificate of authenticity and had to write to Palloy to get another one. He mentioned in this letter that he intended to present his engraved stone to the National Assembly, but in fact it ended up on display in the *Salon de Cire*.*

In spite of the general relaxation of tension people were made aware from time to time that violence was never far distant. Even in her old

* Madame Tussaud brought the stone to England with her in 1802. It survived in the exhibition until 1925 when the premises were destroyed by fire. Palloy was imprisoned in 1794, for misappropriating most of the money he got from selling material from the demolition of the Bastille.

age Marie still had stamped on her memory the scene at the public hanging on 11 February 1790, of a certain Marquis de Fabras with whom she had been acquainted at Versailles. Then he had been a young officer in the detachment of the Swiss Guard which acted as bodyguard to the King's eldest brother, the Comte de Provence.

The Marquis was travelling abroad during the dangerous months of 1789, but returned to Paris. He was then accused of plotting with foreign powers to gain support for a possible abduction of the King and the assassination of Lafayette and Bailly. De Fabras admitted to having tried to influence 'certain parties' and to having received 100 *louis* towards his expenses abroad.

Many believed that the Marquis was acting on behalf of the Comte de Provence, but there was no evidence to prove this. The aristocrat would not speak. 'I carry my secret to the grave,' he said, and walked on to the scaffold with great calm and dignity, the first of many of his kind to display such qualities as they went to their execution.

The Marquis was executed in the Place de Grève, where so many felons had met their doom, and so became the source of many portraits of criminals in Curtius's *Caverne des Grands Voleurs*. Marie recorded in her *Memoirs* that the enormous crowd 'showed a savage delight at a Marquis being executed in the same manner as would have been the lowest individual in Paris'.

Incidents like this made Curtius, conscious of former royal connections, feel it necessary to go on underlining his patriotic zeal, and especially his participation in the storming of the Bastille. In March he obtained a paper from a gunner in the Pères de Nazareth district National Guard declaring that it was Curtius who had rallied all those eager to play a part on that occasion, and had led them to the Bastille, in spite of the fact that there were some, including the Sergeant, who did not wish to go.

In May 1790 the National Assembly abolished the old district boundaries, and created forty-eight *sections* in their place. The old Pères de Nazareth district was now incorporated in the *section* of Temple. Each of the new Paris *sections* had its own committee, elected by tax-paying householders, which was responsible for dealing with charity, food supply, and general business in the section.

The *sections* were each allocated a company of *Chasseurs* to supplement the National Guard. The *Chasseurs* had been created the previous September by a decree of the National Assembly. Its members had special duties at the *barrières*, as the gates into Paris were known. Lack of sufficient guards had caused a severe loss of revenue, as dues on commodities being brought in were not properly collected, nor

1. Marie Grosholtz (Madame Tussaud) aged 17, shortly before she went to Versailles as Madame Elisabeth's art tutor. (Madame Tussaud's Archives.)

2. Dr Philippe Guillaume Mathé Curtius wearing his National Guard uniform. (Portrait by Gilles Louis Chrétien. Bibliothèque Nationale).

3. Tableau of 'The Royal Family at Dinner' in the *Salon de Cire*. (Madame Tussaud's Archives.)

4. Outside the *Salon de Cire* in the Boulevard du Temple. The crowd includes workers wearing trousers, as well as better-off men in breeches (*culottes*). (Madame Tussaud's Archives.)

5. The Palais Royal Gardens. The people who frequented them became increasingly raffish in the 1780s. Curtius moved his exhibition from this location to the Boulevard du Temple. (Lithograph after Debucourt.)

6. 'Changing the Heads in the *Salon de Cire*'. A French cartoon of 1787, mocking Curtius's rapid up-dating of his exhibition. (Madame Tussaud's Archives.)

7. Fashionable promenade on the ramparts of Paris. People of all classes enjoyed strolling on these boulevards, with their many entertainments. (Engraving after A. de St Aubin.)

8. Voltaire on his deathbed. Wax miniature by Curtius. (Madame Tussaud's Archives.)

9. Wax miniatures by Curtius of Louis XVI and the Duc d'Orléans. (Madame Tussaud's Archives. The originals were lost when the exhibition burned down in 1925.)

10. A Revolutionary orator harangues the crowd at the Palais Royal. (Gouache by Le Sueur. Musée Carnavalet.)

11. 12th July 1789. The wax heads of Necker and the Duc d'Orléans seized by the mob from the *Salon de Cire*, for a protest march after Necker's dismissal from his post as Controller-General of Finance. (Gouache by Le Sueur. Musée Carnavalet.)

12. 12th July 1789. Rioting in the Place Louis XV after the protest march with the wax heads of Necker and the Duc d'Orleans taken from the *Salon de Cire*. (Auber. Collection Complète de Tableaux Historiques de la Révolution.)

13. The opening of the newly convened States General at Versailles in May, 1789. Louis XVI presided over the three Estates, the Nobility, the Clergy, and the Third Estate. All the Deputies were elected. (Contemporary engraving.)

14. Louis XVI, Marie Antoinette, and the first Dauphin, Louis Joseph, who died in June 1789. His brother Louis Charles then became Dauphin. (Engraving after A. de St Aubin.)

15. 10th August, 1792. The storming of the Tuileries by *sans-culottes* mobs. The Royal Family had escaped, but nearly all their loyal Swiss guards were killed. (Madame Tussaud's Archives.)

16. 21st January, 1793. Louis XVI on the scaffold of the guillotine in the former Place Louis XV, now Place de la Révolution. The ordinary carriage which brought him from the Temple prison drives away. (Madame Tussaud's Archives.)

17. The assassination of Lepeletier, a Deputy who had voted for the King's execution. Curtius reproduced the scene as a tableau in the *Salon de Cire*. (Auber. Collection Complète de Tableaux Historiques de la Révolution).

18. Maximilien Robespierre who instituted the Terror of 1794. He always dressed elegantly, and often carried a bouquet at public ceremonies. (Madame Tussaud's Archives.)

19. Antoine Fouquier-Tinville. During his term as Public Prosecutor in 1794 Marie Grosholtz and her mother were arrested and imprisoned. In 1795 he was guillotined and she modelled his severed head. (Madame Tussaud's Archives.)

20. Guillotined death heads modelled by Marie Grosholtz: Carrier, Fouquier-Tinville, Robespierre, Hébert, Louis XVI and Marie Antoinette, with her portrayal of the murdered Marat lying in his bath. (Madame Tussaud's Archives. All these can still be seen in the Chamber of Horrors.)

21. Full-size model of the guillotine constructed in 1854 by Joseph Tussaud, son of Madame Tussaud. He purchased scale drawings from the grandson of Charles-Henri Sanson, executioner of Louis XVI, and a blade, lunette, and chopper, used by Sanson and his son during the Revolution. (Madame Tussaud's Archives.)

smugglers apprehended. The establishment of the *Compagnie des Chasseurs Nationaux Parisiens* was designed to combat this situation.

The nomination of captains, lieutenants and sub-lieutenants was the privilege of the Municipality, also referred to as the Commune under the new circumstances. In spite of previous complaints about duties encroaching on his working-time, Curtius was flattered to be chosen as Captain for the *chasseurs* of his section, with the name *Bataillon de Nazareth* allocated to his Company. Curtius was, of course, an old friend of the Mayor, Bailly, and it would have been difficult to refuse the compliment to his zeal and efficiency.

The uniform of the *chasseurs* was similar to that of the National Guard, except that the hat had large and small green tufts and tassels; there was additional green ornamentation on the jacket, and instead of wearing gaiters the *chasseurs* had smarter, laced half-boots coming six or seven inches above the ankle. Curtius was proud of his uniform, and had a head-and-shoulders portrait of himself in profile, drawn by an artist who specialised in this type of likeness.

By now the bragging of the 'Volunteers of the Bastille', as those who had taken part in the conquest liked to call themselves, was beginning to annoy many citizens who had not actively participated. Such people, said Curtius, were viewing the Volunteers with a *mauvais oeil* (an unfavourable eye). They were jealous, and also a little frightened lest their own patriotic enthusiasm at the time should be questioned.

The Volunteers, however, thought that the moment had come when they should make representation to the Commune that their services had not received due official recognition. They were delighted when, on 19 June 1790, a Decree sanctioned by the National Assembly gave them the right to assume the title 'Conqueror of the Bastille'.

Curtius's numerous 'proofs', so carefully gathered, which he backed up by a printed brochure entitled *'Les Services du Sieur Curtius'* which gave a detailed account of the part he had played, of course gained him a place in the illustrious band of patriots.

Awards accompanied the title. These consisted of a *brevet* or certificate, a badge with a victor's wreath to be worn on the left arm or left lapel, and also a gun and a sword. These weapons each had an inscription 'Presented by the Nation to a Conqueror of the Bastille'.

All those 'Conquerors' whose health permitted were expected to serve in the National Guard, but there was a promise of pecuniary compensation for any who had suffered loss on account of their service. In spite of a number of grumbles expressed in his brochure, Curtius did not apply for any compensation for the money he claimed he had lost through curtailment of his work-hours while on National Guard duty.

[89]

Not everybody was pleased at the distinctions conferred on the 'Conquerors'. When it became known that they would have a special area allocated to them at the forthcoming celebrations in the Champ de Mars for the anniversary of 14 July 1789 there was, as Curtius wrote gleefully, 'almost another revolution'. However, trouble was staved off when the 'Conquerors' went in a body to the Mayor, and waived this concession.

Curtius was extremely gratified at the honour he could now claim, and henceforward signed his letters 'Conqueror of the Bastille'. He also greatly valued his inscribed gun* and sword which remained on display in the *Salon de Cire* until Marie brought the gun with her to England in 1802.

While the citizens of Paris were now able to occupy their minds with such trivialities as the official recognition of the 'Conquerors of the Bastille', the National Assembly, sitting in the old Tuileries riding-school, were pushing ahead with reforms. Already, the previous November, the Church's vast estates had been transferred to the State and become 'national' land, though the royal estates were not yet confiscated.

The National Assembly not only needed money urgently, but wanted to create a new class of property owner which would be pledged to the new order. Early in May, municipalities throughout France were ordered to sell off 'national' land in lots, sometimes as small in value as 600 *livres*, with generous instalment terms.

The former ecclesiastical lands were apportioned out among thousands of peasants and simple *bourgeois*, the new landowners who could be relied on to support the government which had given them this opportunity, never before available to them, to acquire their own land holdings.

The clergy had already been divested of their tithes. In future they were to be paid by the state, while both bishops and priests would hold office through election by 'politically active' citizens. The National Assembly's Declaration of Rights laid down that no man should be penalised for his religious beliefs, and full citizen's rights were granted to Protestants and Jews. Finally, all clergy would be required to take an oath of loyalty to the State, the Civic Oath. The King countersigned the National Assembly's decrees relating to 'national' land and the clergy with the utmost reluctance. He really had no choice.

The clergy themselves seemed ready to accept their new circumstances as State-paid employees more or less passively. There was no

---

* The gun remained on display in Madame Tussaud's exhibition until it was destroyed in the fire of 1925.

official protest from the Pope. The devout were distressed, but in general the clergy, with the vast wealth the Church had acquired over centuries, were not held in great popular esteem. Most people felt it was a good thing if this wealth were now put to work for the new Nation.

Neither Curtius nor Marie was devout and they did not concern themselves over the new system for the clergy. Curtius regularly attended meetings of the Jacobin Club, feeling secure in his title of 'Conqueror of the Bastille'. The Club met in the old library of the former Jacobin convent, an imposing room with its high, curved, barrel ceiling. The Club was already noted for its debates, but in spite of its radical aims the subscription of 24 *livres* excluded poorer and less educated people, no matter how enthusiastic they might be for revolution.

Curtius also frequently visited the public gallery of the Manège, the riding-school, where he listened intently to the Assembly's proceedings. But Marie, fully occupied with her work at the *Salon de Cire*, kept herself detached from politics as far as she could, and only went to the public gallery when she needed to observe some deputy whose portrait she was modelling.

The main source of public excitement was the preparations for the 'Solemn Festival of the Federation', planned to mark the 14 July anniversary of the storming of the Bastille, which had become a symbol of the new revolutionary era that had dawned.

The site chosen for the festival, the Champ de Mars, was across the Seine, near the spot where the Invalides stands now. Although it was within the city walls, this area was so deserted it was a favourite place for fighting duels. Some twelve thousand workmen were put to work on levelling and preparing the site, and erecting stands round it. Paid work was welcome and the labourers toiled, but as the month of July drew near, it was obvious the huge Champs de Mars would never be ready in time.

The citizens of Paris, of every type and grade, were called on to help, the city *sections* organising contingents. From the highest to the lowest, Parisians came forward voluntarily, civilians of all ranks, ecclesiastics, military, offered their service. There were even nobles, who had recently been deprived of their titles and escutcheons by the National Assembly, and ladies who, though they might have hunted vigorously, had never lifted a finger, were eager and willing to join in and do their inexperienced best.

Curtius stayed at home to look after the *Salon de Cire* and sent Marie alone to the Champ de Mars. It was an excellent opportunity for her, as for many others, to demonstrate by this willing service their patriotic loyalty. Marie, of course, had already given evidence of hers when she

[91]

modelled without visible flinching the decapitated heads of de Launay and Flesselles, but additional proof, Curtius considered, was always prudent in the present climate.

This, at least, was an occasion she could enjoy, for, though tiny in stature, she was strong and wiry, and accustomed to physical work as well as modelling in her daily life. While others wielded pick, spade or hammer, Marie cheerfully trundled a barrow.

It was a brilliant scene, for many of the contingents from the *sections* carried bright flags and banners, and were accompanied by a drummer. 'Perhaps never before nor since', recollected Marie, 'was seen such a gay and animated assemblage of labourers.' Foreign visitors came to witness the extraordinary scene on the Champ de Mars. The toilers worked on till sunset, when they departed home to their *sections*, banners still flying and drums still beating, to encourage aching limbs.

On 14 July, the actual day of celebration, this mood of enthusiastic joy still prevailed. The processions began gathering early, some on the site of the demolished Bastille. As yet there was no bridge across the Seine from the Place Louis XV at the bottom of the Champs Elysées, another gathering-place. Hundreds of participants and spectators picked their way across a specially constructed bridge of boats. This was Marie's shortest route so she too made the novel crossing.

Three triumphal cars were the *pièces de résistance* in the huge procession that marched into the Champ de Mars. The first carried a woman dressed as the Goddess of Liberty. Some said she was a prostitute hired for the occasion, but others, including Marie, maintained that she was a respectable person. Wherever she came from she filled her part well, having an imposing stature and fine features.

The other two cars bore effigies of Voltaire and Rousseau. These cars were followed by dozens of deputations with National Guardsmen from all the provinces, their flags and banners bright, their bands playing loudly. There was group after group of women all dressed in white with tricolour sashes, and those men who were not in uniform displayed tricolour scarves.

All converged into the Champ de Mars, surrounding the central spot where the ceremonies were to take place. The stands were packed with spectators. It took three hours for everyone to assemble, during which it began to pour with rain. But this failed to dampen the general spirit of gaiety, even hilarity. Never before had there been a people's spectacle like this. All previous parades and processions in Paris had been connected with royalty or the royal armies.

On this occasion the President of the National Assembly and the King sat as equals, side by side, on chairs ornamented with gold fleurs de lys. They sat in a splendid pavilion erected to shelter the representatives of authority. The Queen, the Dauphin, and members of the royal family and Court were accommodated in an elevated balcony.

It was the first time Marie Grosholtz had seen Marie Antoinette since she left Princess Elisabeth's household. She noticed that the Queen had tricolour ribbons in her hair. She could not clearly distinguish Madame Elisabeth on the crowded special balcony.

When the 'Conquerors of the Bastille' group arrived, they marched to the altar that had been set up in the centre, and laid on it ribbons that they had earlier been awarded for their services. Curtius was proudly among them. The *Salon de Cire* would not open that day, and Marie's mother was left in charge of the shuttered house. There was a remarkable atmosphere of fraternity and goodwill when Talleyrand, Bishop of Autun, took his place at the altar, surrounded by clergy in white surplices, to conduct the Mass which opened the ceremonies.

After the Mass, Lafayette, former royal general and now commanding the National Guard, rode on a fine horse to the pavilion where he received a command from the King. He turned his horse and rode to the altar, carrying a parchment inscribed with the words of the Constitutional Oath. He dismounted and placed it on the altar. Louis XVI rose and stretched his arms in the direction of the altar while he pronounced the words of the Oath. As he finished all the deputies of the National Assembly shouted, 'We swear!'

It was a moment of high drama. The sky had cleared and the altar of Liberty was sunlit. Marie could see that the Queen's face, up to now sad, had lighted up. Caught up in the general enthusiasm, she seized the Dauphin in her arms and held him out to the people. 'Vive la Reine!' thundered in her ears, the last time she would ever thus be greeted by her subjects. No such occasion would ever be witnessed again.

Although there were reported to be 400,000 people present, the processions and the whole ceremony had gone off without a single instance of disorder. 'Now the future of France is bright and secure,' thought the people as they began to disperse. 'Bloodshed, oppression, misery and hunger are past.'

They wended their way back to their *sections* to celebrate the future in their own localities. Marie spent the night dancing with friends, neighbours and visitors who joined in, on the site of the demolished Bastille. 'Happy illusion,' she wrote in her *Memoirs*. 'Pity that it could not longer have endured!'

Royal Disaster

SOON after this highly successful festival a number of deputies in the National Assembly thought it would be a good idea to set up a tableau of Curtius's royal wax portrait figures in the palace gardens at Versailles. The King and Queen seemed to have regained public approbation. Though neglect was fast overtaking the once-glorious parterres, fountains and groves, many Parisians still resorted there during the summer. A royal group might be an attraction, for without the bustle of richly dressed courtiers and liveried servants everywhere, the gardens were lifeless and dull.

Portrait figures that Marie had modelled during her time with Madame Elisabeth were chosen, the King, the Queen, Madame Royale and the Dauphin. Of course the little boy she had modelled was now dead and his brother was Dauphin, but no-one was likely to notice this, as the general public had scarcely had a glimpse of either child.

It was a depressing task for Marie. The royal group was arranged just inside the empty Petit Trianon, once Marie Antoinette's jewel-box of a retreat, where even her husband could not go without invitation. The royal family looked forlorn, immobile in their satin clothes, with a few pieces of gilded furniture arranged as a setting.

Before she took the road back to Paris, Marie managed to take a brief look at the great palace, empty and abandoned apart from a few servants, now in shabby clothes. Some of the furniture had been taken to the Tuileries to make the royal accommodation there a little more comfortable. The rest was in store. No-one really knew what to do with the vast château. Some deputies had suggested it should be sold to raise money for the Treasury, but there had been violent protests from the residents of Versailles.

So many of these had suffered financially since the departure of the Court, which, since the time of Louis XIV, had been the source of their livelihood. It seemed incredible now that the place, once thronged with people, the scene of glittering ceremony and entertainment, had all been eclipsed in the space of a single year. Whatever people thought would be the future of the monarchy, none believed that the King and Queen would ever return to live in splendour at Versailles.

The harmony between the King and Queen and the people, expressed by the enthusiastic cheering at the festival of 14 July, did not last more than a few weeks. It was rudely shattered. A number of regiments and many generals still remained staunchly loyal to Louis XVI. One such officer was General the Marquis de Bouillé whose headquarters were at Nancy in north-eastern France. In August a Jacobin mutiny erupted among his hitherto Royalist soldiers. General Bouillé crushed this revolt immediately and decisively, executing a number of the 'Patriot' mutineers.

When this news reached Paris there was a wave of popular fury. Orators and pamphleteers accused Marie Antoinette of having encouraged, if not instigated, the severe reprisals against these patriotic men. People belived this. There was no more 'Vive la Reine'. Marie Antoinette was again the prime object of her subjects' hostility, for all believed it was the Queen's influence which had prevailed over her hesitant and now bewildered husband, who could not cope with the events that had overtaken him.

Nor was it all harmony in the National Assembly. Although the deputies had shouted 'I swear' in unison when the King took the civic oath on the Champ de Mars, unison was now increasingly absent between the extremist Left, whose members sat on the left side in the Tuileries riding-school, and the moderate liberals, such as Lafayette, and those who took their seats on the right side of the hall, supporters of a constitutional monarchy. These included conservative deputies who wished the King to retain a number of his rights, possibly even the hated Right of Veto. Debates were heated, and political watchers like Curtius found it difficult to assess whose views would ultimately prevail.

Curtius was also worried because Mirabeau, his friend and patron, was becoming increasingly discredited. Mirabeau made no attempt to conceal the fact that in May 1790 he had made a deal with the King and his close advisers. It had not been difficult to win a promise of stronger royal support from Mirabeau. He was deeply in debt, and in acute financial embarrassment. When the King offered to pay off all his debts and give him a substantial annual pension, Mirabeau agreed to protect the monarchy to the utmost of his ability. On 10 May he sent Louis XVI a written declaration of 'loyalty, zeal, activity, and courage'. But Mirabeau prudently added the proviso that 'success never depends on one person alone'.

Marie Antoinette had always refused to receive Mirabeau on account of his professed liberal views. 'I think we shall never be reduced to the painful extremity of having recourse to Mirabeau,' she had said. Now she was forced to recognise that he was indeed perhaps the only hope of saving the monarchy. In July she reluctantly met Mirabeau in the park of the palace of St Cloud. He noticed that though she spoke to him graciously, her eyes were filled with tears of humiliation.

The deputies of the Left accused Mirabeau of treachery. Moderate Lafayette cynically remarked, 'He only betrays in the direction of his convictions!' Mirabeau ignored accusations and criticisms. He continued to work prodigiously and exercise his gift of eloquence, but in December 1790, when the Jacobin Club elected its President for the coming year, Mirabeau met with overwhelming defeat. Robespierre became the new leader of the Jacobins. Curtius's political acumen had not failed him, Marie reflected when she heard the news. From first acquaintance Curtius had picked out Robespierre as a man of the future and had cultivated his friendship. Now Robespierre was beginning to win power.

Curtius was not only worried about Mirabeau's growing unpopularity as a representative of the people. With his medical knowledge he was anxious about his friend's health. Though Mirabeau's energies seemed undiminished, he was obviously ill. Curtius was convinced that Mirabeau would not live much longer, and his portrait figure in the *Salon de Cire* was out of date. It would never do if Mirabeau were to expire and his portrait in wax, which everyone would want to see again, was no longer an accurate likeness. While Curtius's *Salon* might have become more of a political portrait gallery than the splendid exhibition of general current interest that it had originally been, Curtius refused to lower his standards of 'the closest approximation to life'.

At the turn of the year he was able to persuade Mirabeau to give another sitting. Marie was allocated the job of modelling the new likeness. It was only just in time. Though Mirabeau retained his mental forces to the last, and in January 1791 blocked the Abbé Sieyès's proposal that if the King died, the regent should be elected by the National Assembly, his health worsened rapidly and he expired on 2 April 1791.

Marie, who had been observing Mirabeau for years, thought privately that he had probably been poisoned by some of his many enemies, but others considered it was his wild early life and debauchery that had brought about an early death at forty-two. With him died another of the royal family's hopes.

Directly Mirabeau was dead pamphlets condemning his 'treachery' flooded the streets. Ironically, he was more mourned by the King and the nobility than by the people whose rights he had so strongly supported.

With Curtius still spending a great deal of his time in political venues and frequently absent on his duties with the *Chasseurs*, Marie was hard pressed to keep the *Salon de Cire* updated. There were continual shifts of interest in the National Assembly, personalities emerging and then fading away. Newspapers and broadsheets carried sketches and carica-tures, but if citizens really wanted to know what a newly prominent deputy looked like, they went to the wax exhibition on the Boulevard du Temple. Interested bystanders outside the riding-school could easily identify deputies as they went in and out if they had scrutinised their lifesize and lifelike portrait figures in the *Salon*.

There always seemed to be someone new in the forefront. Now it was Barnave, who had become alarmed at some of the actions of the deputies on the Left. He felt uneasy that they had insisted on giving political freedom to the negroes and mulattoes in the French possession of San Domingo. Other deputies were disquieted too, and Barnave formed a new 'conservative' group on the Right. Their aim, if the King could be persuaded into proper co-operation, was to end the Revolution and establish the much talked-about constitutional government which so far had taken no definite shape.

To keep pace with the public's demand to see new faces all the time, Marie herself was obliged to pay frequent visits to the public gallery in the riding-school in the Tuileries. Even though most deputies were pleased enough to be asked to sit for a life-mask to be taken, she still had to observe the 'subject's' stance, gestures and personality in order to provide the kind of likeness for which Curtius's *Salon* had always been famous.

It was not an easy time for Curtius and his household. Money was short. Those willing to give sittings did not expect to pay for them. There were no more lucrative private commissions for portraits in wax, nor for decorative or licentious little groups, as there had been from a rich and aristocratic clientèle. Foreign visitors still came to Paris, of course, but they were not the kind likely to leave a handsome acknowl-edgement that they had enjoyed touring the exhibition.

Madame Grosholtz had to devote the whole of her time to finding the best sources of food for the table at which Curtius still liked to welcome political guests. The whole entertainment area around the Boulevard du Temple was suffering from revolutionary austerity, though nearly all the shows managed to keep going, keeping a wary eye the while on political trends. No-one had forgotten how the mobs of the previous year had several times threatened to burn down the theatres, showing that French people should not enjoy themselves while their country was in distress.

In the Tuileries the Queen was cut off from all her old diversions, occupying herself in her apartments with embroidery and playing with the Dauphin. She had been considering for some time whether flight from Paris might not be the best, perhaps the only, hope for the future. She began taking steps in this direction as early as December 1790, when her brief popularity after the Champ de Mars anniversary had completely vanished.

Her admirer, the still faithful and still infatuated Swede, Axel Fersen, had managed to find a way of access to the royal apartments through a secret entry. Through him Marie Antoinette decided to order a special travelling carriage. Axel Fersen should have had enough sense and firmness to dissuade the Queen from insisting on the kind of vehicle that she deemed suitable for the royal family to flee in.

His blind obedience to her wishes resulted in a large coach, the type known as a berlin, which would have been conspicuous even in the days when nobility and aristocracy travelled in great splendour and ostentation. The enormous green-and-yellow berlin was designed to seat six people, and was upholstered in white velvet. Its interior was lavishly fitted out, complete with food containers, canteen of plate, and chamber-pots.

The coach also carried a heavy load of spares against breakdowns on the road. Six horses were required to draw this equipage, and even then it could travel at only a slow pace. This, with the time needed to change six animals at every posting-stage, meant that haste was an impossibility.

Axel Fersen himself was convinced that the royal family should leave France, and even Mirabeau, now so unfortunately deceased, had supported the idea. He had thought it very likely that if the King informed the National Assembly that he and his family intended to leave the country on a specified date, the Assembly would agree to let them go. After all, in February 1791, two aged royal aunts who had left secretly were stopped three times by zealous National Guards but, instead of arrest and punishment, were in the end allowed to go by a special decree of the Assembly. Many deputies would probably be relieved to be rid of the royal family. But the King would not agree to any such plan.

However, as the year progressed, Louis XVI became more and more despondent. The clergy had now been obliged actually to swear the Civic Oath, as laid down in the Civil Constitution for the Church which the King had so reluctantly signed. Priests who refused to do so were banned from their ministry. This had at last aroused the Pope to activity. In March 1791 he issued a Papal Bull condemning the Civil

Constitution which the King had signed, and condemning revolutionary principles.

Louis, sincerely pious, was greatly distressed. On Palm Sunday he heard a mass from a cardinal who had taken the Civic Oath, but refused to take Communion from his hands. Popular opinion declared that the King should have accepted the entire mass from a 'Constitutional' cardinal, and news of his refusal to do so was immediately carried outside. When the King left the chapel, the National Guardsmen on duty refused to line his path.

The following day Louis wished to leave Paris for the palace of St Cloud, as he had done the previous year, but there was a demonstration as the royal family's coach moved off from the Tuileries. Men seized the horses' bridles, but the National Guard made no attempt to intervene. To the Paris mob it was clear that the King was leaving Paris in order to perform his Easter religious duties with a priest who had not sworn the oath, away from the watching eyes of the citizens.

The coach and those following it were surrounded by a now frenzied mob. 'He shall not leave,' they screamed. Commander Lafayette and Mayor Bailly ordered the National Guardsmen to clear a passage for the royal coach, but Louis intervened. The mood of the milling crowd was ugly. He did not want the bloodshed that seemed inevitable if a way through were forced.

For two hours the royal party sat in their carriages, besieged in a menacing silence. Finally, the door of the royal coach opened. The King stepped out and with his ponderous gait made his way back on foot into the Tuileries. There was still dead silence as the rest of the party followed him. After this episode the King gave way to Marie Antoinette's pressure and agreed to flight from Paris, though he would not hear of leaving France.

The secret plans for escape were masterminded by Axel Fersen. The objective was for the King, the Queen, the Dauphin, Madame Royale and Madame Elisabeth to join General Bouillé, who had dealt so drastically with Jacobin mutineers and who commanded all the forces in Lorraine. There, it was hoped, a sufficient force of loyal troops and *emigrés* from across the eastern frontier could be mustered. Thus supported, the King could march back to Paris, or, if this proved impossible, be safely escorted across the border and out of France, no matter how unwilling he might be to go.

The detail was carefully worked out. Using Axel Fersen's clandestine way of entry and exit, the royal party, plus the children's governess and two loyal waiting-women, would slip out from the vast and now almost empty Tuileries palace to a secret rendezvous in a quiet street beyond the courtyard, the Carrousel. Each would leave separately, except of course the children, and at the rendezvous Axel Fersen would be waiting, disguised as a coachman.

He had obtained a kind of small omnibus called a *citadine* which would hold them all. Fersen would then drive them through one of the *barrières* or gates. Hopefully there would be no trouble with the customs at an early hour of the morning, since the party would be plainly dressed and without heavy baggage. Once past this hurdle he would drive to a place where the green-and-yellow berlin would be waiting, probably beyond the Porte St Martin on the road to Metz.

With almost incredible luck the entire royal party succeeded in leaving the palace without detection. It was said later that Lafayette must have connived, as it was his National Guardsmen who were responsible for guarding the Tuileries. At the rendezvous there was anxiety when everyone had appeared except the Queen. Finally she turned up, agitated and upset. She had been escorted by a loyal courtier, and neither of them had ever been in the small streets of Paris before. They missed the way and had great difficulty in locating the arranged meeting-place.

Hurriedly they scrambled into the *citadine*, and Fersen drove it by a roundabout route to the *barrière*. At such an early hour the customs official did not bother himself over this undistinguished-looking family in the shabby omnibus. They passed through the gate, already later than planned because of Marie Antoinette's late arrival. There was further delay when Fersen could not find the berlin, discreetly hidden down a by-way. At last the royal party clambered into the heavy vehicle, with the two waiting-women in a light cabriolet which would drive a little way ahead of the berlin.

They said goodbye to Axel Fersen, who was worried that they had already lost so much time. Tears welled in Marie Antoinette's eyes as they made their rapid farewell, but the King had refused to allow Fersen to travel with them any further. It was after two o'clock in the morning when the green-and-yellow berlin moved off on a journey that was doomed from the start.

The heavy coach moved at a very slow pace, even with its six horses. Every change of horses necessitated a long stop. The King insisted on putting his head out of the window to look around whenever they passed through villages, and the flamboyant vehicle attracted attention all along the route. Twenty-four hours later at Varennes the King and Queen and their family were arrested.

All along the way the rumour had flown, 'The King and Queen have passed!' When their flight from the palace was discovered, it was not difficult for pursuers on fast horses to find out their route. Even empty, the green-and-yellow berlin had attracted notice when it passed through one of the gates on its way to the rendezvous on the Metz road. How could anyone fail to notice such a conspicuous vehicle?

Marie Grosholtz never forgot how news of the royal family's escape from the Tuileries was received in Paris. In her *Memoirs* she said, 'The sensation throughout Paris was indescribable: all the shops were shut, the tocsin was sounded, and the drums beat to arms: a general apprehension seemed to invade the populace that Louis would soon return with an army formed of emigrants and foreigners and wreak a dreadful revenge on the people of Paris for all the indignities with which they had overwhelmed the unfortunate Monarch.'

Curtius, as a Captain in the *Chasseurs*, was called out at once. Marie had to conceal her agitation and dismay. She prayed that the royal family, including her former employer, Madame Elisabeth, might reach safety, but common sense told her they would certainly be overtaken by the pursuers, who had been despatched with the utmost promptitude.

Marie heard that Barnave was one of the three deputies riding post-haste to Varennes, to conduct the arrested royal family back to Paris. His hopes of getting the King's co-operation to act as head of a proper constitutional government had vanished with the monarch's flight. His 'conservative' group, that so feared the Left's extremism, could be dismissed as uselesss now.

During the return journey to Paris, Barnave sat in the berlin with the King and Queen, Princess Elisabeth and the two children. Progress was terribly slow, matched to the pace of the National Guardsmen, hastily rounded up in Varennes and the neighbourhood, who marched alongside. Barnave was courteous to his prisoners. It was told later that Madame Elisabeth had even seized his coat-tails to stop him getting out of the royal coach when it was stopped by a hostile mob in one village, as she feared he might get hurt trying to protect them.

When the royal family finally reached the Tuileries again, Marie Antoinette's suffering was obvious and Louis, whose brown plush, sober suit was covered with dust that had come through the lowered windows of the coach, seemed dazed and uncomprehending. On arrival the Queen went straight to her rooms. When she took off her hat her attendants saw that her ash-blonde hair seemed to have turned white.

To Marie the whole disastrous episode seemed ridiculous as well as tragic, and typical of the folly and lack of common sense of which she had witnessed so much at Versailles. The actual escape of the royal family from the Tuileries, though highly dangerous, had been carefully planned and successful. Had they not then travelled in so conspicuous a fashion and at such a slow pace, with such long and noticeable halts—six horses had to be changed—Axel Fersen's hope of getting Marie Antoinette and her family to a safe haven might have been realised.

Emergence of the Sans-culottes

THAT same summer of 1791 saw Curtius achieving an ambition he had pursued for twenty-one years. He successfully entered a coloured wax bust for the annual exhibition put on by the Academy of France. Hitherto he had met with failure, and had been obliged to content himself with exhibiting in the Académie St Luc, the gallery in which artists of sufficient merit, but who had failed to make the grade with the Academy's selectors, could put their work on display.

Curtius was helped in this triumph by his friendship with the celebrated painter Jacques-Louis David. David had been a member of the prestigious Academy of France since 1780 and though he painted portraits of members of the aristocracy he made his name with his pictures of historic scenes from classical antiquity.

In 1789 David threw himself enthusiastically into the revolutionary cause. The picture he painted that year was called 'Brutus condemning his Son'. It showed the legendary hero, Lucius Junius Brutus, who established a Republican government in Rome in 509 BC. Subsequently, Brutus condemned his own son to death for conspiring to restore a monarchy. The picture was a great success in Paris for its revolutionary theme.

Curtius wanted to add a portrait of David to the *Salon de Cire*. The artist visited his house frequently, and though Marie was not always pleased with his rough manners, he was good-natured and pressed her to visit his studio and inspect his paintings whenever she liked. Curtius wanted Marie to model the portrait, and she had some difficulty in persuading him to sit. David was very conscious of his ugliness and particularly of the disfiguring wen on one side of his face, almost like a tumour. In the end David yielded, and was complimentary about the likeness she produced. He admired Marie's talent, and later on would use it for his own purpose.

Meanwhile the King's attempt at flight began to have serious consequences, though at first it seemed as if the whole affair might be

[103]

dismissed as a sort of escapade. Then the National Assembly concluded that an enquiry must be held. The moderately inclined deputies, who wanted to keep the King at the head of the government, claimed that Louis had not gone willingly, but had been 'abducted' by enemies of the Revolution. They succeeded in convincing a sufficient number of their fellow-deputies for the King to be declared innocent of any hostile intention against his people. This decision incensed the far more violent deputies on the Left, members of the Cordeliers Club, and the more extreme elements in the Jacobin Club, to which Curtius belonged.

These anti-Royalists combined to organise a great demonstration against the decision to absolve the King. It was held on the Champ de Mars, scene only a year before of so much goodwill towards the monarchy. Lafayette called out the National Guard to disperse the demonstration. There was resistance, and the Guard opened fire. Fifteen of the demonstrators were killed. 'A massacre!' screamed the leaders of the Left. The only result of the massacre of the Champ de Mars on 17 July 1791 was an even wider split between the moderate Right and the extremist Left in the National Assembly, and uneasy apprehension among the many uncommitted citizens of Paris.

In the Jacobin Club the moderates decided to withdraw. The membership had become far too revolutionary for their taste. They formed a new Club in premises not far away, which was called the *Feuillants*, as it met in the former *Feuillants* monastery, no longer functioning.

Curtius did not join the *Feuillants*. He remained in the Jacobin Club, with Robespierre as its President. All the Jacobin Clubs that had sprung up in the provinces declared their allegiance to the parent club in Paris, and feeling against the King increased.

Louis XVI accepted the helplessness of his position. Without demur he agreed to a revised Constitution which the National Assembly had drawn up. It was quite clear that the King of France was not going to get any active support from fellow European monarchs. On 25 August the new Emperor Leopold of Austria and the King of Prussia met at Pillnitz and made a declaration of their general wish to protect the King of France. They went no further than that.

Even such a feeble announcement was, however, sufficient to arouse the fury of the Jacobins. It was an attempt, they claimed, to interfere with the affairs of the French nation. Extreme Leftists, with the exception of Robespierre, demanded war. Barnave's group, and the moderates, opposed any opening of hostilities. They were not eager to embark on what the Left regarded as a crusade of liberation to free countries oppressed by monarchy.

For the first time the King and Queen found themselves in harmony with the Left. They thought that a declaration of war by France, and a subsequent defeat of the Revolutionary army by other European powers, was the only hope of putting the French monarchy back in its rightful place. Louis appointed a new Foreign Minister, General Dumouriez, who was also strongly in favour of war as a solution.

For the moment, however, in the last months of 1791, the National Assembly had other matters to occupy its attention. It was a new Assembly, for after the revision of the Constitution the old one had been dissolved, and an entirely new set of deputies elected, some retaining their old seats, some newcomers. Among the latter was Curtius's artist friend, the famous David, who was one of those representing the people of Paris. In this new Assembly the balance of power was uncertain. There were three hundred uncommitted deputies, two hundred and sixty moderates or *Feuillants*, and one hundred and thirty-six Left-wing Jacobins.

The new people's representatives had grave problems to consider. The fall in the value of the paper banknote, the *assignat*, was creating acute problems which affected the entire populace. In purchasing power it was now worth only five per cent of its original value. The 1791 harvest had been quite good, but the farmers refused to sell their grain for such a rapidly depreciating currency. They preferred to hoard it. Other commodities were in short supply too, especially those imported from the French colonies, such as coffee and sugar.

The measure giving political freedom to the negroes and mulattoes of San Domingo, which had so alarmed Barnave and his colleagues in the previous National Assembly, resulted in widespread slave revolts. The crops were not harvested and shipped to France in the quantities expected. Marie recalled in her old age the reaction of the people of Paris, 'the scarcity of coffee and sugar . . . gave rise to many violent scenes, the people insisting that it was [due to] a monopoly. They broke open and pillaged the shops of many grocers when at last it was proved that throughout Paris there was a total deficiency in the supply of these articles.'

The fear of monopolies such as there had been during the bad harvests and shortages under the monarchy was widespread throughout France. In this situation a movement began, a movement that was spontaneous, springing from the grass-roots of the entire country, owing nothing whatsoever to the deputies of the National Assembly. Just as the people of Paris had banded themselves together entirely of their own volition to storm the Bastille and to march on Versailles and fetch Louis XVI back to Paris, so now the people in all the provinces of France came together to voice their wishes and demands.

It was not a movement confined to the very poor. Joining in it were peasants, working men earning a wage, even quite highly paid craftsmen. They were united in their fear and hatred of monopolies, and those who grew rich through them. They demanded fixed prices. They called themselves the *sans-culottes*. It was not a name meant to imply that those who formed the movement were ragged and half-naked. The name merely expressed the common people's contempt for all those—the noble, the aristocratic, the wealthy merchants and manufacturers—who marked their superior status by always wearing *culottes*, knee-breeches, never trousers of any kind.

The *sans-culottes* movement, increasingly vociferous, was extremely disturbing to the moderates in the National Assembly. Their aim was a free economy: they did not want fixed prices for commodities. They felt this new movement was a dangerous one, seeking to impose its will on the elected representatives, the deputies, who now formed the nation's government.

All the *sans-culottes*, women as well as men, adopted as their badge a red Phrygian cap. This distinctive bonnet, which any woman could run up from an oddment of red cloth, or knit more quickly than a stocking, would become, all too soon and for all peace-loving citizens, the symbol of revolutionary violence and terrible bloodshed.

The King Humiliated

IN this time of financial stringency, scarce and expensive food, and unpredictable public temper, all proprietors of theatres and places of entertainment in and around the Boulevard du Temple were feeling the pinch. Curtius's *Salon de Cire* was attracting plenty of visitors, but entrance charges had to be kept low so that all good patriots could afford them. His profits suffered and his costs rose.

The exhibition's wardrobe in particular required constant outlay, and cloth was expensive. There were still good stocks of silks and satins in the cupboards—Marie had never had any difficulty about dressing suitably while she was working at Versailles—but these were now useless. All notabilities now had connections with the Revolution, so portrait figures could no longer be clothed in silk or brocade. Sober materials had to be found and purchased at inflated prices.

Anxious about his finances, Curtius renewed, in January 1792, his efforts to lay hands on a family inheritance he had been chasing since 1788. The difficulty was that the lawyer handling this family affair was located in Mayence (Mainz) in the Rhineland, and since the outbreak of the Revolution with the fall of the Bastille in 1789, communications had become chaotic, making the conduct of business outside the capital, and particularly outside France, extremely difficult.

Soon after Curtius had put in his original claim to the inheritance the lawyer concerned died. He then addressed himself without success to the Secretary of the French Legation in Mayence. The documents requested by this official, and promptly despatched by Curtius, appeared never to have arrived. In the political upheavals of 1789 and 1790 it was impossible to pursue this matter, but with his ever-tightening purse strings, Curtius decided he must make a further effort.

He sat down and wrote again to the Secretary of the French Legation in Mayence. 'The Revolution which has occurred in France', he complained, 'has not permitted me to write to you, having sent several other letters which I suppose were intercepted, since I received no answer.' Under the circumstances this was hardly surprising.

Even under the *ancien régime* the postal services had not been outstanding in their efficiency. Organised by the tax-collecting officials of each area, the mail was carried in two-wheeled vehicles, protected by a tarpaulin hood. The boxes and baskets into which the letters and parcels were packed were stored in the wagon by the courier, whose duty was to stop and distribute the mail in each town or village in the district through which his mail-cart passed.

In 1790 the National Assembly had removed responsibility for mail from local tax officials, and transferred it to the newly formed local municipalities. These authorities had no experience of organising a mail system. With general disturbances in the countryside and a pervading atmosphere of suspicion among Jacobin patriots, not only was the service now erratic or almost non-existent, but letters and packages were apt to be opened, inspected, and then destroyed or mislaid.

It was almost to be expected that Curtius's earlier correspondence with the French Legation at Mayence would vanish en route. Inherited wealth was not favoured by the Jacobins. The inheritance he was seeking was a dubious one in any case. A relative, a cleric whose residence was in Mayence, though he had died on a visit to Hungary, had willed his estate to be divided between Guillaume Mathé Curtius and his brother Charles.

Curtius had duly received his share some five years earlier, and was now trying to obtain his brother's portion, for Charles had not been heard of for fifteen years, and the lawyers' efforts to trace him had failed. He might be dead, he might have sailed for one of the colonies. Whatever his fate, Curtuis felt he was now entitled to claim his brother's share of their relative's estate. He needed it.

Curtius did not trust this letter to the mail. He had been recommended a reliable person who was travellling to Mayence, and who agreed to carry the missive. It was a somewhat dangerous service, for if the carrier were stopped and searched, a letter claiming money from the estate of a cleric, even if that cleric were deceased prior to the Revolution, would cast suspicion on the patriotic fervour of both sender and carrier.

The letter was delivered to its destination, but did not produce any response, though a certain Count O'Kelly who had been in Mayence at the time, told Curtius, with whom he was acquainted, that the Legation's Secretary had seemed favourably impressed by the claim. However, the official took no action, sensibly being unwilling to involve himself in so trivial a matter. Curtius gave up his efforts, realising that revolutionary conditions and private financial claims did not mix and, moreover, could be dangerous if pressed too far.

In Paris there was a new excitement. The humane Dr Guillotin's pressure on the Assembly to sanction a more reliable and less painful instrument of execution finally succeeded. A guillotine was built according to his plans, and trundled into the Place de Grève, a favourite spot for carrying out the death penalty. It was not set up as a fixture, for gallows and other instruments of public punishment had always been portable and moved around the city as convenience dictated.

On an April day in 1792 an enormoous crowd gathered to see the heavy knife drop for the first time on the neck of a mugger who had snatched a purse. People roared approval as the head tumbled into a basket, and the body was rolled into another basket alongside. Curtius could feel confident that, whatever the turn of events, his *Caverne des Grands Voleurs* would never lack new subjects or interested visitors.

On the twentieth of the same month of 1792, the National Assembly finally decided to declare war on Austria, the Queen's native land. It was a disastrous move, for the rapid campaign planned by Generals Dumouriez (the Foreign Minister), Dillon and Biron failed completely. The French army was in no state to embark on battles likely to lead to swift victory. Nearly all its most able officers had emigrated, and its organisation was miserably broken down.

Lafayette, even though he had been amongst those who favoured a declaration of war, wrote, 'I cannot conceive how war was declared without any kind of preparation.' All three generals retreated ingloriously, outnumbered by superior troops. On 20 May hostilities ceased, though there was no treaty or formal peace agreement offered by either side.

The people of France were furious at the ignominy that had befallen the Revolutionary army which had hoped to liberate oppressed nations from their absolute monarchies. They turned their anger, not on the deputies who had instigated the brief, humiliating campaign, but on their Queen, 'the Austrian' Marie Antoinette.

Though popular fury was concentrated on the Queen, the deputies who had ordered war found that public esteem for them had waned considerably. To restore it, and to pacify hostile feeling, particularly among those who sported the red bonnet of the *sans-culottes*, the Assembly passed three new decrees.

The first decree, published on 27 May, threatened banishment to all those priests who had not sworn the oath to the Civil Constitution of the Clergy. The second, a personal insult to Louis XVI, dissolved his personal bodyguard, the Household Guard, and the third proposed that, for the second anniversary of the storming of the Bastille, 20,000 patriots from the provinces, *fédérés* as they were called, should be invited to camp, for the duration of the festivities, outside the walls of Paris.

The King swallowed the personal insult, and agreed to the dissolution of his loyal bodyguard, but for once exercised immediate decision and authority by vetoing the other two decrees. He was deeply religious and had already refused Communion from the hands of a cardinal who had taken the oath which the Pope had condemned. The dangers of a 20,000-strong mob of revolutionary fanatics camped at the gates of Paris were obvious. There would certainly be trouble, and probably the bloodshed he abhorred.

In Paris itself discontent had been fermenting since the failure of the Austrian campaign. Many citizens had allied themselves to the *sans-culottes* whose numbers in the provinces continued to grow in considerable strength, particularly around Marseilles in the south of France.

Here extremists were increasingly strident, demanding the total abolition of the monarchy, and the election of a new Assembly by universal suffrage. Hitherto voters had to have qualifications as householders and taxpayers. The Marseilles *sans-culottes* wanted none of that.

Trouble in Paris seemed inevitable, and it came on 20 June. The pretext was the celebration of the Tennis Court Oath taken at Versailles in 1789 by the original deputies of the Third Estate. On this anniversary crowds, under the leadership of a local brewer called Santerre, began to gather in the Faubourg St Antoine, always a hotbed of dissension. The brewer, Claude Santerre, was described in contemporary memoirs as 'bloodthirsty, brutal, and without education', but he was popular and wielded great influence in the restive Faubourg St Antoine.

There was no special call-out of the National Guard, but news of the gathering came quickly to Curtius's ears. Always fearful of the safety of his exhibition, too near the Faubourg St Antoine for comfort, he and Marie went out to see what was happening. They were appalled by the size of the mob, which had begun to march in the direction of the Tuileries.

Men were armed with every kind of weapon: old muskets, pikes, pieces of sharpened iron tied to poles, staves and brickbats. The mob was a sea of red bonnets, the *sans-culottes* badge, and there was a continual roar of 'Down with Veto!'

Horrified, Marie saw a calf's heart impaled on top of a pike, with a dangling placard, 'Heart of an aristocrat'. She saw a miniature gibbet being carried along, a female doll hanging from it, symbolising the Queen. Citizens who stood watching as the crowd streamed past realised, as Marie said later in her *Memoirs*, that they were witnessing 'a dreadful warning of what might be expected from the future'. But, she added, 'None dared voice their sentiments.'

Curtius decided to follow the mob at a discreet distance, while Marie, filled with alarm and apprehension, went back to the *Salon de Cire*. The exhibition must stay open even though there would be few visitors this day. She could only hope that it would not end with the arrival of dripping heads on pikes. She could still hear the strains of the revolutionary song, *Ça ira*, mingled with the shouts, as she turned towards the Boulevard du Temple.

When the rabble, with Santerre at its head, reached the Tuileries the vanguard surged noisily into the riding-school where the Assembly was in session. They were shouting for the King's veto on the two decrees to be ignored. The deputies were alarmed and angry at this invasion. With some difficulty the demonstrators were persuaded to leave the hall, and a more orderly delegation was readmitted to present their petition formally to the representatives of the Nation.

This objective achieved, the mob smashed its way into the Tuileries gardens, heading for the palace. No-one was on duty there except the usual small number of National Guardsmen. No reinforcements had arrived, and there was no sign of any official from the Paris Municipality.

Faced with this menace, the duty Guards opened the gates leading into the palace forecourt, and the crowd rushed in screaming, 'Down with Veto!'

Groups of men led by Santerre converged on the great doors of the palace, yelling to the helpless National Guardsmen to open up or they would smash down the doors.

Inside the palace the King was in a vast anteroom, whose windows looked out on to the forecourt. When the invaders swarmed into this room, such was the press that he was forced back into one of the window embrasures to face the sea of hostile faces, red bonnets and brandished weapons.

Others in the mob headed up the great staircase, hunting for the Queen. When Marie Antoinette realised that a hostile crowd was going to break into the palace, she wanted to go downstairs and join the King, but Madame Elisabeth and her ladies persuaded her that this would only make the situation worse. Madame Elisabeth said that she herself would go down and join her brother, but it was too late. The noise of heavy feet on the stairs, and crashes as some of the rioters tried to drag a small cannon up them, made instant flight imperative.

The Queen, her sister-in-law, and her two children, with a few attendants, fled from room to room as the search for them began. They

[111]

used the concealed passages through which they had escaped for the doomed flight to Varennes.

While Marie Antoinette was being chased from room to room, the King stood calmly in the window embrasure, facing his subjects. For two hours he was hemmed in. A red *sans-culottes* bonnet was clapped on his head. A bottle and glass were thrust into his hands with orders to drink to the health of the Nation. This he did cheerfully, but he made no response to threatening demands that the veto he had given on the two decrees be reversed.

Now, at last, the Mayor of Paris, Pétion, who had succeeded Bailly in that office, appeared on the scene. He had, he said, only just learned of the disturbance. Hoisted on the shoulders of two National Guardsmen, he addressed the mob, asking the demonstrators to withdraw quietly.

Then the King made an extraordinary suggestion. Why not, he said, open the doors of the enfilade of state rooms that led off the anteroom, and let people pass through and look at them before they went home? The doors were thrown open.

The result was astounding. The pushing, jostling, hostile crowd became quiet and formed itself into orderly lines. The people began filing through the splendid rooms, examining their surroundings with lively interest. The men who had been crashing about on the upper floors in search of the Queen came downstairs and joined them.

When they reached the council chamber an astonishing sight met their eyes. Marie Antoinette's flight had ended in the state apartments. Now she stood in the council chamber, flanked by two hussars, with Madame Elisabeth, her children and a few attendants. They stood by a long table, on the end of which the little Dauphin was sitting.

No-one attemped to assault the Queen. A few insults were hurled, and someone put a red bonnet on her head. This she took off and placed on the head of the Dauphin. Most of those filing through the room just stared at the royal group, standing so still they might have been in Curtius's *Salon de Cire*.

By eight o'clock in the evening all the crowd had passed through the state apartments and departed for home. The splendid rooms were untouched, though upstairs, where the hunt for Marie Antoinette had gone on for two hours, rooms were wrecked, doors smashed, floorboards stove in and carpets littered with broken mirror-glass and ornaments. When at last Louis XVI was able to join the Queen, she saw that a red bonnet was still perched on his head. He had forgotten that it was there.

Curtius arrived back late at the Boulevard du Temple, having seen as much as he could without involvement. He told Marie that the door-man, or barker, who invited passers-by into the *Salon*, calling out its attractions and prices of entrance, had better be dressed immediately as a *sans-culottes*. It had always been his policy to have the doorman dressed appropriately for the time. Since the fall of the Bastille his uniform had resembled that of a National Guardsman. Now a red bonnet, trousers and a pike might help to keep the exhibition safe from mob attack.

Royal Prisoners

MANY who supported the King, publicly or privately, were heartened that he had managed to defy the mob by refusing to reverse his two vetos. After all, a dangerous situation had ended without violence, apart from the smashing up of a few rooms in the Tuileries palace. They were soon disillusioned.

Egged on by the ranting of such newssheets as Marat's '*L'Ami du Peuple*', and Hébert's '*Le Père Duchesne*' and inflamed by continual haranguing by street-corner orators, the committees of the forty-eight Paris *sections* decided to disregard the King's veto. All the provincial municipalities, under increasing Jacobin pressure, followed suit. The Assembly, swimming with a tide that seemed ever stronger, agreed to sanction this decision. The *fédérés* of all the provinces of France were officially invited to converge on Paris for the 14 July anniversary celebrations of the fall of the Bastille. The second matter, that of the recalcitrant priests, was left more or less in abeyance for the moment. Some of them were arrested and imprisoned, some managed to get out of the country, and many abandoned their parishes to go underground, under assumed names, wherever they could find a safe refuge. There was nothing they could do for their parishioners. Non-juring priests were forbidden to exercise their ministry, charity was now the responsibility of the municipalities, and anyone who tried to see them privately for religious consolation was put in danger.

Then a devastating shock hit Paris and the whole nation. Prussia, joining forces with Austria, turned the tables by suddenly declaring war on France. Though the hostilities of France's earlier declaration of war on these two nations had ceased with the rout of the French generals, no peace terms had ever been discussed, so no treaty was broken. The King of Prussia had been a co-signatory with the Emperor of Austria on the Pillnitz declaration of support for Louis XVI nearly a year before, but this had been dismissed as a totally ineffectual document by the Assembly. No-one had expected this action by Prussia.

Panic gripped the country. The Assembly issued a proclamation, 'The Motherland is in Danger!' and a call to arms, '*Aux Armes, Citoyens!*' All the *section* committees of Paris and all the provincial municipalities went into permanent session. The National Guard was put on permanent alert throughout the country.

Inspired with patriotic zeal, men rushed to respond to the call for all 'viable' citizens to enlist. 'As many as fifteen thousand men enlisted in one day,' recalled Marie, 'at amphitheatres that were erected in various public places.' The *Salon de Cire* was badly affected by this flight to the army. There were a number of men on the regular staff, for maintenance, for moving heavy figures and fittings. All disappeared. Marie was obliged to call on the help of any older men she could find who were able-bodied enough to handle these tasks. Curtius could give little active help, for he was on permanent duty as a National Guard officer.

With Paris in a state of frenzied excitement, the *fédérés* began arriving on 8 July with the Marseilles contingent, already notorious for extremism, bawling a song that would become famous as the *Marseillaise*. It was a song originally composed by a young man, Rouget de L'Isle, for the French army in the Rhineland. It was first sung in the Strasbourg drawing-room of a Madame Lietrich, and the stirring words and rousing tune appealed to the popular patriotic mood. Soon it was heard everywhere, and when the song reached Marseilles it was adopted by the *sans-culottes* as their own.

They also brought a dance to Paris, called the *carmagnole*. A resident of Paris, Monsieur Thibault, described how he first heard the song and witnessed the dance, roared and capered by about five hundred men and women from Marseilles. He wrote, 'You cannot imagine anything more horrifying. These five hundred fanatics, three-quarters of them drunk, almost all wearing a red bonnet, bare-armed and dishevelled . . . We left them moving towards the Champs Elysées where they indulged in devilish dances before joining the orgy to which Santerre invited them . . . they howled the airs of *Ça Ira* and the *Marseillaise*.'

The Bastille anniversary celebrations for 1792 went ahead on 14 July in spite of the tense atmosphere. Curtius and Marie again repaired to the Champ de Mars. Amongst the emblematic monuments erected there they saw an immense tree, 'The Tree of Feudalism', rising from a funeral pyre. On its branches were hung ermine-lined mantles, tiaras, escutcheons, and a jumble of other objects symbolic of the *ancien régime*.

During the opening ceremonies it seemed to Marie that the Queen was weeping, and she shrieked in terror when there was some confusion and jostling around the King, fearing that he had been assaulted. But Louis' calm remained unshaken. When he was asked to put a torch to

[115]

the pyre beneath the Tree of Feudalism, he quietly declined, saying that as feudalism no longer existed there was no sense in burning it.

No-one insisted that he take the torch and he was allowed to rejoin Marie Antoinette and the royal party, cheered by a few loyal troops who were present. The royal family regained the Tuileries without any hostile demonstration. It was the last time the King, Queen and Madame Elisabeth were seen in public till Louis, Marie Antoinette and the Princess in turn mounted the scaffold of the guillotine.

Meanwhile Curtius visited the public gallery of the Tuileries riding-school as often as possible, trying to assess the political temper. Within the Assembly, renamed in September the National Convention, numerous factions were disputing and sparring. Some demanded the King's deposition, some his banishment and a regency for the little Dauphin. Others clamoured that he should be brought to trial or even assassinated.

There were very few now who clung to the concept of a constitutional monarchy, once the objective of the first National Assembly when it proclaimed itself at Versailles in 1789.

Anxious not to imperil his household and his exhibition, Curtius agreed to have nine *fédérés* billeted on him. Marie and her mother were dismayed but they were fortunate for, in the event, their lodgers proved to be respectable men, representatives from various provinces. 'They behaved well,' Marie recorded, 'and were very polite.' These particular *fédérés* even showed consideration, always letting Madame Grosholtz know when they would be out for meals. Food, now organised by the *section* committees, was still scarce and expensive.

After the 14 July celebrations of 1792 only a few *fédérés* departed for home. Paris remained swarming with provincial *sans-culottes* mingling with its own groups of the same movement. When the Duke of Brunswick, commanding the Prussian and Austrian armies and the *emigré* forces, headed by the King's brothers, the Comte de Provence and the Comte d'Artois, which had joined them, issued a manifesto, this threw the whole country into a state of panic. Parisians were particularly alarmed and agitated.

The Duke's manifesto proclaimed that unless the royal family of France were treated with respect, France would suffer 'military execution' and its capital, Paris, 'total destruction'. In spite of the thousands of volunteer soldiers who had strengthened the French army, terror spread. There were rumours that the Prussian forces were already marching on Paris, and would massacre the wives and families of those now dong military service.

An almost hysterical reaction was immediate. All the *section* committees got together and marched on the Hôtel de Ville. There, alongside the Commune that regularly ran the municipal affairs of the city, they set up another Commune to liaise with the *fédérés*.

This new Commune at once planned a day of demonstration to take place on 10 August. Lafayette, the original Commander of the National Guard, was now back in the army, and the *sans-culottes* did not like his replacement. They regarded him as a monarchist and believed that, if trouble arose, he would do his utmost to protect the King. He was arrested by the new Commune and promptly executed.

In his place Santerre, the brewer from the Faubourg St Antoine, was put in command of the National Guard. Marie hastily finished his portrait in wax, on which she had already started work, and re-arranged the grouping in the *Salon de Cire*. Many *fédérés* were visiting the exhibition, and they wanted to see their heroes of the day. Voltaire, Rousseau and Mirabeau were now background figures, Lafayette and Bailly less important. Pétion, the current Mayor of Paris, must be brought forward, and Marat, Danton and Robespierre have precedence over more moderate deputies from the Assembly.

During the nights of 9 and 10 August, while Curtius was out with the National Guard, Marie, alone with her mother, heard the sound of the tocsin, the bell that was rung to signal trouble. It was impossible for her to leave the house. Like her neighbours and so many other peaceable citizens of Paris, she had no idea what was happening and could only wait for someone to bring news.

The tocsin was warning that a rabble had assembled. It formed a pincer movement encircling the Tuileries, one arm marching from the nearby Faubourg St Antoine, one from the left bank of the Seine, led by the men from Marseilles and another extremist group from Brittany. Soon the palace would be surrounded by a menacing mob, hundreds, if not thousands, strong.

Inside the palace Louis XVI received warning. He knew too well that revolutionaries like Marat and Hébert had been calling for his death. The attitude of the National Guardsmen on duty made it clear that he and his family could not look to them for protection. The Assembly, in this moment of emergency, was sitting in session in the riding-school. This seemed the only possible refuge for the royal family. The loyal Swiss Guard in the palace would be hopelessly outnumbered by the horde of fanatics closing in on it.

For the second time the King and Queen, with their children and Madame Elisabeth, and a handful of trusted attendants, made their way secretly out of the Tuileries palace. They crossed the gardens unhindered, and entered the riding-school. If any National Guardsmen were aware of the escape they took no action. The devoted Swiss Guard were now virtually the only protection left in the Tuileries. Very few of the National Guard could be counted on to give them support.

Inside the riding-school there was consternation. The deputies had known what was happening, but had been powerless to halt the marchers, powerless to defend the royal family. Hurriedly they decided that the royal party must be transferred at once to a safe place where they could be guarded—guarded as virtual prisoners.

Quickly the refugees were smuggled out of the riding-school and taken to the prison keep of the Temple, part of the vast complex where the Prince de Conti, Curtius's first patron, now many years dead, had once held court in his glittering apartments, inviting artists like Curtius to join his guests.

No-one in Paris slept after the tocsin began to toll on that night of 10 August. Marie, shut up in the house on the Boulevard du Temple, was racked with anxiety. She could not go out to seek information from neighbours, leaving her mother alone and the exhibition unguarded. She did not know in what part of Paris Curtius was on duty with his *Chasseurs*. Among the Swiss Guard were companions of her early childhood in Berne, men she regarded almost as uncles and brothers. During her eight years at Versailles she had seen much of them and made friends with others. Since Curtius had brought her back to Paris she had been out of touch with them. What would happen now if there was trouble at the Tuileries? The Swiss were the only loyal troops left in the palace to try to protect the King. No-one yet knew that the King and his family were now incarcerated in the Temple, only a short distance from the *Salon de Cire*.

Before dawn Marie's agonising vigil was interrupted by a neighbour. This woman's husband was with the National Guard, she thought on duty at the Tuileries. She had learned that there was fighting there, but could get no definite news, only reports that the gardens were littered with bodies. She begged Marie to come out with her so that she could search among them, and find out if her husband had lost his life in the bitter battle people were saying had taken place.

Marie knew that if Curtius were at hand he would forbid her to go on such a dangerous venture. But all night she had been desperately anxious. She must find out what had happened. 'I will come,' she told her distraught neighbour, and what she saw when they reached their destination was stamped on her mind for the rest of her life.

They walked by a devious route along the *boulevards*. In her *Memoirs* she recalled it as if she were living it again. 'The weather was intensely hot: the sun was just beginning to throw his deep red light on the highest buildings and trees of the Boulevard: an awful stillness

[118]

pervaded the scene. . . . Not a breath was stirring, not a leaf was ruffled as we entered the gates of those gardens which had so often been the scene of innocent joy and revelry, where happy thousands had appeared in holiday attire . . . but now, alas, how bitter was the contrast. Wherever the eye turned it fell upon many a mangled corpse, and in some places heaps of the slain were thrown indiscriminately together.'

Marie and her companion saw that the beautiful gravel walks were stained with gore. The statues, though spotted with blood, were undamaged, for such was the extraordinary respect manifested by the mob for these works of art that, when their victims sought refuge by climbing up the statues, even these murderous men would not fire their guns at them, but pricked the clinging figures with their pikes until the unfortunate wretches were forced to the ground and killed.

In spite of her fear and horror, and impelled by her torturing anxiety for Curtius and the Swiss Guards she knew so well, Marie helped her neighbour search through the mangled bodies. Had they been noticed they would have been arrested at once, but the gardens were now deserted. Discovering no-one they recognised among the 'appallling objects' they inspected, the two women fled the scene as unobtrusively as they had arrived. Over 370 had been killed in the 'demonstration' of 10 August, including nearly all the loyal Swiss Guards, but a quarter of the dead were *fédérés*.

After the slaughter the Assembly, menaced in the riding-school where they had been trapped by *sans-culottes* with pikes, guns and other weapons, agreed to suspend the monarchy. The King would be replaced by an Executive Council until such time as a new Assembly could be elected by universal suffrage, as the *sans-culottes* had demanded.

The September Massacre

BY the end of August of 1792 the mood in Paris was divided. Some of the forty-eight *sections* seemed bleak, the streets almost deserted as the inhabitants kept to their houses as far as possible. Other *sections* were jittery and restless. Fear was everywhere. The French armies had sustained two more reverses in the Austrian Netherlands, and how soon would the joint armies of Prussia and Austria and the *emigré* forces be marching over French soil to capture Paris?

To citizens like Curtius, trying to assess the present and gauge the future, the Assembly seemed to be in total confusion. The triumph of the *sans-culottes* on 10 August had destroyed the moderating influence of the Feuillants.

Jacobin, republican-orientated deputies now seated themselves high high up on the left at the back of the Tuileries riding-school. Known as Montagnards, or the Mountain, these deputies were opposed by a group known as the Girondins, because they were led by four men from the Gironde department in south-western France, though its members came from a variety of provinces. These Girondins sat in the middle of the hall, 'the Plain', and were committed to democracy. They had little use for the clergy. This group was made responsible by their fellow deputies for the conduct of the war.

Curtius had friends in both camps. Many of the still uncommitted deputies supported the Girondins. Others simply did not attend the sessions and stayed away from the riding-school. They were frightened by the rantings of such as Marat, who demanded the slaughter of all nobility and clergy, and Danton, whose orations, delivered in his huge, bellowing voice, made him appear an alarming embodiment of republican fervour. The King, a prisoner in the Temple, had ceased to play any part at all in government.

The Assembly, now called the National Convention, and the new revolutionary municipal Commune set up by the *section* committees before the assault on the Tuileries on 10 August, appeared to most people to be two rival authorities, though Danton strove to bring about unity in face of the threat of an invading army.

The new municipal Commune had instituted patrols, which circulated the streets picking up anyone suspected of favouring the King. These victims were taken to the Hôtel de Ville, and then distributed among the prisons of Paris on both sides of the river Seine. All the prisons were becoming crammed with royalist suspects and non-juring clergy, as well as the common run of criminals arrested every day for serious or minor offences.

Dangerous rumours began to circulate in the city. It was whispered that all these royalists and priests in the prisons were plotting a mass escape and insurrection, when they would take bloody revenge on those who had incarcerated them.

Tension grew, and matters finally erupted on 2 September when a bloodthirsty rabble set upon six hackney coaches which were taking recalcitrant priests to the Abbaye prison of St Germain south of the river. All but one of the clergy were murdered. Then the cut-throat gang, numbering about a hundred and fifty men, burst into the prison itself, killing the inmates indiscriminately. Most of the attackers were *sans-culottes*, many of them butchers by trade, but ordinary tradesmen and workpeople were caught up in the bloodlust and turned into vicious, merciless mass-killers.

After the massacre at the Abbaye, the mob turned its attention to the many other prisons. The various *section* authorities seemed stupefied at the outbreak of violence. Not a National Guardsman was seen. People living in the vicinity of the prisons or happening to be on the spot, who saw the slaughter going on, stood watching, silent, stunned by what they saw, hardly able to comprehend what they were witnessing.

The murdering gang moved relentlessly on from prison to prison, among their leaders the former soldier Maillard, who had led the march on Versailles when the King was brought back to Paris. It was hot work covering the distance between the nine prisons, and killing so many suspects, priests and ordinary criminals alike. None was spared. In one of the prisons the inmates were the dregs of the city, guilty of petty or habitual offences, many suffering from disease. Locked away in this place nicknamed 'the Sink', these wretches too were murdered brutally. The mob called for wine as they raged through the streets. *Section* committees hastened to open up shuttered wine-shops, setting out tables and bottles so that the killers could slake their thirst.

At mid-day a cannon was fired off on the Pont Neuf, one of the bridges across the Seine, and a black flag was run up at the Hôtel de Ville. Marie heard the cannon-shot. Word of bloody rioting around the prisons had reached the Boulevard du Temple, but there was none in the vicinity, although the prison of La Force was not far off. Curtius was out and Marie hoped that he was in no way involved. No-one around really knew what was happening, for there had been no general mustering of a crowd from the Faubourg St Antoine, as on previous occasions.

When the murdering rabble reached La Force prison they found the Princesse de Lamballe among the packed-in prisoners. Marie had heard that the Princess, once Marie Antoinette's closest friend, had been arrested at the Tuileries. She had managed to leave France after the royal family were taken from Versailles, but she had returned to the side of her royal mistress when she heard of their disastrous flight to Varennes.

At the Tuileries she had resumed her title of Superintendent of the Queen's Household, though there was no longer a household left for her to superintend. But at least she could give Marie Antoinette devotion and support in this time of distress. Marie had no idea where the Princess had been taken after her arrest.

When Maillard and his blood-soaked mob discovered the Princesse de Lamballe in La Force prison, she was dragged into the courtyard and ordered to declare her love of the Nation and liberty and to swear hatred for the King and Queen. The former she did willingly, but refused to swear the second oath even though offered safety if she did. Her fate was as rapid as it was horrible.

The Princesse de Lamballe was struck down with a stunning blow, her body revoltingly and degradingly mutilated, and her head cut off and stuck on a pike. 'Take it to the Queen!' someone yelled. 'Let the Queen see it!' A group seized the pike and set off to the Temple, the head aloft, the mutilated body dragged along behind.

Then somebody in the mob recollected the other severed heads that had been taken to Curtius's *Salon de Cire*. If Curtius were away his niece would surely be there and could make a good job of it, as she had done before.

Marie's shock and horror when she saw this head were almost uncontrollable. She had managed the heads of De Launay, Flesselles and Foulon, but they, as individuals, had meant nothing to her. The Princesse de Lamballe she had known well during her years with Madame Elisabeth at Versailles. She had personally experienced her sweet nature and kindness to everyone, even if she had found Madame de Lamballe's extreme sensitivity, which caused her to burst into tears so frequently, a trait with which she could not sympathise. Now she was forced to take this head on her lap, though she could not control the trembling of her hands as she did so. She always remembered it. 'The features, beauteous even in death, and the auburn tresses, though smeared with blood . . . shone with all their natural brilliance and lustre.'

In spite of Marie's shrinking horror and revulsion, once she had cleansed the delicate features the artist took over. She determined, since she was forced to perform this task, that she would make sure this portrait was as beautiful as the original. No matter in what guise it would have to appear in the *Salon de Cire* to satisfy the likes of Santerre and Maillard, she would make for herself a 'souvenir' of this kind and gentle lady. Marie kept her resolution. When, many years later in 1802, she took her wax exhibition to London, the recumbent portrait figure of the late Princesse de Lamballe was one of the most admired examples of her art, showing the lovely face in sleep, not death.

Pleased that the head of the Princess would take its place among other 'criminals', the mob stormed off to the Temple keep, but the Queen was spared the horror of a terrible last look at the head of the woman who, though displaced in Marie Antoinette's fondest affection by the calculating Duchesse de Polignac, now safe in Vienna, had returned loyally to her mistress's side at risk of her own life. The Queen fell unconscious to the floor when told why a screaming mob outside was demanding her presence at the window.

Madame Elisabeth managed to get the fainting Queen carried to another room. Fortunately she was slow to recover consciousness and 'though for a considerable time the Temple rang with the horrid yells of the brutal mob', the men finally gave up and departed, to parade the head and body of their blameless victim elsewhere along the streets of Paris.

The slaughter in the prisons carried on for two days. No-one could calculate the exact death-toll of clergy, aristocrats, royalist suspects and common criminals, but somewhere between twelve and fourteen hundred prisoners were brutally murdered. Neither the authorities nor the citizens themselves had made any attempt to halt the bloodshed. Some whispered, but dared not say aloud, that Marat, with his ferocious calls for all anti-Jacobin opposition to be annihilated, bore the greatest responsibility for the massacre.

The deputies of the Assembly brushed aside the whole affair, stating that it was the result of fear engendered by the enemy invasion of French soil, and a belief that those incarcerated were plotting an outbreak and would attack and kill the families of all those men who had rushed to enlist in the French army. Most Parisians seemed to wish only to forget the whole bloody occasion, but Curtius was seized with apprehension.

[123]

He realised that Marie's revulsion and trembling hands, which she had tried so hard to conceal as she modelled the dead head of the Princesse de Lamballe, could have put the whole household at risk. He felt, as he had felt after the fall of the Bastille, that his patriotism must be emphasised and underlined, for he was after all German-born. If someone chose to investigate, they would find this defined in the documents he had been obliged to get certified by the French pre-revolutionary authorities, in order to back his claim to his brother's inheritance. They would find that his father had been in the civil service of the Holy Roman Empire, that nominal collection of states whose monarch was the Emperor of Austria. Curtius still spoke fluent German, in spite of so many years' residence in Paris.

The action he took in his state of momentary fear and panic was peculiar. Curtius had never interested himself in matters religious or clerical, but now he chose to write to the President of the Assembly on the subject of the remaining rebellious clergy who would not take the Civic Oath. He made an extraordinary proposition in his letter:

> Everyone is embarrassed, it seems to me, in coming to a conclusion about the refractory priests whose conscience and ridiculous theology cause so many troubles and massacres in this empire, also in those where these lions in sheep's clothing steal money, wine and women of feeble character whose confidence and protection they gain.
>
> Here is what I propose in respect of these. We have in the hands of the Dey of Algiers and that of Tunis a number of good sailors and good soldiers, and above all good Frenchmen, who would be in ecstasy to learn on their return to their homeland of the marvels that have taken place here. . . .
>
> Let us therefore make an offer to our neighbours, the Deys of Algiers and Tunis, to make an exchange of three to one, that is to say three refractory priests for one good patriot.
>
> If they lose on account of the bad merchandise we send them, how much shall we gain by reason of the spirit of citizenship with which our enslaved brothers, become free, will be animated!

After signing this remarkable missive Curtius added to his name 'Capitaine de la Bataillon de Nazareth', to underline his continued devoted service in the National Guard. The letter, dated 16 September, was annotated by an official and included in the Assembly's Order of the Day.

Marie made no comment on the letter. Any measures Curtius took for the safety of household and exhibition she regarded as necessary. Possibly some remark of hers might have inspired his unpleasant idea. The piratical Deys, rulers of Algiers and Tunis (not to be confused with

Beys who were governors of Turkish provinces) had for years organised raids against French shipping and coastal villages on the Mediterranean, taking captives who were then used as slaves, but whose freedom could be purchased by ransom.

Marie remembered how, when she was with Madame Elisabeth at Versailles, the monks of the Convent of Maturin located in the Vielle Rue de Temple near the *Salon de Cire*, used to march through the streets of Paris, continuing in procession to Versailles to seek alms towards the ransom of French subjects captured by the Deys. Some, whose relatives or charity had managed to find the required ransom, used to march with the monks, carrying fetters similar to those they had worn as slaves. Madame Elisabeth's heart was invariably touched by these unfortunates.

Curtius felt that he had made his point, though the Assembly took no apparent notice of his letter. Large numbers of recalcitrant priests had been massacred anyway and at the moment they were not considered an urgent problem. It was over a year since the last of the religious orders had been abolished. Municipalities took care of charity. Religious buildings throughout the country were being put to more patriotic uses, such as housing Jacobin Clubs in the towns, or were being gradually demolished, the stone and timber carried away for secular building projects. Curtius had been somewhat over-apprehensive. After the savage violence of the prison killings, a comparative calm returned to Paris.

Then, on 20 September, came great good news. The French Generals Dumouriez and Kellerman had clashed with the Austrian, Prussian and *emigré* forces under the command of the Duke of Brunswick as they were on their march towards Paris through the valleys of the Argonne. The French infantry and artillery stood firm in their path at Valmy. After an exchange of fire the invading forces withdrew in the face of this stubborn opposition, and began a general retreat.

At the same time General Custine, with whom Curtius would later become embroiled, advanced from Alsace into Germany and reached Mainz (Mayence) and Frankfurt. General Adam Philippe Custine, *ci-devant* Count, had served with the French forces in the American War of Independence. While courageous, he was severe and despotic, sometimes to the point of brutality. Subordinate officers and his men alike feared him: he was generally unpopular, not at all the type of man to get along with the easy-going and flexible Curtius when their paths ultimately crossed.

None the less, when General Custine's armies appeared in their midst the Rhinelanders seemed to awake suddenly to the new concept

[125]

of freedom symbolised by the tricolour flag of the Republic of France. They put up little resistance to the invasion of their territory.

Immediately after the French victory at Valmy the Assembly disbanded itself for re-election. The new representative body, comprised of many who had sat before as well as newcomers, immediately introduced measures which eased the surveillance, repression and controls which had made the people's lives miserable. At the end of September decrees were also introduced by which births, deaths and marriages had to be registered at the Hôtel de Ville. Under the *ancien régime*, when the Church was supreme in these matters, the local church registers recorded baptisms, funerals and nuptials, but though these religious ceremonies were not actually forbidden, they were frowned on and few took place. Divorce was made possible and legal.

People were confused and bewildered when the National Convention introduced a new calendar with Year One of the Republic starting on 22 September 1792. All the months were renamed and religious festivals such as Easter and Whitsun had no place in the new Republican layout of the year. Ordinary citizens found it difficult to adapt to these sudden changes, but it really did seem as if the new era was now firmly established, with prospects of victory abroad and peace at home.

None the less Curtius thought it prudent to continue making his supportive patriotism known to those in power in the new Assembly. Once again he addressed himself to its President. He forgot, however, to make use of the new calendar, dating his letter 5 October in the old style, instead of the republican 14 Vendémiaire.

With the epistle he sent what was his second donation of two hundred and twenty *livres* towards the expenses of the war, and took the opportunity to grind a personal axe:

> I have learned with all the interest the Cause of Liberty should inspire of the complete victory gained by General Custine, who could, if you requested, do me a very great service in Mayence by enabling me to receive the inheritance of my elder brother of whom there has been no news for 60 [?] years . . . to give orders to the Town Hall of Mayence that the inheritance of Charles Curtius should be sent in francs to his brother Guillaume Curtius. . . . I should have much more to offer the country.'

Not surprisingly, General Custine, even if he did receive such a request, refused to be pestered with the affairs of the proprietor of the *Salon de Cire* in which his portrait in wax was prominently displayed with those of the other victorious generals. His acquaintance with Curtius was of the slightest.

[126]

Curtius, like so many others, was finding money a problem. Cash was short everywhere, with so many men in the army instead of pursuing their normal peacetime trades. Although entrance fees had to be kept low, it was difficult now to attract visitors to the exhibition on the Boulevard du Temple in the numbers that had once flocked there. The scope of the *Salon de Cire* was virtually limited to political figures, though the criminals in the *Caverne des Grands Voleurs*, augmented by the grisly array of death-heads, never failed in its popularity. It was hard for Curtius to find the money to keep up his high standards, and impossible to maintain former profits. Marie had to do most of the work, since Curtius's civic duties kept him away so much of the time.

Madame Grosholtz's housekeeping problems were augmented too. In October 1792 the Jacobin Club appointed Curtius as *defenseur*, or protector, of all Austrian or Prussian deserters who applied to the Society of Jacobins for assistance and refuge. They were accommodated in Curtius's house on folding beds that were set up at night, even in the exhibition area when there was an influx.

Curtius had let himself in for this burden in July when, attending a meeting of the Club, he had volunteered to take into his house a Tyrolean deserter from the Austrian army. As the French forces became victorious, more and more enemy soldiers decided to desert and made their way to Paris to enjoy, they hoped, the benefits of Liberty and Equality. They were turned over to Curtius for food and lodging until such time as they found the means of fending for themselves. Marie and her mother could well have dispensed with this responsibility, though some of the men could give help with the heavier tasks in the exhibition, and their presence did give to the household a measure of protection from suspicion.

[127]

The Inevitable Penalty

WHILE many ordinary citizens were optimistic that bloodshed and terror had finished, others felt apprehensive about the rabidly left-wing 'Mountain' in the National Convention. Out of the seven hundred recently elected deputies, some 150 were comparatively moderate Girondins. People were not uneasy about them, but the leaders of those who opposed them caused alarm among citizens who longed for a peaceful life.

Danton, with his huge head and thunderous voice, dominated the Montagnards, with Marat whose violent influence was undiminished even though he was now a sick man. His body was covered with a repulsive skin disease, to relieve which he spent his time at home, whether writing or resting, in a bath. This was fitted with a writing-board so that he could use his still intense energy pouring out anti-monarchist invective for his newspaper, *L'Ami du Peuple*.

Robespierre also sat with the Montagnards, but, ever cold and detached, held himself aloof. Invariably seated near him was his close friend and ally St Just, who declaimed fanatically 'that which constitutes a Republic is the destruction of everything that opposes it!' These were the men who made many ordinary people feel frightened and insecure. They were the men that Curtius was always watching, and Marie distrusted.

The future of Louis XVI was continually under discussion in the Assembly. The Constitution drawn up in 1791 declared that the King was inviolable, but some deputies argued that since the attack on the Tuileries on 10 August, and the subsequent incarceration of the King and his family in the prison keep of the Temple, he had become merely an ordinary citizen, and thereby subject to the same laws and justice as anyone else.

The imprisoned royal family's only means of getting fresh air and exercise was strolling on the battlements of the keep. Landlords whose property had windows overlooking the battlements quickly found a source of profit by charging interested people for a private viewing during the family's exercise periods.

Marie was invited to go along with some neighbours. She dared not refuse, and caught a glimpse of Madame Elisabeth along with the others. The sight caused her distress which she found hard to dissimulate. However she managed never to repeat the experience, pleading that her work and responsibilities at the *Salon de Cire* made it difficult for her to get away. In any case, she told her friends, there was nothing new to be seen even if she did take time she could ill spare for further visits.

At the end of November 1792 the optimistic calm in Paris was shattered. Officials who were still rummaging through and clearing out the Tuileries palace found a box. It contained papers that implicated the King in counter-revolutionary plots. Whether this box had been overlooked when the remains of the Court made its hurried and confused exodus from the Tuileries after the King was lodged in the Temple keep, or whether it might have been planted with forged documents, was immaterial. The King's trial by the deputies of the National Convention was now inevitable.

The Girondin deputies did their best to procrastinate but to no avail. The power of the Montagnards was too strong. Robespierre and his crony St Just declared that a trial was not even necessary. Louis XVI was guilty by the mere fact of being King. Marat refused to support this. He declared that a public trial was essential for the benefit of the people, so that every member of the Nation would be convinced of the King's criminality.

Curtius, who was normally on hand at every hour of crisis, was on this occasion out of France, away in the Rhineland. His second letter to the President of the Assembly had not been entirely without effect, for it was arranged for him to go to General Custine's headquarters at Mayence on some sort of official mission. As a German-speaker he could perform a useful service, and this would enable him to pursue in person his request for General Custine to intervene in the matter of laying hands on his brother Charles's inheritance.

Curtius usually had a gift for getting along with everyone, but when they met there turned out to be little *rapport* between himself and General Custine. However, Curtius was able to write to the Jacobin Club in Paris that he had been very warmly received by the local Society of Jacobins which had been founded after the arrival of the French army. His letter was read out, welcomed and duly minuted in the proceedings of the Paris Jacobin Club on 2 December.

The King's trial by the deputies of the National Convention began on 10 December 1792. Louis had been allowed to choose three 'defenders' to argue his case, and one of these had been quite well known to Marie when she was at Versailles. He had briefly held office in the King's Ministry in 1787. He had resigned his post when Louis dismissed the then Finance Minister, Turgot, who was detested by Marie Antoinette on account of his efforts at reform.

This man, Malesherbes, was one of the few at Court who had won Marie's genuine respect. She wrote of him in her *Memoirs*, 'The highest respect is ever associated with every recollection of this upright Minister.' She knew that once, under Louis XV, Malesherbes had been exiled to his country estate because he protested at the abuse of royal prerogatives. He had returned with the accession of Louis XVI, and accepted office, but when his liberal views were again unpopular, he returned of his own accord to the life of a country landowner. Marie was glad he had now come back to stand by his King.

The royal defence, though impeccably conducted and argued, was useless. It was a foregone conclusion that the accused would be found guilty, even though Louis XVI declared that he had never acted against his own high principles, and his lawyers argued the King's inviolability under the Constitution of 1791.

The pressure exerted by the Montagnards on uncommitted deputies was enormous, and in the end the vote was almost unanimous. Malesherbes' loyalty did him no service. After the trial he was arrested, together with his daughter and son-in-law. All three lost their heads under the guillotine blade the following April.

The fate of the 'criminal' King had still to be decided by the deputies. Was he to be executed? The Girondins wanted a referendum before any decision was made. It was the people's Constitution which had declared him inviolable, so it should be the people who decided his punishment.

This idea was voted down, as was another that the King should be condemned to death, but with a stay of execution. Finally, on 13 January 1793, after four inconclusive votings on the stay of execution, the King's death was decided by a majority of some seventy votes. Among those who voted for regicide was the King's cousin, the former Duc d'Orléans, now Philippe Egalité, still a welcome visitor at Curtius's dining-table. When titles had been abolished, the one-time Duc had coined his new name. Marie remembered how Madame Elisabeth had once called him 'a disgrace to the family'.

Louis XVI was given just twenty-four hours' notice of his execution. There was no great public demonstration when the day and time of it were cried in the streets, no gatherings, hardly any reaction.

Since the Place de Grève was estimated too small to hold the crowds expected, the guillotine was trundled to the Place de la Revolution, formerly the Place Louis XV, and today's Place de la Concorde. The scaffold was set up facing the Tuileries. The authorities arranged that the crowds would be controlled by huge contingents of National Guardsmen, backed up by *fédérés* from the provinces and representatives from the Paris *section* committees.

Curtius had received his orders as Captain of his company of *Chasseurs*, and he had also received orders regarding his 'niece' Marie, whose work on five decapitated heads had been noted and admired by many of the left-wing deputies. Curtius told her what she must do, and it was unlikely he would be able to get away from his National Guard duties to help her.

Once the procession of death had left the Temple area, which she would know by the fading noise of drums, Marie was to slip out of the house on the Boulevard du Temple and make a discreet and devious journey to the cemetery of the church of the Madeleine, a short distance from the Place de la Revolution. She would take with her a bag containing the plaster and other material required for taking a death mask. Officials in charge of the cemetery had their instructions, and her skilled fingers could take a mask in a matter of minutes from Louis' severed head when his remains were brought to the cemetery for perfunctory and unceremonious interment. The hole would be ready.

The strictest secrecy was imposed on Curtius and Marie by those members of the National Convention who issued the orders. The modelled head would not be publicised, nor would it be exhibited in the *Salon de Cire*. Such a thing would cause additional shock and hostility in other European countries, and as for French people, the sooner Louis XVI was forgotten the better. No-one wished to focus attention on the past, with the great republican future ahead.

The King was allowed a brief, last private meeting with his wife, children and sister. He was also permitted to have a non-juring priest, the Abbé Edgeworth, who had been Madame Elisabeth's confessor, to console and support his last hours and accompany him to the scaffold.

The morning of 21 January 1793 was dark, wet and misty. In No. 20 Boulevard du Temple, Marie and her mother moved uneasily through the shuttered rooms. Every building in Paris was closed and shuttered. Marie prepared for her gruesome errand, but she was calm. After the shock and revulsion she had experienced over the Princesse de Lamballe's head, nothing she was asked to do would affect her deeply.

It was about half-past eight in the morning when Santerre the brewer, now Commander of the National Guard, went to the Temple prison keep to collect the King of France and put him into a carriage which was waiting in the courtyard. As it rolled out it was joined by an enormous crowd of men, thousands strong, armed with muskets and pikes. They marched along the route to the Place de la Revolution in silence. There seemed to be no sound at all but the rolling of drums as Louis XVI went to his death in an ordinary carriage.

The procession took about an hour and a half at a slow pace to reach its destination. The drums beat louder as the King, helped by the Abbé Edgeworth, ascended the scaffold. He made an attempt to address the dense crowd, but the drums beat louder still and his words were drowned in their rolling. It was twenty minutes past ten when the chief executioner, Charles-Henri Sanson, carried out his duty. The heavy blade of the guillotine fell and Louis XVI's head rolled into the basket with no more ceremony than when it had dropped for the first time to cut off the head of a common mugger.

But then the hitherto silent crowd burst into noise, screaming patriotic slogans. As the King's head and body were quickly dumped into a cart, which at once set off towards the Madeleine, this mass of people began to dance as well as yell, circling the scaffold with a wild farandole.

In the not-far-distant cemetery of the Madeleine, Marie could hear the tumult, but when the cart with the King's remains arrived there was no-one following it. The attendants had their orders and there was no interference or hindrance as Marie rapidly completed her work. Soon she was on her way back to the Boulevard du Temple through still empty streets and shuttered houses, the death mask of Louis XVI carefully packed with her materials in the roomy bag she carried.

Outside Paris and throughout the provinces the news that the King's execution had actually taken place caused little stir. The people seemed quite apathetic. There was hardly any public reaction to the end of centuries of absolute rule by the kings of France.

Curtius, however, did find himself in an awkward position. No-one but those who had ordered it knew of the commission Marie had carried out, and nothing relating to the King's actual execution appeared in the *Salon de Cire*. Curtius did, none the less, create a tableau recording an incident that had taken place the day before the guillotine blade had fallen on Louis's neck. A deputy called Lepeletier, who was one of those who had voted for the King's death, was assassinated as he sat dining alone at a small restaurant.

The assassin, who escaped and made his way to England, was a member of the former Royal Bodyguard, a man named Paris, devoted to his monarch. It was a dramatic incident, but the deputy's murder did not cause an uproar. Curtius, seeking a new attraction for his exhibition, used the incident to create an effective tableau. It depicted the moment when the assassin struck his fatal blow as Lepeletier sat eating.

Unfortunately for Curtius, this vivid tableau aroused the fury of one of the most violently revolutionary of journalists, Prudhomme. In his newssheet he made a dangerous attack. Why, howled Prudhomme, does Curtius not show us a tableau of the execution of the criminal King? He went on to point out venomously that Curtius had made plenty of money showing much less important criminals in his *Caverne des Grands Voleurs*.

Any such attack made Curtius nervous, but this one he could afford to disregard. The Montagnard deputies did not want any attention focussed on the defunct King. They wanted him erased from public consciousness. Only a few deputies and officials knew of the portrait Marie had modelled from Louis' death mask. They kept their silence and ignored Prudhomme's taunt. The *Salon de Cire* benefited, as the publicity made more people go to see the assassination tableau.

Every purveyor of entertainment was at risk of denunciation by patriots who took objection to something said or performed. Curtius, though always cautious, did agree to intervene to rescue a friend and fellow-showman not long after the King's execution. This showman, Philipstal, ran a kind of magic lantern entertainment known as the Phantasmagoria. By means of light, likenesses of people were projected on to a screen, where they moved, appearing to advance or retreat.

One of Philipstal's shows was taking place in a large room filled with people when, by mistake, the operator threw onto the screen a picture of the late King which had at one time been used. Realising what he had done, the man hurriedly drew it up to make way for another, but several enthusiastic patriots in the audience took exception to this. It was done on purpose, they accused loudly, as an allegory implying that the guilty King had risen to heaven.

A general uproar ensued. Philipstal was arrested and thrown into prison. Even though the picking up and treatment of suspects had been eased, prison could still be a dangerous threshold to execution. Philipstal's wife tried every means she could think of to get her husband released. Finally she came to Curtius in the middle of the night, and begged him to use his influence with some of his friends among the Montagnards to get her husband set free. The episode was so clearly an accident, she argued.

Curtius agreed to help, but said that money would certainly be necessary. Madame Philipstal had come prepared. She knew her husband was known to be well off, to keep a carriage and to live in some style, all disadvantageous in the present climate. She laid a purse on the table. 'Please ask your friend Robespierre to intervene, and contrive to give him this money as a present.'

The stories about Robespierre's incorruptibility were not believed by everyone. Curtius and Marie had their private doubts. Even though he was putting himself at considerable risk, Curtius called on Robespierre. He wanted to help an old friend and colleague and his friendship with the increasingly powerful Deputy had grown quite close.

In the course of general conversation at Robespierre's lodging Curtius mentioned Philipstal's plight, declaring his personal opinion that his friend was a sincere patriot, and that it seemed a pity he should be locked up for what appeared only a foolish, careless and unintentional mistake on the part of an employee.

Robespierre acquiesced, and wrote an order for Philipstal's release. At the beginning of their conversation Curtius had laid the purse casually on a nearby table. He took his leave without picking it up. It was not returned to him. Possibly, of course, a servant had noticed the purse and pocketed it without his master's knowledge.

Philipstal was set free and his fortunate escape from danger was not discussed. Ultimately it would be responsible for the great turning-point in Marie's life, but for the moment it was wisely forgotten.

The Terror Looms

THE execution of Louis XVI caused profound shock in England, while the French armies' successes in the Austrian Netherlands, far too close for comfort, increased the English government's hostility towards the new Republic across the Channel.

Well aware of this, the National Convention did not wait for their old enemy to take action. On 1 February 1793, France declared war on England and her ally Holland. A month later war on Spain was declared too. France's need for more troops became urgent.

Towards the end of February, three hundred thousand Frenchmen were conscripted. Each *département*, or province, of France was ordered to produce a contingent of bachelors and widowers, making the problem of staffing the *Salon de Cire* even more difficult. Women had to take on heavy jobs everywhere, but fortunately for Marie, Curtius was exempt. Though a bachelor, he was now fifty-six, and still Captain of his battalion of the *Chasseurs*.

The conscripts were needed not only to fight on the frontiers, but to suppress anti-Jacobin revolts which had begun to spring up all over France. Those in the Vendée, on the south-west coast, were particularly violent and widespread.

Then came a shock to government and people, which caused the hurried removal from his place in the *Salon de Cire* of victorious General Dumouriez, whose campaigns had led to the conquest of the Netherlands. Now the tide had turned against Dumouriez. On 18 March he was heavily defeated by the Austrians at Neerwinden. This unexpected setback infuriated the Montagnard deputies, especially Marat. He had always been hostile to Dumouriez on account of his earlier support for the concept of a constitutional government with the King at its head. Curtius had often listened to Marat voicing suspicions about Dumouriez' republican patriotism, even when his armies were winning victories.

The General was summoned back to Paris to explain his defeat to the National Convention, but he knew all too well the fate that would await him there. Instead of returning to Paris to face the Montagnards, Dumouriez defected to the Austrians.

Marat was both enraged and triumphant at this shocking news. 'Dumouriez who you so ridiculously crowned,' he declaimed to the assembled deputies, '. . . four months ago I predicted his defection. My newspapers prove it. This event shows that I was the only man of foresight in the Republic!' His outburst was reported in the official Government newspaper, *Le Moniteur Universel* on 8 April. It had won applause from the deputies and from the public gallery of the Tuileries riding-school where they still sat.

Curtius rearranged his portrait figures of the military commanders. He had known General Dumouriez quite well, and was not entirely surprised at his defection to the Queen's country. Marie recalled her uncle's opinion in her *Memoirs*, 'from his youth a change of opinion seems to have influenced his views'. The once royalist General, turned republican, had reverted to his earlier loyalties and joined the Republic's most bitter enemy, Marie Antoinette's Austria.

Now menaced by enemies without and uprisings within, the morale of the French people ebbed low, particularly in Paris. The purchasing power of the paper currency, the *assignat*, took a further plunge. In Paris the price of bread was now fixed, and wages more or less retained their level, but in the countryside there were no controls as yet and earnings were very low. People went hungry in many provinces.

Inside the National Convention in Paris the power struggle between the Girondins and the Montagnards increased in bitterness, while the *sans-culottes* movement exercised ever greater pressure on the deputies. Repressive measures reappeared after the brief respite. On 6 April a Committee of Public Safety was proclaimed, with a Revolutionary Tribunal for the trial of suspects.

Even more frightening for ordinary citizens was the appointment of a local Watch Committee in each of the Paris *sections*, and in each Municipality in the provinces. These committees were charged with the surveillance not only of any foreigners who might be around, but also of any citizens who seemed not to be giving sufficiently ardent support to the Revolution and the Republic. *Emigrés* who had fled the country were now formally banished, and faced the death penalty if they tried to return and were caught.

A special tax was imposed on everyone who could be assessed as possessing a degree of wealth.

Curtius had some unpleasant and alarming moments when his name was publicised in a report on the National Convention's proceedings, published in *Le Moniteur Universel*. It was the last kind of publicity he wanted, and he had brought danger on himself through uncharacteristic indiscretion.

Although, during his mission to the Rhineland, Curtius had found General Custine unfriendly and unco-operative in his quest for his brother Charles's inheritance, he refused to give up his efforts to win the General's favour and support. Since his return to Paris he had seized every opportunity to declare what a good patriot General Custine was.

Now, to Curtius's dismay, an anonymous broadsheet was in circulation condemning General Custine as a traitor. On 8 April the deputies, severely shaken by the defection of General Dumouriez, began discussing the reliability of Custine. Evidence against him was produced by a deputy named Ruamps, who told the Assembly an odd and Scarlet Pimpernel-like tale: 'I demand', cried Ruamps, 'that the facts should be established. Four months ago we brought before the Committee of Surveillance a porter carrying a basket of apples under which forty letters were hidden! We opened them and found one addressed to Madame de Liancourt, which was unsigned but in Custine's handwriting. He said to her, "I hope, my good friend, you have given no credence to the statement spread around Paris by Curtius!" Everyone knows that Curtius has said that Custine is a very good patriot. That is the fact.'

At best Curtius was made to look foolish with his enthusiastic praise, at worst he stood in danger for trying to obscure the true sentiments of one who was now openly branded as a traitor. Arrest and imprisonment, if not execution, threatened and Marie trembled for her uncle's safety. Had Curtius not warned her from childhood to guard her tongue? No matter if finances were now difficult, it was not worth risking everyone's safety for the inheritance.

Curtius was fortunate. His friendship with Marat and the help he had given by concealing his friend when on the run from royal arrest warrants before the Revolution, now stood him in good stead. Marat spoke up for him and Curtius's foolish praise was ignored, even though it was decided to call Custine back to Paris to give an account of himself.

After capturing Mainz from the enemy allied forces on 21 October 1792, General Custine failed to hold it or to recapture it after the enemy had reoccupied it in 1793. When he obeyed the summons to Paris, instead of defecting like Dumouriez, he was charged with conspiring with the enemy to bring about a counter-revolution, and went to the guillotine in August. He and his friends believed that Curtius's talk had contributed to the suspicions that led to his fate.

Early in May the National Convention moved out of the riding-school and into the Tuileries palace itself where the former theatre had been converted for the Assembly's sessions. It was here that the Girondin deputies met their downfall in attempting to break the power of the revolutionary Commune, the current Paris municipality, which the Girondins found too greedy for both money and power, and too little attentive to decisions taken by the elected representatives of the nation.

The revolutionary Commune won the battle. The Girondins hoped support from uncommitted deputies would carry them through, but the Montagnards were powerful. Even though Marat and the infamous Hébert of *Le Père Duchesne* and a few other extremists were arrested, they had to be quickly released, and the climax of the power struggle came with yet another *sans-culottes* uprising.

On 28 May one of the more violent *section* committees, that of the *Cité* district, called on all other *section* representatives to join them at the archbishop's palace, no longer the residence of that prelate. Only thirty-three of the *section* committees responded to this call, but those who did gather elected a shadowy Committee of Six whose members were later increased to seven. They were all agitators who had worked unobtrusively, and their names were not generally known. They were from the artisan and shopkeeper class, not from the city's rabble. The very anonymity of this committee aroused fear in those citizens who still hoped for peace and quiet in which to get on with their work and livelihood.

Danton, and indeed many of the Montagnard deputies, did not want any more riots, but their efforts to forestall trouble failed. On 30 May the new Revolutionary Committee, as it called itself, appointed a new Commander of the National Guard, one of their own choice, to supplant the brewer Santerre.

His name was Hanriot, and he was little known. Hanriot, born near Paris of humble parents in 1761, had started work as a servant in Paris, progressing to various low-grade jobs including that of a clerk at one of the *barrières* of the city. He joined the revolutionary mob on 12 July 1789, when the wax busts of Necker and the Duc d'Orléans were seized from Curtius's exhibition, but remained only one of the crowd until the September massacres of 1792. Then, during the slaughter in the prisons, he emerged as a leader and an ardent supporter of Robespierre.

Though Santerre was replaced, his services to the Revolution were not overlooked. He was given a command of troops sent to the Vendée to suppress anti-Jacobin uprisings there. However, he suffered defeat in a battle with the rebels and returned to Paris, but took no further active rôle, retiring as proprietor of a piece of land in the vast Temple complex.

On 31 May, as day dawned, Curtius and Marie again heard the tocsin sounding, the drums beating. A cannon boomed from the Pont Neuf, fired by Hanriot and his men. Hours of tension and sporadic disturbance followed until five o'clock in the evening when the mob again converged on the Tuileries, surrounding the former theatre building where the National Convention was in session. Petitions were handed in, mostly for extreme demands. One petition called for all deputies who had voted for a referendum on the late King's execution to be put under arrest immediately. Another demanded the formation of a special *sans-culottes* army to hunt down suspects, and that only *sans-culottes* should have the right to vote in the election of deputies.

The majority of deputies would not consider voting upon such measures, so the Revolutionary Committee took matters into its own hands and ordered the arrest of all suspects, which included those Girondin deputies who had supported the idea of a referendum before deciding the King's fate. Some of them managed to escape, including Roland, one of their leaders, so the Committee had his wife arrested in his place.

Marie was upset when she learned that Madame Roland had been hauled off to the Abbaye prison across the river. She feared for the consequences, with good reason. This highly intelligent and charming woman had dared speak openly against the brutalities of the September massacres. Now she found herself in the prison where the killing had started. Madame Roland was to stay in prison for five months. She spent the time writing her *Memoirs*, which she did not finish, as she was guillotined on 5 November.

Not only did Madame Roland face her final ordeal with exemplary fortitude, but she supported and helped another victim in the same tumbril on the way to execution, whose spirit was less able to face the scaffold with calm and dignity. Nine days after Madame Roland's death her husband, who had reached the safe refuge of Rouen after his escape, killed himself by thrusting his swordstick into his body.

The critical day of this *sans-culottes* revolt came on Sunday 2 June, when the mob was swelled by many workers who had remained at their jobs on the previous days. The National Convention was still in session and once again the mob besieged the Tuileries. This time the deputies decided to leave the building. To their shock and consternation they found themselves faced not only by the mob, now thousands strong, but also by a ring of Hanriot's cannon, primed ready to fire.

The horrified deputies beat a retreat back into their chamber. It was a crucial moment for the future of France. This *sans-culottes* uprising, masterminded by the nebulous figures of the Revolutionary Committee, brought no bloodshed: not a shot was fired, not a head decapitated and carried on a pike. At the same time it demonstrated that not only had all the original revolutionary ideals vanished with the Girondins, but also that the Nation's elected assembly, the National Convention, no longer wielded power. Its deputies were at the mercy of mob rule.

The June revolt and the rout of the Girondins did not make life any easier for the citizens of Paris, short of bread, short of money and under constant surveillance by the Committee of Public Safety and its local *section* watch committees. A triumph for the *sans-culottes* but of no visible benefit to anyone else, so it seemed to those who secretly harboured fears of a future under the government of the 'Mountain'.

Under these circumstances, Curtius thought it prudent to catch up on his promised voluntary contributions to the nation's war effort, which was costing huge sums, while revenue flagged. On 27 June 1793 he despatched another letter to the current 'Citizen President' of the National Convention. This epistle earned him some useful praise, for it was annotated officially 'Honourable Mention and insertion in the Bulletin, 27 June, Year II of the Republic'.

Curtius had written in his usual fulsome style:

> I have the honour of sending you herewith the sum of one hundred livres of my voluntary contribution whose despatch has been retarded on account of my absence, occasioned by the mission with which I was charged by the Executive Power, of visiting the storehouses of the army of the Rhine. I beg you to ask the Convention to accept my respects as one most feeble mark of my gratitude for their labours.
>
> I am, with fraternity, Citizen President,
> Your co-citizen
> Curtius.

Even if Curtius's mission was confined to acting as German interpreter, he was a natural busybody, and the appointment of such a civilian to make the rounds of army storehouses cannot have pleased colleagues of former commander General Custine, who had found Curtius's presence irksome and in the end dangerous.

It was time Curtius devised something new, reflected Marie, as she worked in the studio and supervised groupings in the exhibition so that nothing could give offence to those now enjoying power. Another crowd-puller was needed. Attendances were dwindling. Heaven forbid there should be any more severed heads, but it was difficult to give any kind of glamour to the new leaders, such as Hanriot, Commander of the National Guard. Marie had been to take his life-mask at his wine-shop near the Hôtel de Ville. Hanriot had married the widow of its previous owner who had gone to the guillotine for some crime. She found no pleasure in modelling his portrait figure. Though Hanriot was a well-built man she considered he had 'a vulgar and brutal aspect'.

It was very different from the old creative days of glittering tableaux such as 'The Royal Family at Dinner', with Marie Antoinette in her Rose Bertin gown. The waxworks' wardrobe had produced fine raiment and superb uniforms when Curtius made his portraits of foreign monarchs or noble ministers. No-one could voice such nostalgic regrets. In the present climate of suspicion no-one could be trusted; walls did indeed seem to have ears pressed against them and the slightest indication of a hankering for any aspect of the *ancien régime* could land everyone in prison, and probably on the road to the guillotine.

Very soon, however, Curtius's *Salon de Cire* would again be besieged by eager crowds, pushing to get in. It was late evening of 13 July when Madame Grosholtz told Marie that a messenger from the National Convention had arrived and urgently wished to see her. She thought it was probably something for Curtius, who was out, and was surprised when the man handed her a letter addressed to herself. When she read it she was dumbfounded.

Marat was dead! Marat had been assassinated in the house in the Rue des Cordeliers that he used both as his home and his office. Marie was commanded to go at once with the man who brought the letter, to Marat's house, take a death-mask and record the scene in detail. The order was instigated by David the painter, one of the deputies who had sat for some time as a Paris representative. He had always admired Marie's skills.

Hurriedly collecting her materials, Marie was on her way in a matter of minutes to a scene that seemed almost unbelievable. As she went into the house she had a fleeting glimpse of a young woman being hustled away through a menacing crowd that had already gathered, held back by National Guardsmen who were about everywhere.

Marie had never been in Marat's house, though Curtius often called in there. She was taken upstairs to a small room and there she saw Marat, his face even more repellent to her in death, slumped over the edge of a covered bath, pen and writing-materials still on the board that covered it. There was a bleeding wound in his chest and a large, sharp knife had fallen to the floor by the bath.

Marie was not allowed any questions. She was told to get to work immediately, take the mask and sketch the scene so that it could be reproduced exactly in detail. She could only assume that David, unable to come himself, intended to use her work as a basis for a painting. No doubt Curtius, if he could get permission, would find it an admirable subject for a tableau.

Marie was beyond being shocked by dead faces now. She opened her bag, called for water and began to mix the plaster. Later she would discover the circumstances of this murder. She had always found Marat's appearance repulsive, and had to conceal her distaste as, with hands perfectly steady, she smoothed the plaster over the 'demon's' features. They had been familiar to her for so many years, since the days when Marat held a royal appointment as physician to the Comte d'Artois' bodyguard.

The young woman she had glimpsed as she entered was the assassin. Her name was Charlotte Corday and she came from a family of minor aristocrats living at Caen in Normandy. Charlotte was an intelligent and well-educated girl of twenty-five, whose fiancé, an officer in one of the regiments of the Royal Guard, had been killed in the disturbances of 1789.

She had read the classics and imbibed the ideas of Voltaire, and, in spite of her fiancé's royal sevice, was inspired by the concept of a pure and idealised Republicanism. Charlotte identified these ideals with the views of the Girondins, to whom she gave enthusiastic support, developing a corresponding hatred for the policies of the Jacobin 'Mountain'.

As the power of the Montagnards increased and *sans-culottes* pressure grew, she believed the Revolution was being blown off course. After the September massacres she became convinced that, unless Marat was eliminated, her cherished ideal of a Republican France was doomed to disaster and destruction. She brooded on this for a long time.

Early in July 1793 she took a coach for an unaccompanied visit to Paris. When she got there she delivered a letter she had written to Marat's house. She also purchased a long, sharp carving-knife. Twice she called at Marat's house, asking to see him, but was turned away by his housekeeper/mistress. Making a third attempt, she said she had important information from Caen, which she would give only to Marat himself. Marat, who at this time of day, about seven o'clock in the evening, was in his bath relieving his itching skin while he wrote for his newspaper *L'Ami du Peuple*, was informed of this call. He was, after all, a journalist, and he said he would see the young woman who might have something of interest to say.

The room in which Marat sat in his bath was only small, with just two chairs in it. The strange and persistent young woman came in, moved one of the chairs close to the bath and closed the door. It was only a short time later that those in the adjoining room heard Marat's cry for help through his closed door. Four people rushed into the bathroom. One was Citizen Laurent Baz who had been busy folding copies of *L'Ami du Peuple*, another Marat's sister, and a couple of other women who had been helping them.

They saw Charlotte Corday standing near the bath, a perfectly composed figure in her plain but elegant spotted dress and tall hat with a black cockade. They were horrified to see Marat's body with a stab-wound, drooping over the rim and a large knife lying on the board. Citizeness Marat ran and put her hand over the wound, knocking the knife to the floor. 'It was', wrote Citizen Baz in his description of the scene, 'the weapon with which the murderess had deprived the Nation of one of its Representatives!'

Charlotte Corday accepted her arrest with unruffled calm, and made no fuss or protest as she was hurried out of the house just as Marie was entering. Marie had hardly seen her and when she had finished taking the death-mask and making sketches and notes of the room, she was uncertain what to do. If the painter David wanted a complete record of the murder scene, she must have access to the young woman.

No problems arose over this. Marie was allowed to visit Charlotte Corday in the Conciergerie prison where she awaited her inevitable execution. Marie was impressed by her deportment and total acceptance of the fate that she had brought on herself. 'Her countenance had quite a noble expression,' Marie recalled. 'She conversed freely, even cheerfully, and ever with a countenance of purest serenity.'

Charlotte maintained this serenity through her trial, where she admitted everything, on her journey to the scaffold, and when she laid her head on the block and the guillotine blade fell. The crowds in the streets and round the scaffold watched her noble demeanour, and made no hostile demonstration. When the executioner picked up the head and slapped the cheeks as he showed it to the people, a groan of horror and protest was heard. This young woman might have murdered Marat, but no-one who saw her could doubt the idealism of her motive, however misguided it might have been. A perfect Republican France was a dream people still cherished in their hearts, even if reality was proving different.

Marie did not watch the execution. She waited in the Madeleine cemetery, as she had done before, to take a death-mask from Charlotte Corday's still serene features. Curtius had got permission to create a tableau of the assassination scene and it would be useful for the striking painting that David planned.

Curtius's tableau reproduced exactly Marat's body in the bath and the room as Marie had recorded it, with the addition of the figure of Charlotte Corday standing beside the bath. It was a sensation, attracting crowds 'loud in their lamentation'. Among those who came was

Robespierre. As he left the house he stood on the steps and harangued passers-by and the queue that was waiting to get into the *Salon de Cire*.

'Citizens!' he cried, 'follow my example and enter! See the image of our departed friend snatched from us by the demon of aristocracy ... let us fortify our minds with the resolution to avenge his death by extirpating his enemies who must be ours and those of our country!'

People did follow his example and enter. They poured into Curtius's wax exhibition again, and for many days Marie did not have to worry about the takings. Curtius felt some genuine regret for an old friend of whose faults he had always been tolerant, while admiring Marat's furious energy and sharing many interests with him. Marie, remembering the September massacres and the roughly decapitated head of the Princesse de Lamballe, could not share her uncle's feelings. She had heard too many whispers about Marat's responsibility for that terrible slaughter.

Robespierre's Reign Begins

THE dead Marat became quite a cult figure. Members of the violently extremist Cordeliers Club, of which Marat had been so vociferous a supporter, got possession of his heart. At the end of July the Cordeliers arranged a well-attended civic ceremony to raise an altar to the heart of 'the incomparable Marat'. It was generally agreed that the tableau of the death scene was one of the most striking Curtius and Marie had created.

While Marie could not inwardly share all this emotion, she recognised that Marat had, before he plunged into revolutionary activities, made a contribution to the success of the *Salon de Cire* through his researches on light and optics which he had shared with his friend Curtius. She had read Marat's translation of Newton's *Optics* and his own book *Découvertes sur la Lumière*, and learned lessons that greatly influenced the presentation of the exhibition. She hoped violence would decrease with his demise.

Curtius realised that good relations with Robespierre were now even more essential. His fluent German, and willingness to undertake missions where this was useful, helped win the favour and friendship of this now-risen political star. Curtius felt comparatively confident and secure, but, though normally of robust health, he had returned from inspecting the army storehouses in the Rhineland with some kind of illness.

Marie was immediately suspicious. She thought her uncle's food might have been poisoned during his stay there. The now disgraced General Custine had always disliked him, and many of his friends believed Curtius's untimely braying around Paris about the General had somehow helped bring about his denunciation as a traitor. To them Curtius could appear a dangerous figure whose missions to the Rhineland and troublesome personal demands were unwanted.

It was this undiagnosed illness that had symptoms akin to poisoning, together with continued food shortages and an unerring premonition of

[145]

even more difficult and dangerous times ahead, that decided Curtius to scrape together his money and buy a house outside Paris. While he, Marie and Madame Grosholtz had always been city-dwellers, access to fresh food and a refuge where Curtius could take some rest from the tensions of Paris seemed a sensible idea.

There were plenty of vacant houses around Paris, for many people had moved away, feeling they were safer in more remote regions. However, private transactions over house property had long been banned. Those who wished to sell or buy did so through *L'Agence National*, the national housing bureau of each district.

Curtius found what he wanted at Ivry-sur-Seine, now an industrial suburb, but then a quiet country place on the river. The property included a poultry yard, a garden, and a loft for storing fruit. Marie recalled in her *Memoirs* how glad they were to have this country house from which supplies of fresh produce, unobtainable in Paris, could be brought to the Boulevard du Temple.

It was only a small dwelling on two floors, with dining-room, kitchen and three other rooms. Curtius did not have enough cash to buy the place outright. He paid a first instalment to the official at the housing bureau, Citizen Junot, of five thousand and ten *livres*. Remaining instalments could be spread over several years, a convenient arrangement when finances were so uncertain. Soon the house was crammed with furniture and bits and pieces from the Boulevard du Temple. Ivry-sur-Seine was a reasonably short journey from Paris by carriage or cart.

There were no valuables either in the Paris establishment or in the little country retreat. All citizens had been ordered to turn-in their plate and jewellery to the National Convention, to be sold towards the expenses of the war. *Section* watch committees instituted a search of every household to make sure no valuables were being concealed. The searchers pounced without warning, and any guilty hoarder was taken off to prison.

When this decree was issued Curtius promptly packed a large hamper with all the plate and valuables he possessed and despatched it forthwith to the National Convention. He made his immediate patriotic action known, and Marie and her mother were spared the sudden knock on the door and searchers rummaging through all the cupboards, the exhibition wardrobe and the cluttered studio, to say nothing of the exhibition rooms with their carefully set-out portrait figures, groups, mirrors, pictures and curiosities.

The summer of 1793, when Curtius bought his country house, was a desperate time for France. Her enemies—Austria, Prussia, Italy, Spain and England—besieged every frontier. The people suffered. In March,

Fouquier-Tinville, a dreaded and ruthless figure, who seemed to have no interest beyond sending unfortunates to the guillotine, had been appointed Public Prosecutor. The Committee of Public Safety was reconstituted under the direction of Robespierre, while the Cordeliers Club increased is violent pressures. Since Marat's death the Club was led by the even more venomous Hébert. His scurrilous newspaper, *Le Père Duchêne*, had a wide circulation and he nourished a particular hatred of the Queen, still imprisoned in the Temple keep with her children and sister-in-law, Madame Elisabeth.

Hébert was among Curtius's visitors. Marie was always especially careful to guard her tongue when he was around, yet he was a man of agreeable manners, and anyone might find it hard to believe the part he had played in instigating the September massacres and the rabidly revolutionary invective of his newspaper.

Fragments of news about the royal prisoners in the Temple came to Marie's ears. She refrained from discussion or comment. Since its new session had started early in April, the Revolutionary Tribunal had issued sixty-three death sentences on suspects. It was murmured that judges and jurors had become weary and pronounced the penalties without any pretence of interest or concern. Anyone's life could be forfeit for a triviality, so the prudent did not chat about anything they might hear.

At the end of June, Marie learned that the Committee of Public Safety had removed the little Dauphin from the care of his mother, aunt and fourteen-year-old sister, Madame Royale. The boy was not yet twelve. Marie thought of his elder brother, whose portrait she had modelled at Versailles, and who had died so sadly just before the Revolution broke.

The Committee of Public Safety handed the Dauphin over for 'education' to a *sans-culotte*, Antoine Simon, a former cobbler. The boy was still kept in the Temple prison and Simon received five hundred francs a month for his duties. The new room allocated to the Dauphin was the one his father, Louis XVI, had occupied. Soon there were rumours circulating that the child, so tenderly reared, was learning to use appalling language under Simon's tuition.

A week later the 'case' of the Widow Capet, as Marie Antoinette was now called, was referred to the National Convention. She was removed from the comparative comfort of the lodging in the Temple, and the supportive company of her sister-in-law, to imprisonment under humiliating conditions and degrading constant supervision in a cell of the Conciergerie prison.

There she remained until October, the month of her son's birthday. There were delays and hesitations about her fate. Some thought she could be usefully kept alive as a prisoner-hostage, others demanded and petitioned the Convention for her execution.

Hébert was one who screamed for her head. 'I promised it to the *sans-culottes*.' On 4 October the former Queen of France was led from her cell to her trial in what had once been the Great Chamber of the Paris *parlement*. Public Prosecutor Fouquier-Tinville, impatient to be rid of her, prepared the indictment. It was the despicable Hébert who insisted that a charge of sexually debauching her son in the Temple should be included in the list of Marie Antoinette's 'crimes'.

From Brussels the former Queen's devoted admirer, the Swede, Axel Fersen, wrote in despair, 'Her fate is certain.' How could it be otherwise? Much had happened in the weeks since Marie Antoinette had been taken to the Conciergerie. In September, Hébert had organised a further outbreak of rioting in Paris. *Sans-culottes* and other extreme elements once again threatened the deputies of the National Convention as they sat in the former Tuileries theatre.

Alarmed, the Committee of Public Safety persuaded the deputies to agree to new measures which initiated the period of wholesale bloodshed known as the Terror. Only by an organised and controlled Terror, declared Robespierre, could bloody outbreaks like the September massacres be avoided and a stable post-revolutionary France be established.

A new Law of Suspects came into force on 17 September, bringing in its wake an ever-swelling flood of accusations, perfunctory trials or no trials at all, and sentences of death from the Revolutionary Tribunal. The people trembled, for the Law of Suspects covered not only Paris but the whole nation: any person able to satisfy the Tribunal about their own 'patriotism' had the right to accuse a fellow-citizen of anti-revolutionary sentiments or feeble support of its glorious principles. Some accusers wanted to curry favour, some hoped to save their own necks, others paid off grudges or vented personal antipathy. It did not matter how trivial the charge was.

The guillotine began to work overtime. There was no need to cry public executions in the streets, as had once been the custom. An execution was almost permanently available for those who wished to enjoy the spectacle. The Place de la Révolution, where the guillotine remained after the execution of the King, became a rendezvous, a place for diversion, a kind of club for the population to which women brought their knitting.

The situation was not so different outside Paris. There was a guillotine in every sizable town in France. Nor was it only aristocratic heads that rolled, though there was a plentiful supply of those. Dozens, even hundreds, of ordinary people were denounced by their fellow-citizens. Every knock on the door was a knock of dread.

What hope, in this terrible climate of wholesale execution, had the hated 'Austrian woman'? Frivolous, extravagant, heedless of the miseries of her subjects, for many years Marie Antoinette had dug the abyss into which her mother, the Empress of Austria, had repeatedly warned her she would plunge if she did not mend her ways. Now it was inevitable that what her brother had called her 'little feather-head' would be parted from her shoulders.

16 October was the day decreed for the execution of the former Queen of France. It would not be the same executioner who had lopped the King's head. Chief Executioner Charles-Henri Sanson was stricken with illness soon after he had guillotined Louis XVI and, though he retained his title, it was his son and ultimate successor who carried out the work.

Marie received similar secret, official instructions as she had when the King was executed: she was to go to the Madeleine cemetery and take a death-mask. No-one must discover this and it was not going to be easy for her, for she had been invited to watch Marie Antoinette pass in the tumbril along the Rue St Honoré. Someone had managed to book a window that would give a good view of the two-wheeled open cart as it rattled over the cobbles, shaking the royal victim as she sat upright on a plank fixed across the cart.

Apart from the fact that a refusal to go might be dangerously misinterpreted, Marie had to admit to herself that she felt an over-whelming curiosity to see for the last time the Queen whose path she had so often crossed at Versailles, whose portrait she had modelled there. It seemed as if it had been in another world that Curtius had set up his famous tableau of 'The Royal Family at Dinner' with the portrait figure of Marie Antoinette resplendent in a Rose Bertin dress that had cost a great deal of money.

Marie remembered the Queen as a charming and elegant woman, with a graceful, voluptuous figure and a naturally regal carriage. Was it possible she was now, as people whispered, a gaunt, emaciated creature, her blonde hair quite white, although she was only thirty-eight years old? Once so vivacious, she was, they said, a woman who seemed drained of all feeling. 'Nothing can hurt me now,' she had said when she knocked her head sharply on a low arch as they took her into the Conciergerie prison.

Marie took her place in the window looking on to the Rue St Honoré at the appointed time. She would have to find some excuse to leave immediately the Queen's tumbril had passed. In fact, Marie never saw the Queen. Normally in complete control of herself, she suddenly felt overwhelmed and faint as the sound of the tumbril wheels approaching came to her ears. Briefly she lost consciousness, blacked out, and missed observing the unrecognisable figure so cruelly depicted in a sketch by the painter David, the head held proudly high, and seemingly unseeing and unhearing as people raised fists and hurled abuse. Marie Antoinette went to her execution with hands bound, humbly clad in a worn dress with a fichu, her roughly scissored hair protruding in white spikes beneath a muslin bonnet which left her nape bare for the blade.

The Queen went to her death still totally uncomprehending the hatred of her subjects. She had obeyed too well her mother's instructions that she must never forget she was an Austrian at heart. Marie Antoinette never identified with her new people, never attempted to understand the miseries and poverty most of them endured, while she spent vast sums on pleasure and jewels, and disastrously dominated her kind, weak, dull and equally uncomprehending husband.

In the room looking on to the Rue St Honoré, Marie rapidly recovered herself. The spectacle had passed, and she could claim still feeling shaky and unwell after her brief faintness, brought on by patriotic stress, as an excuse for leaving. She hurried to the Madeleine cemetery, picking up her materials on the way. She arrived in time and no longer felt any particular revulsion. It was just a job that circumstances forced her to carry out.

She encountered no problems. When the cart with the Queen's bloodstained remains arrived at the cemetery no-one was about the place. The blade had fallen at fifteen minutes past twelve. Crowds had applauded when executioner Sanson held up the head, but there was no unseemly dancing as they had been at Louis XVI's execution.

At the cemetery it was the hour of the midday break. The men who unloaded the cart could not see any officials around, no coffins, no grave prepared. They wanted to get off to their own lunch, so they dumped the Queen's body, putting the head between the legs. Marie was able to do her work undisturbed.

She departed unnoticed, with Marie Antoinette's tragic death-mask in her bag. The call to arms on this day of execution had sounded at five o'clock in the morning. All the National Guardsmen were on duty and it was quite late when Curtius returned to the *Salon de Cire*. The crowds had dispersed without trouble. The detested Austrian Marie Antoinette was no more, and no-one was interested in her any longer. When she got back to the studio Marie began the task of modelling the head. When it was finished it was hidden away with that of the King. The National Convention wanted no publicity that could be avoided over the death of the Queen of France.

The Guillotine Rules

AFTER Marie Antoinette's execution, heads began to fall 'like roofing tiles' as the Law of Suspects really began to bite. Yet a curious kind of calm seemed to spread over Paris. Marie wrote of it in her *Memoirs*, 'Accustomed as they had become to scenes of carnage Parisians were paralysed with horror to the point of stupefaction.'

The people who passed through the *Salon de Cire* were a silent crowd now. It was unwise to make remarks about the portrait figures. An admired personality of today might be an enemy of the Republic tomorrow in the present political climate. Opinions expressed aloud might be overheard and members of the local watch committees were always on the alert, eager to keep up the rate of denunciations.

In the National Convention the Montagnards split into two factions. Curtius was watching especially the actions of Robespierre. Would this detached, ruthless enigma of a man come out on top and control the government of France? Opposing him were the Hébertists, an extreme faction popularly called the Enragés ('the Rabids'), who wanted ultra-revolutionary violence like the September massacres and the cannon that had forced the Convention to bow to the *sans-culottes* during the recent rioting that Hébert had instigated. The Enragés also demanded that churches must be de-Christianised and turned into Temples of Reason.

Robespierre managed to rally a wearying Danton to his side to oppose the Hébertists, get rid of them and pursue his own plans of an organised Terror instead of spontaneous mob massacres. He also wished to impose fixed prices throughout the country, to combat the soaring cost of food and commodities.

All was not well on the military side either. The Committee of Public Safety sent emissaries, who included Robespierre's fanatical supporter St Just, to the French armies fighting on the northern and eastern frontiers, with instructions to stimulate morale and rouse the soldiers to greater efforts. They were to evaluate the generals who commanded these troops for ability and 'patriotism'.

[151]

General Dumouriez's defection, and the so-called treason of Curtius's enemy, General Custine, rankled and no general could feel safe unless his display of Jacobin zeal was equal to his military ability. The mission appeared to meet with some success in stimulating the military, for two minor victories removed at least the immediate threat of invasion, which had caused so much popular alarm.

The Vendéean counter-revolutionary outbreaks were in process of being crushed too, with a rebel force smashed at Cholet on 17 October. This defeat inspired Curtius, six days later, to despatch another of his regular contributions of two hundred *livres* for the war effort to the 'Citizen President' of the National Convention, but this time he was unable to deliver the letter and the money in person. 'My illness,' he wrote, 'has deprived me of the pleasure of bringing them to you myself. I should have performed this action with the more satisfaction since I could have joined my applause to that of the representatives of the people on the happy news from La Vendée, the fruits of the labours of the Committee of Public Safety.' Curtius signed himself 'with fraternity', determined to underline his own patriotism in the dangerous atmosphere of suspicion and surveillance.

The illness he had picked up in the Rhineland, whatever its cause, was proving persistent, exacerbated no doubt by the nervous tension of his situation, demanding unceasing watchfulness to keep the *Salon de Cire* both a popular attraction and out of political trouble. He was not the only one in the entertainment area of the Boulevard du Temple whose livelihood and personal safety were constantly at risk.

With the political in-fighting in the National Convention, even deputies were being arrested, accused of corruption and despatched to the guillotine. Not everyone was easy at the licence allowed to those who flaunted their revolutionary sentiments. At a meeting of the Paris Commune, the municipal authority, one of its members, called Chaumette, complained about the way in which the guards at the Madeleine cemetery stripped guillotined bodies and sold the clothes. Such attitudes did not meet with favour and Chaumette himself finished up under the blade during the period of the Terror.

Philippe Egalité, once Duc d'Orléans and long-time friend of Curtius, and the people's hero on 12 July 1789 when the mob carried his wax bust with that of Necker from the *Salon de Cire*, was in prison. His eldest son, fighting with the French army, had defected to Austria at the same time as his commanding officer, General Dumouriez. All the remaining members of the royal family who had not fled France were arrested after this.

The former Duc d'Orléans, cousin of the late King, was accused of having encouraged General Dumouriez to defect. On the general proscription of members of the royal family, he was officially declared a traitor and all his property and possessions confiscated. Arrested on 7 April 1793, he was sent to prison in Marseilles in the south of France. In September he was brought back for trial by the Revolutionary Tribunal. On 6 November the once-royal Duc, who had voted as a deputy for the execution of his cousin Louis XVI, himself climbed the ladder to the guillotine platform. At one time he had hoped to reign as a constitutional monarch, or at least act as regent for the little Dauphin.

Marie found it frightening to contemplate how many portrait figures, once the focus of popular attention, had to be removed and consigned to oblivion. One of them was Bailly, first Republican Mayor of Paris and first President of the National Assembly in its early days at Versailles. Marie remembered how Curtius had gone to the Place de Grève when Bailly, as Mayor, had received Louis XVI when the mob brought the King and his family to Paris, never to see Versailles again.

Bailly had become sickened and disillusioned by the increasing violence and carnage of the Revolution he had once so enthusiastically supported. He left Paris to live with a friend at Mélun in the country-side not far from the capital. The Committee of Public Safety brought him back and the Revolutionary Tribunal condemned him to death in spite of his services to the cause of Liberty.

The Committee of Public Safety decided that Bailly's execution was to be an exemplary occasion, ramming home the fate that awaited backsliding former 'patriots'. It was to take place on the Champ de Mars, scene of the brilliant festival on the first anniversary of the fall of the Bastille. Bailly had presided in his glory on that occasion, and after the ceremonies were over all Paris had danced. Now people had almost forgotten that happy period when the revolutionary ideal seemed trimphant and peace and justice lay ahead for France.

In the event the exemplary execution was a disastrous failure. The guillotine in the Place de la Révolution was dismantled and trundled across the river to a site on the vast Champ de Mars. Crowds had gathered there as anticipated, both regular attenders and those who lived south of the river and did not normally bother to tramp across the bridge to the Place de la Révolution to watch the guillotine at work. But the deadly instrument took too long to reassemble in proper working order. The waiting masses grew impatient, angry, bored. Many wandered off, and when the unfortunate Bailly finally climbed on to the platform there was no more than routine interest from the remaining spectators. The idea of moving the guillotine from its permanent site on the Place de la Révolution to appropriate spots for special executions was not repeated.

[153]

Marie had liked Bailly, and she also secretly regretted the execution of the moderate Barnave. He had once been prominent in the *Salon de Cire* as one of the deputies who escorted the royal family back from their ill-advised flight to Varennes. He had sat between the King and Queen and behaved 'with such gentleness and politeness', Marie recalled, that Madame Elisabeth had seemed, it was said, quite taken with his conversation, 'full of talent'. In contrast, the second deputy in the royal coach, Pétion, who succeeded Bailly as Mayor of Paris, showed rough manners.

Barnave's services to the Republic were of no consequence as far as the Hébertists were concerned. Moderation must be obliterated. It was not surprising that Curtius felt it essential to maintain his prestige as a 'patriot' by every means he could. He had some welcome publicity on 23 November 1793, when the Jacobins, the 'Society of the Friends of Liberty and Equality', accepted his offer of a wax bust of one Lajouski, a 'homage' that was received with applause by members gathered at a session.

Lajouski was one of many foreigners who had joined the French revolutionary movement, and been accepted into its ranks. He was a Pole of extreme and violent radical opinions. He had been obliged to flee his own country and take refuge in Paris in 1784. There he early espoused the revolutionary cause, and when the National Guard was formed, he was elected Captain for the Finistère *section* in which he lived, and subsequently led the Breton contingent of *fédérés* at the march on the Tuileries in 1792. Madame Roland said in her *Memoirs*, which she wrote in prison, that Lajouski had been seen cutting priests' throats at one of the prisons during the September massacres the following year.

Though acclaimed as an outstanding patriot, the Pole had enemies. Vergniaud, an extremist Montagnard, was one of them. He denounced Lajouski for setting up a local revolutionary committee in a district in the provinces with which he had connections. This, said Vergniaud, was unnecessary and in defiance of the National Convention with which it was in competition. He should be arrested.

Lajouski's friends were strong and rallied to his support. Vergniaud was publicly reproached for being motivated by personal animosity in putting forward this denunciation. Cleared of the accusation, the Pole left Paris for the country, but there he became suddenly ill with 'an inflammatory fever' and died. His body was brought back to Paris and buried with full revolutionary honours at the foot of a tree named as the Tree of Liberty in the Place du Carrousel, the great courtyard of the Tuileries. Hanriot organised the funeral and Robespierre delivered one of his orations during the burial. Curtius hastened to model a wax bust of this 'patriot', like himself of foreign birth. He was glad to see that the presentation to the Jacobin Club was reported in the official government newspaper, *Le Moniteur Universel*. This helped to ensure his own safety, when denunciation was always round the corner for everyone.

Even if the hard-working guillotine did provide diversion for those who liked to watch its victims, from all walks of life, climb the ladder and lose their heads, existence for most Parisians was drab and anxious. They were starved of the spectacles which they had enjoyed so much in the days of the *ancien régime*.

With more cheerful news from the war fronts and La Vendée, and under pressure from the Hébertist Enragés for the de-Christianisation of churches, the deputies decided that the ancient cathedral of Nôtre Dame, scene of so many splendid royal and religious occasions over the centuries, should now become a republican edifice, a Temple of Reason.

The event was celebrated on 10 November under the guidance of the painter David who, as well as being an outstanding artist, excelled at and enjoyed the designing of impressive if somewhat flashy pageants. As friends of the artist, Curtius and Marie had no difficulty in getting good places from which to watch proceedings. Marie always retained a vivid memory of this festival. She was not a religious woman, but she recalled it with a contempt that she dared not show at the time, and joined in the applause with as much enthusiasm as was prudent.

She described the principal figure in the ceremonies, 'the wife of a printer . . . impersonated the Goddess of Reason. She appeared in white drapery, an azure blue mantle hung from her shoulders, and from beneath the Cap of Liberty her hair flowed in rich profusion.' Marie's artist's eye had to admit that the printer's wife chosen by David for the rôle was indeed a beautiful woman, 'though modesty might be lacking'.

The Goddess of Reason was enthroned upon an antique seat borne by four strong male citizens, for David's choice was a statuesque woman of considerable weight. The Goddess's arrival in the cathedral was heralded by bands of young girls dressed in white and crowned with roses and, as Marie remarked scornfully, 'a bust of Marat heightened the disgrace of the occasion!'

Quite in the old royal style, musicians, contingents of troops and uniformed Civil Guards added martial splendour to the procession. Once everyone was inside the cathedral, speeches were delivered and hymns of a non-religious nature sung by choirs. The crowds of spectators were delighted. Wild applause came from the colour-starved public. 'The Republic for ever! Reason for ever!' they shouted.

Many deputies from the National Convention joined in what Marie called 'this cavalcade of mockery', of which, she said, most of them seemed half-ashamed, though they had to go along with the popular enthusiasm. Robespierre was one who did not wholly approve of the campaign for de-Christianisation of churches. A month after this festival of the Goddess of Reason he persuaded the deputies to reaffirm the already sanctioned principle of free worship.

At the end of 1793 an execution took place in the Place de la Révolution in which Curtius had a particular interest. The head that was severed was one which he had modelled years ago and was determined to model again after death. On 10 December, Madame du Barry, last mistress of the old King Louis XV, mounted the ladder to the guillotine. Marie remembered, from her arrival in Paris as a child of six, the beautiful wax head, bust, arms and the graceful recumbent body that Curtius had modelled when Madame du Barry was only the twenty-two-year-old Jeanne Vaubernier. She had not yet caught the King's eye and was the mistress of rascally Jean du Barry. When she did attract royal attention she was hastily married to his brother, the Comte du Barry, because only married ladies were received at court.

Jeanne had never collected the portrait figure, but Curtius had always kept it as an example of his best work, showing to perfection the turn of the long neck and the oval face with its delicate arched eyebrows. It became known as 'The Sleeping Beauty' and is still in Madame Tussaud's exhibition.

When Curtius learned the date of her execution it was not difficult for him to gain entry into the Madeleine cemetery, though this time there were no official orders. Bodies of guillotine victims were still being tossed into common pits, though space was rapidly getting filled. Curtius and Marie were both well known to the officials there. This time Marie did not accompany her uncle, but in fact anyone who could pay could gain access. Many relatives of guillotine victims sought to obtain some last relic before the remains were thrown into the quick-lime.

Marie had heard with a shudder the story of one such seeker. A young woman of aristocratic family bribed the guardians of the cemetery to allow her to rescue the head of her executed lover. She carried it away bundled up in her skirt, the way working women carried firewood or vegetables if they had no basket. As the girl was crossing the bridge over the Seine to the south bank, she was seized with faintness, her legs gave way and she let go her skirt. The head rolled in the road. Unfortunately other people were crossing the bridge at the same time and it was not long before she herself made the journey to the guillotine.

Curtius took some slight risk in going to the cemetery, but he was not to be put off. He had not seen Madame du Barry for many years; Marie had never seen her in the flesh, but she was said to be still beautiful, though stouter in figure. It was her own fault that she faced execution, for she could have lived to a comfortable old age abroad had she not cared too much about her possessions.

In 1789, when the Bastille was stormed, Madame du Barry was living tranquilly on her country estate of Louveçiennes. She enjoyed a yearly income of some 50,000 *livres* secured for her by Louis XV, who had also given his last mistress this country property as well as much valuable jewellery. She loved diamonds as much as did Marie Antoinette.

Madame du Barry was considered a kindly and generous landowner, appreciated by her tenants and benevolent to the poor. She was happy in the devotion of her lover, the Duc de Brissac, and loved her estate of Louveçiennes. The outbreak of the Revolution did not affect her unobtrusive lifestyle in the country, where her tenants seemed to realise they could go further and fare worse than under their present mistress.

Early in January 1791 Madame du Barry spent a night in Paris at the house of the Duc de Brissac. While she was away her jewellery was stolen from her château at Louveçiennes. She went to great efforts to try to retrieve it, and in spite of prevailing political conditions, obtained permission to make several visits to England where some of the stolen jewels had turned up in a London jeweller's establishment. She had not been entirely untouched by the Revolution and its dangers. Her lover, the Duc de Brissac, was briefly arrested, but on his release Louis XVI had appointed him to command the *Garde Constitutionelle* which replaced his disbanded Royal Guard. It was this appointment which led to the Duc's denunciation and rearrest while he was out of Paris, staying in the country.

In September 1792 the Duc was being conveyed back to Paris with other prisoners when a mob attacked the carts in which they rode. Several prisoners were murdered and the Duc de Brissac was one of them. His head was cut off and taken to Louveçiennes, where it was thrown into Madame du Barry's garden. She had the sense to dissemble shock and grief, and still considered herself safe among her devoted retainers and tenants. Unfortunately, she had never been a woman of perspicacity—or even intelligence—in spite of her charm and good nature.

The following month, still in pursuit of her stolen gems, Madame du Barry managed to get official sanction for another visit to London. A law suit against the jeweller, who claimed he had purchased jewels from her collection in good faith and legitimately, was dragging on. It continued to drag and Madame du Barry continued to stay in London, where she enjoyed the society of many French *emigrés* who bore no malice towards their late monarch's wealthy and attractive former mistress.

Madame du Barry was still in London when the shattering news of Louis XVI's execution arrived. She promptly went into deep mourning and attended a memorial service at the chapel of the Spanish Embassy. Such actions, together with her prolonged stay in England and close association with the *emigrés*, were dangerous in a city teeming with spies of the French Republican government.

Further bad and disturbing news from France reached the one-time Comtesse. A French-speaking Englishman, said to have been a friend of Marat, had arrived in Louveçiennes. Madame du Barry did not know this man, had never seen him, nor had he been seen locally before. He was violently Jacobin, a convincing orator, and managed to sway local opinion against her. Of low birth their landlady might be, but Louis XV had squandered fortunes on her, which she had accepted while the poor starved.

Madame du Barry was appalled to learn that the local authority had placed seals on her beloved château, and the National Convention had declared her an *emigrée*, which meant all her property was forfeit to the State. Such was her indignation, since her absence in London had been given official sanction, that in March 1793, ignoring the pleas and warnings of her French and British friends, Madame du Barry returned hot-foot to France to rescue her property. She refused to believe that there was not some dreadful mistake, that her tenants and servants who had protected her had turned against their kind and generous mistress.

The immediate arrest and trial of 'the du Barry' were a foregone conclusion, but through the long months of her imprisonment she continued to delude herself that she would never be found guilty, that she would return to her estate and that everyone there would welcome her as they had always done. She was wrong.

When the date of Madame du Barry's execution was announced Curtius felt impelled to make another portrait of the face he had found so beautiful in youth, and which was still comely. He did not go to the Place de la Révolution to join the crowds round the guillotine. It was a terrible execution. Immense mobs had gathered to watch the end of a royal mistress, the last of a line of such women who had drained the Treasury and battened on the taxes paid by the poor.

Even when actually on the scaffold, Jeanne du Barry, once Vaubernier, simply could not believe the fate that had overtaken her. She screamed and screamed most piteously. The massed onlookers were deeply disturbed. They had become accustomed to prisoners, no matter what their rank, facing the guillotine blade in stoical silence and dignity. This shrieking and struggling was most unbecoming and people did not like it. It was a relief when the blade fell.

Curtius slipped almost unnoticed into the Madeleine cemetery. In the chilly, damp December dusk he awaited the cartload of bodies and heads that was on its way. Madame du Barry's head was soon sorted out from the grisly pile. Curtius's skilled fingers made short work of smoothing the distorted features into calm and regularity. He oiled the face, applied the mask, took a clipping of hair and handed the head back to the waiting men.

Like the death-mask portraits of Louis XVI and Marie Antoinette that Marie had modelled on official command, Curtius's private last portrait of Madame du Barry was never put on public exhibition. Even when Marie, then Madame Tussaud, took her exhibition to London nine years later, she did not take it. She took only the youthful Jeanne, recumbent in sleep, that Curtius had modelled before she became a royal mistress.

The year 1793 had proved more profitable for the *Salon de Cire*, thanks to the tableau of 'The Death of Marat', and the acquisition of the country house at Ivry-sur-Seine had already proved its worth as a source of produce and a place of rest, as Curtius's health was still impaired, though he gave up none of his activities.

While Robespierre continued to proclaim that the basic principles of the Republic of France must be 'Virtue and Terror', the plight of the people, in Paris and in the provinces, grew worse. At the end of the year 1793 the paper banknote, the *assignat*, was worth less than half the value of its equivalent in the old metal currency. Marie said she used *assignats* to paper over cracks in the wall, their purchasing power was so low. But at least Robespierre had managed to impose fixed prices, which controlled profiteering on shortages of food and commodities.

Climax of the Terror

THE year 1794, when the Terror reached its climax, and the course of the French Revolution changed, was also the most shattering year in the life of Marie Grosholtz. During it she and her mother narrowly escaped the guillotine, and Curtius, the man she called uncle, her lifelong guide and teacher in whom she had implicit trust, died at the comparatively early age of fifty-seven. It was a natural death, though Marie believed till the end of her life that his illness had its origin in some poison administered at the instigation of the guillotined General Custine.

As the new year began Robespierre was preparing to destroy those factions of the Montagnards which were hostile to his own policies and ambitions. Curtius was preparing to send his work abroad for the first time; he and Marie were getting together an exhibition of wax portrait figures to be taken to India by an experienced showman, Dominic Laurency, an Italian by birth. Dominic Laurency planned to sail in the summer for Calcutta and Madras, taking with him 'The Cabinet of Curtius and the Optic of Zaler'.

The gathering together of the twenty portrait figures that were to make this long voyage was a dangerous operation, and had to be handled with great discretion. The figures included 'Kings and Princes who have been at Paris and were modelled by Curtius, the unfortunate Louis XVI and his family, as well as Voltaire, Rousseau, and members of the first National Assembly, all clothed in the costumes they usually wore.'

Secretly unpacked from the wardrobe's store was the Rose Bertin dress that had adorned the figure of Marie Antoinette in the tableau 'The Royal Family at Dinner'. Also unearthed were rich silk suits, the uniforms and decorations of 'visiting' kings, Voltaire's long cravat and striped stockings, all re-creating something of the *Salon de Cire*'s old splendour.

It was risky work and only Curtius's pride in the artistic value of his work, together with financial need, could have induced him thus to recall the *régime* that had vanished. The republican authorities might not object to likenesses of Voltaire and Rousseau and some of the early deputies being sent across the world, but the inclusion of the royal family of France and other 'Kings and Princes' was something that must be concealed, though these were the highlights of the collection.

There was no doubt that the 'Cabinet of Curtius' would arouse a great deal of interest among the gentlemen and their ladies of the East India Company and other nationals such as the Danes, who maintained trading-posts in Calcutta and Madras. For them the execution of the King and Queen of France was comparatively recent news, as sailing-ships from Europe took about six months to reach the east coast of India.

They would also see some of the horrors of the French Revolution. Curtius had included a model of the Bastille before and after its fall, and the decapitated head of Foulon, once in the King's Ministry and Curtius's neighbour, a grisly representation: 'the blood seems to be streaming from it and running on the ground', Dominic Laurency advertised it on arrival, having sailed in a Danish ship. He publicised his attractions in flamboyant style in the *Calcutta Gazette* and later, as he moved on, in the *Madras Courier*.

The Optic of Zaler, which completed the exhibition, was an optical illusion very popular in the entertainment area of the Boulevard du Temple, involving as it did no political risks. It was 'an Optic Glass representing the rising of the Sun and the Capitals of Europe in their Natural State and Size ... the illuminations in the houses are represented exactly'. Curtius had always been interested in optics, often having discussed them with Marat, so the Optic of Zaler was a fitting complement to his own wax portrait figures. In the end the collection he sent to India survived two hot seasons and two monsoons before Laurency ceased to exhibit it.

By the time the portrait figures and other items for India were packed, in early summer, drastic changes had taken place in the government of France. Robespierre, the man Curtius had always backed, was in complete control. In February and March the demands of the Hébertists and ultra-Left Cordeliers Club had intensified. They insisted on a complete redistribution of property and public offices. They were not satisfied with the suggestion put forward by St Just, Robespierre's closest associate, that instead of this measure there should be a confiscation of the property of all suspects. The State had already confiscated church land, and all the property of *emigrés*, much of which had been put up for public sale.

The violent elements responded to this comparatively moderate suggestion by threatening to raise another insurrection, another outbreak of bloody rioting, the complete antithesis of Robespierre's policy of a ruthless but strictly controlled Terror. He determined that a series of purges in the National Convention was the only way to clear out those who opposed his concepts.

On the pretext of preventing further rioting, Robespierre made a sudden swoop on his enemies. On the night of 13–14 March 1794, Hébert, his followers and a number of members of the Cordeliers Club were arrested, immediately put on trial and condemned to death by the Revolutionary Tribunal. Robespierre had demonstrated his power and influence over the deputies of the National Convention who were not Hébertists.

Hébert, the man who had accused Marie Antoinette of sexually abusing her son and promised her head to the *sans-culottes*, did not acquit himself with the dignity of his royal victims when he himself mounted the scaffold. Experienced guillotine-watchers said he screamed even louder than Madame du Barry. Marie received an official order, no doubt emanating from Robespierre, to take a death-mask from this man who had often visited Curtius, and whom she had always particularly feared. She no longer had any feelings about handling decapitated heads.

Danton, who not long before had rallied to Robespierre's support, now found himself regarded as an enemy. He and his followers were arrested and went to the guillotine on 1 April. Danton was now a very weary man, deeply disillusioned by the course the Revolution had taken. 'I prefer to be guillotined than to guillotine,' he said, but when he heard his death sentence he cried out, 'Infamous Robespierre, the scaffold claims you . . . you will follow me!' Danton died with fortitude. He had made no attempt to fight back against Robespierre. Some called his death almost a suicide.

Robespierre was now supreme ruler of France. His government intensified repression and relied on the Terror to keep a hold on power. Robespierre called for heads and still more heads, yet, contrary to the former Hébertists' efforts for total de-Christianisation, he decided to proclaim the official existence of a Supreme Being. A decree to this effect was issued two days before Madame Elisabeth, Louis XVI's sister and Marie's former employer at Versailles, followed her brother to the guillotine.

Marie suffered much distress, while preserving outward indifference, when she heard that the good and harmless Princess had been brought to trial. She had remained a prisoner in the Temple keep in company with her niece, Madame Royale. Little King Louis XVII was never permitted to see his aunt after the cobbler Simon took charge of him.

No accusation could be less justified than that brought against Madame Elisabeth. She was charged with conspiring against the 'Safety and Liberty' of the French people, and was automatically found guilty. Marie was able to avoid seeing her former kind mistress as she was taken through the streets in the tumbril, bare-headed because the wind had blown her kerchief away. The furniture Marie had been given when she left Versailles had always been hidden away. Curtius had considered this prudent, and ever since her return to the *Salon de Cire* she had avoided discussing her royal service as far as possible.

Twenty-three other victims preceded the Princess on the scaffold. When her turn came to climb the ladder the crowd, many still remembering Madame Elisabeth's generous charity and simple, retiring life, fell silent. There were no cries of 'Vive la République!' as the blade descended on this innocent royal neck. Madame Elisabeth did not flinch.

Fortunately the Princess was of no political importance, so there was no call on Marie's skills to take a death-mask. Madame Elisabeth died with noble serenity, but her body was not allowed to lie in the Madeleine cemetery with those of her brother and sister-in-law. Her remains, together with those of the others who had been executed on the same day, were accommodated in a piece of ground specially designated for guillotine victims, not far from what is now the Parc Monçeau. Danton, and Malesherbes, whose integrity Marie had admired when at Versailles, were among those who were already interred there. The Madeleine cemetery was becoming over-full, and it was not easy to find suitable locations that were not too far from the Place de la Révolution. Marie could only hope she would not be required again to make official visits to cemeteries.

At the beginning of May the National Convention, under Robespierre's direction, having recognised a Supreme Being and the immortality of the soul as republican concepts, decreed that there would be four annual republican festivals, as well as a celebration of civic virtues. This last celebration would take place regularly, but not every seven days like Sunday worship. Every tenth day of the new calendar was designated for this new celebration.

The painter David, now a member of the Committee of Public Safety, proclaimed 8 June as the date for the first Republican Festival of the Supreme Being and Nature. He again exercised his artistry in designing the ceremonies. Robespierre, holding a bouquet of flowers, presided. The procession stretched from the Tuileries to the Champ de Mars.

Curtius and Marie watched in the Tuileries, where effigies of Atheism, Discord and Selfishness were displayed in an amphitheatre specially designed to accommodate all the deputies of the National Convention. Marie could not help reflecting that it was just a month since the pious, amiable and charitable Madame Elisabeth had passed by the gardens on her way to execution. At an appropriate moment Robespierre advanced and set fire to these effigies. Unfortunately the figure of Wisdom which arose from the ashes to replace them was completely blackened by the smoke of Robespierre's ceremonial bonfire.

The gladsome mood of the festival proved to be short-lived, however. Two days later, on 22 *Prairial*, which was the old-style 10 June, the dread Law of Prairial was proclaimed, to replace the already infamous Law of Suspects. Under the new decree there was no requirement for even the most sketchy trial of arrested suspects. Persons seized after being denounced as enemies of the Republic could be condemned to death with no more ado than the signing of a death warrant by a member of the Committee of Public Safety. If, for some reason, a name caught the attention of the member signing the daily pile, he might possibly put that warrant aside for further investigation, but otherwise the process was automatic.

The term 'enemy of the Republic' was so vaguely defined that the merest triviality could be a pretext for denunciation: a misplaced tricolour cockade, for instance, a slip of the tongue, or an ill-advised gesture, might lead to the guillotine. Accusations were welcomed, for the local watch committees needed to keep up a display of zeal in their duties, lest members should find themselves denounced for not doing their job properly.

During the period of the Great Terror, from 10 June to 27 July 1794, more than twelve hundred heads rolled under the guillotine blade in Paris alone, and provincial guillotines were kept constantly at work. It was the Law of Prairial that brought about the arrest of Marie Grosholtz and her mother.

In such a climate of fear, when neighbour dared not talk to neighbour and even families harboured suspicions of their own members, Marie felt uneasy when Robespierre despatched Curtius on another mission to the Rhineland where his fluent German had already proved so useful.

When Curtius was absent Marie had no means of assessing how the political wind was veering, and the *Salon de Cire* seemed to have become essentially a political mirror. She was vigilant over every detail of the grouping and the costumes of the portrait figures. It was even necessary to keep a watchful eye on the appearance of her mother and the staff, as well as her own dress. Unbelievable trivialities such as the size, placing or omission of the now compulsory tricolour cockade could be maliciously interpreted as grounds for denunciation. Too fine a material for skirt or fichu could mean a hankering after pre-revolutionary styles.

She took the minutest care, so it was therefore a shock when, one evening, the dreaded knock came on the door of No. 20 Boulevard du Temple. Marie and her mother were put under summary arrest—accused of having pro-royalist sentiments. How had this charge come about in spite of so much discretion and prudence? Could Madame Elisabeth's execution a few weeks earlier have jogged someone's memory about Marie's long royal service, or was it possible someone suspected that the cases despatched to India contained something other than revolutionary portraits?

It was more likely that an unrecognised enemy had used the very discretion she so strictly maintained, for neither Marie nor her mother had shown themselves aggressively republican in speech or demeanour. There was no time for prolonged protest, which was useless anyway. With only a few minutes allowed to check that the already closed *Salon de Cire* was secure, and to push a few necessities into a bag, Marie and Madame Grosholtz were hustled into a hackney coach and taken first to La Force prison, then transferred to the Carmes.

All the prisons were overcrowded with frightened 'suspects' waiting their turn to be carried off to the guillotine, unless, by some miracle, their death warrant was abstracted from the piles which members of the Committee for Public Safety took it in turn to sign. There was hardly a hope, yet hope was maintained.

The room in which Marie and her mother found themselves already contained twenty women. There were bundles of straw for mattresses. The food, brought by warders, consisted of almost uneatable bread, hard peas and beans which they found difficult to masticate, and some soup or broth. Every time the heavy bolted door opened a tremor of fear ran through the room. Was it just food, or would a prisoner or two take the first steps to death? All the women's hair was cut short, so they were ready for the blade.

Marie could hardly hope that someone would lodge a plea on her behalf with the Committee of Public Safety. Curtius was the only one who knew Committee members personally. The news of her arrest would take days to filter through to him. He might be anywhere in the Rhineland, as the unknown accuser must have been aware. Was it possible that Robespierre had turned suddenly against Curtius, had him arrested—even executed—somewhere in the French-occupied Rhineland?

Another name, minor but potentially dangerous, came to her mind.

Her denouncer might be Jacques Dutruy, a man who worked as a *'grimacier'* amusing audiences between the acts of theatrical performances around the Boulevard du Temple by pulling hideous faces. He had known Marie since her return from Versailles, and they had never been congenial. If Jacques was her enemy, Marie knew she had little chance of escape. He enjoyed the patronage of several prominent revolutionaries, and supplemented his income from the theatres by working as one of the 'lads' who helped executioner Sanson with the guillotine. He would gloat while watching Marie's neck being severed!

With such uncertainties racking her mind, Marie did not know to whom she might safely turn for help. In any case she did not have enough money with her to bribe a warder to smuggle out a message. She tried to keep calm and observe her fellow-prisoners. Among the crowd of terrified women there was one to whom Marie felt drawn. She was a pretty young Creole who had been under arrest since March, the wife of General de Beauharnais, who was incarcerated in the same prison. Josephine de Beauharnais had brought her own plight upon herself by her efforts to get her husband released. He had been waiting trial since the previous July, charged with military incompetence when Mayence (Mainz) had been recaptured by the Prussian army.

Marie noticed that this young woman never seemed to give way to despair, and was always trying to comfort and hearten those whose courage was failing. Her own danger was no less than that of the others, although she managed to keep contact with influential friends outside, and had the privilege of occasional visits from her two young children.

Living thus from day to day in the seemingly vain hope of finding some means of saving her mother and herself, Marie could scarcely believe her good fortune when, in mid-July, they were both suddenly released. They were told to go as summarily as they had been arrested and gaoled. Shaken, and still frightened, Marie did not dare return straightway to the Boulevard du Temple. She and her mother took refuge with an advocate friend of Curtius, who worked at the Hôtel de Ville and was in a position to find out how the land lay. Marie had no idea how their release had come about. She wondered if General Kléber might have heard of her arrest and intervened—he was one of Curtius's closer friends. The General had been defeated in one of the Vendéean revolts and recalled to Paris on the grounds that he was too lenient towards the rebels, but had not been charged or punished, and remained influential. More likely it was the painter David who was the saviour. As a member of the Committee of Public Safety he took his turn at signing death warrants. He had always admired Marie's work and if he had noticed her name on one of them, would certainly have withdrawn it. So talented and useful an artist could not be sent to the guillotine for nothing. He had based his famous painting of the death of Marat on the portrait and sketches she had made by official command immediately after the assassination.

There was no news of Curtius's return, and the doors of the *Salon de Cire* must not remain closed indefinitely. After a few days with their advocate friend, it seemed safe for Marie and her mother to go back. She resumed her work as if it had never been interrupted. Marie's thoughts turned to her prison companion, young Madame de Beauharnais, when she heard that her husband, the General, had gone to the guillotine on 22 July. Josephine was said to be still in the Carmes prison, but there was nothing Marie could do to help her. In any case the less said about her own denunciation and imprisonment the better.

On account of Curtius's continued absence and her own incarceration in prison, Marie was not well informed about what had been going on in the National Convention. Though the month of June had brought increasing successes to the French republican armies, Robespierre, having achieved what seemed complete control, was now facing opposition. Moderate deputies were appalled at the ruthless guillotining of 'suspects' and sensed that, in spite of the crowds that still gathered daily to watch the falling blade, the majority of people throughout the country had had enough of the fear and bloodshed which, under Robespierre's rule, had terrorised the whole of France.

The violently left-wing Montagnard deputies, who had escaped Robespierre's purges, still wanted de-Christianisation of churches, and resented the official establishment of the Supreme Being and the resulting festivals. They had always opposed the 'controlled Terror' policy, even if they had no objection to bloody rioting. There was dissension and hostility at the meetings of the Committee of Public Safety. Robespierre ceased to put in an appearance at them.

The end of the Terror was brought about by a triumvirate of deputies, all with bloodstained records, all known to Marie as visitors to her uncle's gatherings at the Boulevard du Temple. She found little to admire in any of them.

Billaud-Varenne had stood and casually watched the slaughter of priests at the start of the September massacres. Collot d'Herbois, as a Revolutionary Commissioner, took his revenge on the people of Lyons. In that city, as a young actor, he had once been hissed off the stage. He repaid that early insult not only with the guillotine, but also with grapeshot which he had poured into the 'enemies of the People'. Billaud-Varenne had originally been one of Robespierre's supporters, but now he moved against him.

[167]

The third of the triumvirate, Barrère, who acted as a link between the Montagnards and more moderate deputies, was notorious for the ferocity with which he had put down an anti-Jacobin revolt in the south of France. Although Barrère had been one of the first members of the Jacobin Club, Robespierre had found it hard to conceal the intense dislike he felt for this man, and no-one was surprised when Barrère declared his opposition.

These three, who conspired to overthrow Robespierre, were able to win support from all the factions in the National Convention. Now that the republican armies were winning victories, none of them wished to pursue the policy of the ruthless and controlled Terror. All desired internal peace and an end to oppression. Each faction hoped that, if this favourable climate could be achieved, their own particular aims might be realised.

Marie found the little information she could gain about the political situation very disturbing. If Robespierre's reign was to be cut short what would Curtius's situation be when he got back to Paris? He had backed Robespierre right through the Revolution, from his first appearance as a deputy at the National Assembly at Versailles.

While she had every confidence that her uncle could pick his way skilfully through political quicksands, she thought it was perhaps a good thing he was still out of the country, even though it was Robespierre who had sent him on his mission. By the time he returned the situation might have been resolved, and then Curtius could choose his path in whatever the new circumstances proved to be.

The Terror Ends: Curtius Dies

SINCE Robespierre was inflexible in his policy of the Terror, a crisis within the National Convention was inevitable. It came on 9 *Thermidor*, old-style 27 July. One of the triumvirate, Collot d'Herbois, who was serving his turn as President of the Assembly, prevented Robespierre and his close supporter St Just from speaking during the session, as both wished and tried to do.

The President drowned Robespierre's protests by ringing a bell loudly. With Robespierre and St Just silenced, deputy Barrère was able to force through a measure depriving Hanriot of his command of the National Guard. He had held this position since his appointment by the Revolutionary Committee at the start of the *sans-culottes* revolt of May 1793. Then his ring of cannon had prevented the deputies from leaving their Assembly in the Tuileries. Now he was thrown out and a new Commander, Barras, took control of the National Guard.

Robespierre now came under direct attack. An indictment against him, St Just, and another supporter was proposed and agreed. Robespierre had a younger brother, Augustin, who also sat as a deputy, though he had not sought any limelight. Now Augustin and a close friend called Lebas asked to be included in this indictment. All five men were put under arrest, taken out and distributed among different prisons. The triumvirate's coup against Robespierre was almost complete. It would end victoriously, but in utter confusion.

Hanriot and the violently revolutionary Paris Commune did not take his dismissal lightly. They set about trying to rouse the *section* committees which had always responded with enthusiasm when called on to revolt. This time things were different, and there was hardly any response. Only sixteen out of the forty-eight *sections* rallied to the call and sent men along. Most of the citizens of Paris were sick of the Terror, sick of revolt, rioting and bloodshed.

Robespierre and his fellow prisoners were not held for long in the separate gaols to which they had been taken. Released, they made their individual ways to the Hôtel de Ville, or Maison Commune as the *sans-culottes* preferred to call it. They had all arrived there by about one o'clock in the morning. Even Robespierre was uncertain, hesitant, not knowing for once the best course to take in the circumstances in which they now found themselves. The few insurgents who had answered Hanriot's call had been declared outlawed by the National Convention, and the National Guard around the Hôtel de Ville disbanded.

At about two o'clock in the morning the new Commander, Barras, arrived with a contingent of the National Guard. The five released men were inside the building when Barras and his force entered it. Whatever Barras's orders may have been, he was unable to carry them out, for his arrival in the Hôtel de Ville resulted in scenes of total chaos.

Before anyone could take action to restrain them, Augustin Robespierre jumped from a window and Lebas shot himself dead. In the ensuing confusion Robespierre himself was either shot by a guard or turned a pistol on himself. No-one was sure exactly what took place during those astonishing minutes. Robespierre did not die but his jaw was shattered by the shot.

He was placed on a table, trying in agony to staunch his bleeding with a woollen pistol-sheath and bits of paper, till a hastily summoned surgeon arrived to bandage the wound. The news of the débâcle, garbled and confused, spread quickly around Paris. Marie soon heard it, and was thankful that Curtius was abroad, and not in the vicinity of the man he had served and who was now doomed.

The following day Robespierre, who had sent so many thousands of innocent heads rolling into the basket beneath the guillotine blade, himself mounted the scaffold. He was given no trial. The mutilated Robespierre did not attempt to speak, but uttered a piercing shriek as the executioner roughly tore the dressing from his shattered jaw. Twenty-one of his followers mounted the ladder to death after him. Hanriot was among them. He was thirty-three, the same age as Marie Grosholtz.

She had already removed Robespierre's portrait figure from the *Salon de Cire* when she received the command she had feared would come. She must obey it with a good show of willingness, for how easily might Curtius, his work and friendship for Robespierre so well known, have been denounced and sent to join his other followers on the guillotine platform. Robespierre's remains were carted to the overcrowded Madeleine cemetery, and there Marie applied her plaster to the mutilated features.

As Marie worked in the studio modelling the death-head, faithfully reproducing the wounded jaw, she thought of the other likenesses of

Robespierre which had stood in the *Salon de Cire* since he first made his mark in the National Assembly of 1789 at Versailles. The latest portrait, which Curtius had modelled and which she had removed directly she heard of his downfall, had stood, by his own wish, next to the tableau of 'The Death of Marat'. Robespierre had provided some of his own clothing, and suggested other deputies might do likewise, for he wanted the portrait figures to be as near to life as possible. Now Marie made no attempt to modify his countenance in death.

The citizens of Paris rejoiced. During the space of five days more than four hundred 'suspect' prisoners awaiting the death sentence were released from the gaols. Among them, Marie heard, was Josephine de Beauharnais, widowed by the guillotine only a matter of days earlier. What would this young woman, brave as she had shown herself, do with the rest of her life? Marie wondered, but did not think their paths likely to cross again.

She waited with some anxiety for Curtius's return, and worked hard to keep the *Salon de Cire* attractive for the people who were celebrating the end of daily fear and bloodshed with singing, dancing and entertainment. Groups of workers, and all the *sections* of Paris, demonstrated their approval of the 'tyrant's' downfall. They sent messages of congratulation to the National Convention, though there were still some deputies who vowed no mercy for aristocrats and any who committed crimes against the State. This minority was disregarded. It was decreed that all revolutionary Commissioners and revolutionary Committees throughout France must henceforward provide proper grounds and evidence for any arrests they thought fit to make.

Paris seemed to give itself up to a mania for celebratory dancing. A lawyer's clerk, George Duval, wrote a description of this dancing craze. He called it 'sudden, spontaneous and frightening'. Marie found it somewhat excessive too. She was thirty-three now and, while Curtius pursued his political activities, she had taken the brunt of several years of hard work, responsibility, anxiety and fear. She felt relief and thankfulness but could not dance as gaily as she had done on the ruins of the Bastille in 1790. There was indeed something 'frightening' in this sudden switch to manic gaiety, while the cemeteries full of guillotined heads and bodies seemed totally forgotten.

It was to this climate of rejoicing that Curtius returned from the Rhineland. But he returned to Paris too ill for politics or gaiety. The new leaders in the National Convention were well known to him, but he made no attempts to seek their favour. Robespierre, for whom he had worked, had met his fate, the new France was here to stay, but he would play no further part in it.

[171]

The crowded premises at No. 20 Boulevard du Temple, housing the *Salon de Cire* and the old *Caverne des Grands Voleurs*, the modelling-studios and overflowing wardrobe and stockrooms, were impossibly unsuitable for nursing a sick man. Marie was already overloaded, keeping the exhibition updated and in running order while Madame Grosholtz's hands were full enough with cooking and domestic arrangements for family and staff.

Curtius left his life's work in Marie's charge and retired to his small country house at Ivry-sur-Seine, where the housekeeper could look after him and doctors from Paris could come to visit him. He did not want political guests in his house now, only a few long-time neighbours from the entertainment area round the Boulevard du Temple, like Sallé who had joined the National Guard with him in 1789. Sallé, the illegitimate son of a dancer, owned a theatre close to the *Salon de Cire*. Now it was called the *Théâtre Patriotique* and, like the *Salon*, had been safely steered through the twists and turns of the Revolution.

The time had come for Curtius to put his house in order and secure the future of the wax exhibition that had always been his passion as well as his livelihood. Everything he had done since his first arrival in Paris under the patronage of the Prince de Conti in the 1760s had been directed towards one objective, the building-up and, since 1789, the preservation of this spectacle, the expression of his sculptor's art in his chosen medium.

To this end he had trained Marie Grosholtz, the child who proved so apt a pupil in developing a skill equal to his own, and to this end he had walked a long and exceedingly dangerous political tightrope. Certainly Curtius had enjoyed much during this period, for he was a man who loved to be—needed to be—where the action was, involved in the contemporary scene, be it *ancien régime* or New France. He was a compulsive journalist with a flair for judging what people wanted to look at, a flair which he had imparted, with his artist's skills, to Marie. Had he not become mortally ill, poisoned as Marie insisted, he would have continued to balance on the tightrope, but now his concern was to make sure his art and his work did not die with him. In revolutionary France there were many new laws regarding inheritance and wills, which had to be registered officially. Curtius summoned his Paris lawyer, Gibé, to come to him at Ivry-sur-Seine.

The lawyer arrived on 31 August 1794, just over a month after Robespierre's head had rolled under the guillotine blade. Marie stayed in Paris. She could not leave the *Salon de Cire*. It was there that Curtius wished her to be, not at his bedside, and Marie had always followed his guidance and instructions.

[172]

Lawyer Gibé found his client in bed in one of the upstairs rooms overlooking the garden. He found him 'weak in body but collected in mind'. Curtius dictated his will in the presence of witnesses as the law required. He left his silver and jewellery to be sold for the benefit of the poor of the *section* of Temple, a nominal gesture as he had already donated his valuables to the National Convention towards the expenses of war. An inventory made after his death showed only half a dozen silver spoons and knives.

Declaring he had no legal heir, male or female, with a claim on his estate, Curtius willed everything else to Marie Grosholtz, 'my pupil in my art'. She was also appointed sole executrix. Marie was the one person who knew his wishes, and he was not going to have anyone else meddling. For Curtius the Revolution was over. He had played his rôle in it and achieved his aim. The *Salon de Cire* and Marie, on whom its future now depended, had come through the worst relatively un-scathed, thanks to his skilful manoeuvres. He could face his death, premature though it was for a man of his constitution, with peace of mind.

Curtius died on 26 September, nearly a month after he had made his will. He went quietly and there was no time to fetch Marie from Paris before he was gone. That was as he wanted it. The *Salon de Cire* must come first in her life as it had in his. He did not die alone, however. His housekeeper was at hand, and Sallé, with another old friend, a grocer from the Boulevard du Temple, was in the house.

These two friends reported the death to the local authority. An official hurried to the house to check that the deceased had indeed passed away before he made out the *Acte de Décès*.

Marie had kept her suspicions about poison to herself. Curtius had had medical attention—there were a few doctor's bills to be paid—and the document gave no indication of anything but natural death.

In accordance with the laws of the revolutionary government, seals were immediately put on the house, while officials began a detailed inventory of the contents. While they were at this task Marie appeared, just arrived from Paris. Calmly and with determination she stated herself to be Curtius's legal heir. It was a point that could not be made too early or too clearly. The government claimed any estate where there was no blood relative, unless the deceased person had willed it correctly to the inheritor of his choice. Though Marie had been known as Curtius's niece, she could prove no blood relationship.

Funerals were no longer religious ceremonies and a decree of January 1794 laid down that they were to be held at midnight, privately and without ceremonial. Curtius was interred as quietly as he had died.

[173]

There were no political figures among the mourners, just members of his household and a few showbusiness and local friends. Marie could not linger at Ivry-sur-Seine, for seals had also been slapped on No. 20 Boulevard du Temple and officials were making the detailed inventory.

She stood by watchfully as the officials worked. The inventory of the *Salon de Cire* took a long time to complete. Every item was listed, including the folding beds and bedding on which Curtius had accommodated Austrian deserters at the request of the Jacobin Club. She was wary and suspicious. There was little to choose between republican bureaucracy and that of the *ancien régime* when it came to grabbing property and possessions.

Though the terms of Curtius's will were clear enough, Marie felt her position precarious since she could not claim even to have been adopted by Curtius, in spite of the uncle–niece relationship which everyone had accepted. She took the precaution of obtaining a paper from the local *section* committee confirming that she had lived in Curtius's household since childhood, and was in fact 'the pupil in his art' who had spent her entire life under his training and guidance, working alongside him as soon as she was proficient. Even so, she had to fight a battle to get possession of an ivory snuff-box inlaid with a medallion, which Curtius had given her, but which the listing officials claimed as 'jewellery'.

Marie had begun taking snuff to calm her nerves during the stress of the revolutionary years. She had left the box lying around in the studio. The officials snapped it up. The medallion was silver and they had found little enough to sell for the poor of the *section* or, more likely, to pocket themselves. Again Marie had to find acceptable witnesses who would make a declaration that they had often seen her using it, before she could wrest it back.

It was November before Curtius's will was officially registered and Marie could be certain of her inheritance, and even this was not without its problems. There were a few small debts owing to 'doctor-surgeon', mason and locksmith, but also the liability for the previous year's taxes. With the exhibition closed for so many weeks till the formalities were completed Marie was short of cash. She could not pay the taxes in full. She also had to consider the house at Ivry-sur-Seine, on which only the first instalment had been paid to the National Housing Bureau.

In spite of these worries Marie had to turn her attention to the *Salon de Cire*. For the past five years it had been so closely linked with the political scene, and, without Curtius's judgements and guidance, she would not find it easy to assess the shifts in the political wind. It was fortunate that he had managed to impart to her not only his skill as a sculptor in wax, but also his journalistic flair for knowing what held people's attention. On this, and the fact that she had heard politics discussed all her life, she now had to rely.

The situation in the National Convention was fraught with confusion. Having toppled Robespierre, all its different factions were jockeying for power in order to pursue their individual policies. New groups had arisen, which Marie had to watch if the *Salon de Cire* was to reflect the trends of the moment as well as retain some of those of the past.

Among these new groups making themselves noticed was one that people called the *Jeunesse dorée* or 'gilded youth'. Many of its leaders were drawn from the artistic professions that were not usually connected with politics. There were actors, musicians, singers and dancers, who gained this nickname on account of their careful attire, so unlike that of previous revolutionary factions. The *Jeunesse dorée* affected long hair, 'sideboard' whiskers, tightly fitting tailcoats with square collars, and boots with long, pointed toes. It was an attire to enliven the *Salon de Cire* after so many years of drab and *sans-culottes* clothing.

This group was not as frivolous as its name and garb suggested. Its members repudiated the excesses of the Revolution. Membership increased and, by the time Curtius died in September, the *Jeunesse dorée* seemed to be everywhere. Right-wing deputies in the National Convention allied themselves with the movement, rejecting the rule of the Jacobin Club that Robespierre had led.

A mob of these young men attacked the premises of the Jacobins and in November the Club was forced to close its doors for ever. The *Jeunesse dorée* smashed busts and memorials to Marat, and threw the pieces into the sewers. Marie hastened to remove any Jacobin elements from the exhibition. She did not wish them to turn their attentions to the *Salon de Cire*. The tableau of the death of Marat was allowed to remain with a changed connotation. Now it represented the assassination of a monster, not the murder of a revolutionary hero.

Marie's involvement with the horrors of the Revolution was not yet over in spite of the direction in which the wheel seemed to be turning now. Those who, as Revolutionary Commissioners, had organised Robespierre's Terror in the provinces were now brought to justice. Among them was Carrier whose ghastly mass drownings of 'suspects' in the Loire at Nantes in 1793 were now regarded with horror. Hundreds had perished, loaded on to lighters, bound and crammed together so that they could not jump. The lighters had holes bored in them, and when they were towed into swift, deep-flowing water, plugs were removed. The victims sank with the lighters, helpless even to try to save themselves.

[175]

In December 1794 Carrier was guillotined and Marie was commanded to take a death-mask from his head. Would she hold any more severed heads in her lap? It was over five years since the mob had faced her with the heads of de Launay, Governor of the Bastille, and Flesselles, Provost of the Merchants, and forced her to take her first death-masks. The Terror was over, but life did not seem to get much easier.

The winter of 1794–5 was terrible. Price controls had gone with the execution of Robespierre, and the value of the *assignat*, the paper currency, collapsed completely. Marie was thankful she could get supplies of food, even if limited supplies, from Ivry-sur-Seine. A bad harvest, grain speculation, shortage of other foods and inflation produced unrest everywhere. There was a growing black market. Fear had gone, but poor people still starved. In April the people of Paris, who had suffered so sorely, began rioting in protest.

By May food shortages were even more acute and some commodities disappeared altogether. Bread was officially rationed at two ounces per person per day, though many pastry-shops still sold it at black-market prices. Malnutrition brought disease to the city and an increase in suicides. Another crisis was inevitable, and on 21 May a mob once again threatened and attacked the former theatre of the Tuileries palace where the National Convention still held its sessions.

It seemed to many that the downfall of Robespierre had brought little real relief. There were alarming reports of a 'White Terror' in the provinces where royalist groups were now in the ascendant. There was a strong resurgence of royalist feeling in many parts of France and violent revenge. Many former Jacobins found themselves, in their turn, mounting the ladder to the guillotine platform.

At the same time, in Paris, those who had organised the arrest and execution of so many innocent 'suspects' were brought to trial and lost their heads under the blade. On 7 May Marie received yet another call to perform the gruesome task to which she had become almost accustomed. The former Public Prosecutor, Fouquier-Tinville, during whose time in office Marie and her mother had been arrested, was sent to the guillotine for his crimes.

She had met this man, for he had dined with Curtius on a number of occasions. From first sight she had been struck by his ugliness, the sallow complexion pitted by smallpox, thin lips, narrow forehead under dark hair and, above all, a most unpleasant expression. Fouquier-Tinville was reputed to live meanly in spite of his money and property. He made no friendships and had no apparent diversion beyond sending people to their deaths, which appeared to provide him with constant satisfaction.

[176]

When his turn came to be executed he smiled, regarding the crowd in the Place de la Révolution with contempt, though his limbs were seen to tremble.

Marie worked on Fouquier-Tinville's death-head in the studio, alone as she always was there since Curtius's death. She was indifferent, even though, under this man's time of power, both she and her mother might have been executed. As an artist she did her work well, no matter what the subject.

Curtius always preserved the mould of a portrait head he thought to be of historic value. The death-heads that Marie had been forced to model would be historic too. None of these moulds would be discarded, Marie resolved. Hidden they might be, if necessary, like those of Louis XVI and Marie Antoinette, but never broken up. That was what Curtius would have decided and, as long as the exhibition lasted, the death-heads would be part of it. These heads, above all, bore witness to how closely Curtius and herself had been involved in these years of terrible upheaval and the emergence of the new republican France.

Marie Grosholtz Becomes Madame Tussaud

HER experiences during the Revolution did not alter Marie's agreeable and attractive manner, but behind it lay a steely fortitude. She was as determined as Curtius that the *Salon de Cire*, to which they had both devoted their working lives, should not close down after its founder had died far sooner than anyone expected.

She discovered in herself the power to assess the contemporary scene and decide, on her own judgement, what new portrait figures would keep the public flocking in. One personality she watched was Barras, the new Captain of the National Guard, whose power in the political arena was steadily increasing. He had been among Curtius's acquaintances and Marie respected him, 'a character of great wisdom and undaunted courage', she said.

It was not only Barras's political activities that interested her, but also his mistress. She was the charming young Creole widow, Josephine de Beauharnais with whom for a short time Marie and her mother had shared the terror of the Carmes prison. She had not, at the time, thought it likely she would hear of this young woman again even if they both escaped the guillotine, but she had not forgotten the courage with which Josephine had tried to cheer and support her fellow prisoners.

People were now saying that Madame de Beauharnais' morals were questionable, that she had been the mistress of General Hoche before transferring to the arms of Barras. General Hoche's low birth made him only a temporary refuge for the aristocratic widowed Josephine. Louis Lazare Hoche had served in the royal army as a corporal, promoted to the rank of general in 1789 after the fall of the Bastille. He had commanded the army of the Rhine in 1792 and held a command in Alsace in 1793, but his origins were lowly.

In spite of Citizen Barras's revolutionary record, which included voting as a deputy for Louis XVI's execution, he was a *ci-devant* Vicomte, member of one of the oldest families of the Var in the south of France, the *département* he had represented in the Assembly. Although

Josephine de Beauharnais was now Citizeness, she did not forget that she herself sprang from an aristocratic family, and her late husband, the guillotined General de Beauharnais, had also been a Vicomte before he embraced the revolutionary cause after fighting in the American War of Independence.

In spite of her preoccupation with the requirements of the *Salon de Cire*, Marie had to concentrate too on her personal difficulties, for receipts were still suffering in the general climate of shortages and uncertainty. She faced financial problems that had to be resolved. There was the balance of the previous year's taxes to clear, and if she wished to retain the house at Ivry-sur-Seine where Curtius had died, something had to be done about completing the purchase. She did not wish to lose the house. Apart from sentiment, it had proved a valuable source of fresh food supplies.

Fifty-five thousand *livres* were needed to clear off debts and pay the balance owing on the house, for Curtius had paid only the first instalment. Private lending was permitted, and Marie decided to mortgage the tenanted house in the Rue Fossés du Temple, unencumbered like No. 20 Boulevard du Temple which housed the exhibition and was the dwelling-place as well.

She found lenders in a Citizen Horry and his sister. The Horrys were a shrewd and cautious pair. They noted that Marie was only thirty-four, vivacious and agreeable, with no relative but a middle-aged mother. Although under republican law a husband did not automatically take control of his wife's property, together with liability for her debts, as in England, it seemed to them that a woman in Citizeness Grosholtz's position might fall prey to a fortune-hunter who would get hold of her assets.

They insisted on a special clause in the contract, to which Marie had no choice but to agree, as lenders were not easy to find. This stated that in the event of Citizeness Grosholtz marrying, her husband would be equally responsible for interest and the repayment of the loan. Moreover, a document certifying the husband's willingness to undertake this must be handed over to the lenders not more than eight days after such a marriage was registered.

The insistence of the Horry brother and sister on this clause made Marie begin to consider whether she should not set about finding a husband. It was not an easy decision. As a young girl Marie had had plenty of opportunities to change her status. There had been numerous young men in minor offices at Versailles, or in one of the Royal Guards, for whom the pretty *protégée* of Madame Elisabeth would have been a good *partie*.

[179]

Marie had turned such propositions aside. Any such marriage would have certainly meant abandoning her commitment to the *Salon de Cire* and to the uncle who had trained her from childhood to work as a full-time professional in his art. Neither had she considered any young men in the showbusiness world of the Boulevard du Temple as a partner. Either Marie would find herself involved in some other type of entertainment, or her husband would want to take part in running the *Salon de Cire*. Curtius wanted Marie alone to work with him. He laid down his own aims and policies and would brook no outside interference with them.

Curtius had died prematurely without expressing any wishes for the future beyond leaving everything to Marie. Who could she train, so that another generation could step into her shoes? There was no-one. But if she had a child, or children, they could be taught, as she had been, from the day they were old enough to mould a lump of softened wax.

Child-bearing was dangerous for a woman already thirty-four. If this was the course she must take, it could not be long delayed. Marie was still vivacious, with the attractive manner that had made her stay at Versailles so easy. Even though encumbered with a mortgage she was still a woman of property, and if she decided on marriage, suitors would not be lacking. For the moment Marie put the matter aside till she had settled her affairs and attracted back the former flow of visitors into the *Salon*. Sometimes it seemed that peace and prosperity for ordinary citizens would never come again.

It was a shock when, on 6 June 1795, the National Convention announced the death in the Temple prison of the former Dauphin, Louis XVII since his father's execution. He was ten years old and had not been seen in public, except glimpsed when taking exercise on the keep, since that day three years earlier when the royal family fled the Tuileries palace and were escorted as prisoners into the Temple. For a long time there had been rumours that the boy, his parents and aunt guillotined, and not allowed to see his sister who was also still in the prison, was not well, would not talk to anyone or reply to questions. But no-one thought his life was in danger.

With the news of his death wild stories began to circulate. Some people muttered that over a year earlier the little King had been smuggled out with the connivance of the cobbler Simon and even that of the scurrilous Hébert, both heavily bribed, and replaced by a deaf, dumb and sick boy from a Paris orphanage. The National Convention had hushed up this rescue, fearing to stimulate royalist opposition, and allowed the sick changeling to die a natural death. The Convention said nothing in their announcement, or afterwards, as to where the alleged dead Louis XVII had been buried.

Marie herself privately believed the rescue of the young King was a possibility, so many of the people guarding him, and so many deputies in the National Convention, being corrupt, but the Comte de Provence, Louis XVI's brother, he whose face Marie had once slapped on a staircase at Versailles, immediately declared himself Louis XVIII, from Verona in Italy where he was staying.

There was support from foreign powers. The English government gave permission for an expeditionary force under the Comte d'Artois, Louis XVI's second brother, to set sail from their shores for Brittany. On 23 June the force landed at Quiberon, but the Comte d'Artois was a disastrous commander. The royalist attackers were miserably defeated by the same General Hoche who was said to have enjoyed the favours of Josephine de Beauharnais on her release from prison.

It was a bloody business. The *emigré* force and their Breton supporters, known as *les Chouans*, were blockaded in the peninsula and few escaped. The Comte d'Artois was safe, but only three of his band of *emigrés* survived the carnage. Their effort was premature and inept, and did their cause no good.

This defeat of royalist invaders brought about a resurgence of revolutionary fervour in France. Once again Marie heard the strains of the *Marseillaise* echoing in the streets of Paris. Many Jacobins, imprisoned for their cruelty during Robespierre's Terror, found themselves released and free again. Visitors crowded into the *Salon de Cire* to look at Marie's portrait figure of the victorious General Hoche.

The situation soon changed. While the deputies in the National Convention were debating a new Constitution supported by all factions, the *Jeunesse dorée* again became intensely active. They wished to combat the resurgence of revolutionary spirit which they abhorred, and to stir up insurrection against it. The shaken royalist movement backed them.

Dedicated revolutionaries and former Jacobins did not sit idle in the face of this threat. They called on Terror supporters released from prison, army officers dismissed as Jacobins in the anti-Robespierre reaction and volunteers from the leftist *sections* of Paris, to form battalions, 'the Patriots of '89'. Civic rights were returned by the National Convention to those deprived of them on account of their activities during the Terror. It seemed to Marie that the dead Robespierre's reign was about to spring into life again. She was unable to assess where Curtius would have cast his lot in this new crisis, and could only wait the turn of events.

On 5 October Marie heard the tocsin ring out, again calling the men of

Paris to arms. Had Curtuis still been there he would have hurried off to muster his troop of National Guard. Alone, Marie closed the doors of the exhibition. No visitors would come this day even if Paris was spared more bloodshed.

In the fierce street-fighting that followed, the aspirations of pro-royalists and anti-revolutionaries were decisively and finally crushed. Seeking all the information she could get, Marie heard that a young Corsican general, Napoleon Bonaparte, had distinguished himself in the fighting. He was a protégé of the now powerful Barras, and Curtius would certainly have contrived to meet him. There was no way at the moment for Marie to do this, but she registered his name as a man whose career seemed in the ascendant, a possible man of the future.

All this unrest was bad for business. With her mortgage Marie had paid off the tax debt and the balance of the purchase price of the house at Ivry-sur-Seine, but she had been obliged to borrow another twenty-thousand *livres* in *assignats*, whose value had steadily declined, to meet the running expenses of the *Salon de Cire* and maintain its standards. This time the lender was Marguerite Salomé Reiss, who lived in the house and worked in the exhibition. In return Marie signed a document guaranteeing Citizeness Reiss an annuity of two thousand *livres*, another unwelcome financial burden.

However, with the prospect of more peaceful and more prosperous conditions in France, Marie's determination to carry on the *Salon de Cire* did not falter. She also decided to embark on marriage. She had found a man for whom she felt affection and who would, she hoped, be of some practical help in the exhibition even if he did not bring much money with him.

There was no-one she could consult about her choice. Since Curtius's death she took her decisions alone. On 28 October 1795 her marriage to François Tussaud was registered according to republican law at the Préfecture du Département de la Seine, Ville de Paris.

One of her witnesses was the theatre-owner Sallé who had been with Curtius on his deathbed. There was no religious ceremony. Civil marriage had been decreed in 1792. All marriages in central Paris took place at the former Hôtel de Ville, still the seat of the Municipality. A dirty and undecorated room was allocated for the purpose, in which brides, grooms and witnesses were crowded on benches to wait their turn for registration. It was a dismal performance. No family or friends were allowed and some twenty or thirty 'marriages' were registered in turn each day. A Parisian citizen, La Rivière Lapaux, who attended one of these ceremonies, noted that a few words from an official and the signing of a certificate by the couple and their witnesses completed a marriage. Marie exercised her right to retain sole control over her property.

It seemed a good omen for the new Madame Tussaud that three days before her wedding the Place de la Révolution where the guillotine had stood till its removal at the end of the Terror, was officially renamed Place de la Concorde. Now she could hope that her relationship with that gruesome instrument of death, and the part she had played in events of the Revolution, could fade into oblivion.

In fact, and through her own initiative, the name 'Madame Tussaud' would in the future become inextricably linked with the French Revolution and the guillotine, and this connotation remained throughout her life of nearly ninety years, and survives at the core of the exhibition today.

Marie certainly chose her husband, who was six years younger than herself, because he was the man she wanted, but the marriage seemed to have good practical advantages too. François Tussaud, who described himself on the marriage certificate as a civil engineer, had come to Paris from Mâcon and lived in the Temple district. His family were small winegrowers and coppersmiths—not rich, but far from being poor. Though bringing no property with him, François Tussaud's profession promised to make him a definite asset in the maintenance of both No. 20 Boulevard du Temple and the country house at Ivry-sur-Seine, leaving Marie able to concentrate on the planning and artistic work of the exhibition. Tussaud was not an artist and would not interfere in these aspects of the *Salon de Cire*, where Marie wished for no guidance except the policies and standards of her late uncle Curtius.

Marie's husband had no knowledge of the former royal Court at Versailles and the ways of the *ancien régime*, nor had he any political bent. She had had implicit trust in Curtius's political judgement and acumen, but did not extend that trust to anyone else. She was becoming a shrewd observer, assessor and recorder of the political and social scene and the personalities concerned in it, but wished no further active involvement in it herself. She would never link herself to a husband with keen political interests.

In spite of the financial burdens under which they started their married life, there seemed no reason why Marie and François Tussaud should not work successfully together to build up the exhibition to its former glory. Unfortunately, as time went by, François proved himself an unreliable support. He liked to gamble, not with cards or dice, but in property speculation. His favourite speculation was in theatrical property, the most risky field of all. There were only the profits of the *Salon de Cire* to make indulgence of this taste possible, for Marie found

[183]

she had married a man who lacked the ability to make solid money, even though he had charm.

Nevertheless she remained optimistic. After proclaiming a new Constitution, the National Assembly dissolved itself, the end of a revolutionary government which had ruled since the first National Assembly of 1789. In its place a Directory of five men was elected, to govern with a Council. The head of the Directory was Barras, former Vicomte and one-time Commander of the National Guard, while the young Corsican, General Napoleon Bonaparte, was appointed Commander of the Army of the Interior.

Portrait figures of the new Directors brought an influx of curious visitors to the exhibition and also a welcome splash of colour. They had adopted a special uniform that was remarkable in its flamboyance. Marie enjoyed setting her wardrobe staff to work on the cherry-coloured cloak, white silk pantaloons, boots with turnover tops and a Spanish-style waistcoat all embroidered with gold. The hat that topped the outfit was Spanish style too, ornamented with plumes. The Directors almost rivalled pre-revolutionary aristocrats in the splendour of their garb.

By the end of spring 1796 civil war in France was virtually finished. The almost valueless paper *assignat* was withdrawn and replaced by a new metal coinage. Food shortages brought a brief resurgence of revolutionary fervour, but the Directory dealt quickly and firmly with this and regained their control. The situation calmed and became easier, but Marie was still glad of her decision to keep Curtius's country house, with its poultry yard, fruit trees and vegetable garden.

She was pregnant now, but did not cut down on her work. Without her uncle to collect political information and gossip, she had to keep her eyes open all the time. It was said that Barras had grown bored with his liaison with Josephine de Beauharnais and that General Bonaparte had met the lady at a party and fallen in love with her. It seemed that Barras was urging his mistress to marry the General, but Josephine, always conscious of her aristocratic background, did not think a mere Corsican good enough for her as a second husband, although Barras promised her that he had a great future ahead of him.

When Barras made General Bonaparte Commander of the French armies in Italy, Josephine de Beauharnais gave way to her lover's advice. She married Bonaparte on 17 March 1797. Two days later he departed to take up his command in Italy. His enormous military success there brought him credit and fame, which reflected on his wife. Josephine relished this, and when she made her frequent public appearances she was hailed as 'Our Lady of Victories'. The former revolutionary prisoner with Marie and her mother in the miserable Carmes gaol became a worthy subject for inclusion in the *Salon de Cire*.

Josephine remained as good-natured, cheerful and charming in her new rôle as she had shown herself in her previous circumstances. When Marie approached her, she expressed herself happy to sit for the artist in wax who had been with her in the shadow of the guillotine. She proved an excellent sitter and was delighted with the portrait figure that Marie produced, which attracted many people to the Boulevard du Temple. Madame Bonaparte was very popular with the citizens of Paris.

Marie Tussaud's daughter was born at No. 20 Boulevard du Temple in September 1797. Marie, though not deeply religious, turned back to the Church and had her child baptised at the nearby St Nicholas des Champs. There was no danger now in such a ceremony. Marie was happy with her daughter. Here was the child who could be trained to follow her mother as a modeller in wax and, in due course, take over the *Salon de Cire*. Marie's hopeful plans were short-lived. Her first child did not flourish and, at the age of six months, the infant Marie Marguerite Pauline Tussaud died at the house at Ivry-sur-Seine.

The first year of Marie's marriage had not proved easy. Her husband's taste for property speculation caused her anxiety, she lost the baby she had hoped would grow up to step into her shoes, the burden of finances weighed on her. In spite of the refurbishment and new attractions in the exhibition, takings were still not high enough to enable her to start paying off her borrowings.

Even so, the outlook was still hopeful, for France's armies continued to be victorious in Europe and some of her enemies were eager to make peace. By October 1797, only England was still at war with France. The prestige of the *Salon de Cire* was still such that Marie had no difficulty in persuading prominent personalities to let her model their portraits. Among these was the former Comte Talleyrand de Perigord, whom she remembered from her time at Versailles. Then, as Bishop of Autun, he had been elected as one of the representatives of the clergy to the States General summoned by Louis XVI in 1789.

Of course Curtius had been acquainted with him. When the first National Assembly was declared Talleyrand sat as a deputy and was its President in 1792. Then Talleyrand disappeared from the scene. He was sent to London to try to conciliate the English Prime Minister, Pitt. Prudently he had not hastened to return, was declared to be an *emigré* and exiled. He spent the next two years in England and America, returning to France when Robespierre fell. Then he attached himself to Barras, and when he was made Foreign Minister under the Directory, Marie modelled him for the *Salon*.

Then her most cherished hope for the future was realised. In 1798 Marie Tussaud gave birth to a son, Joseph, and a second, François, followed two years later. She kept the children at her side from their infancy. She herself had no recollection of life without the studio, and the glamour and excitement of the *Salon de Cire* with its ever-changing population of wax portrait figures and people stopping to gaze and inspect as they promenaded through it. She wished her sons to be the same. Joseph was precocious from the start, as she had been, and was playing with wax before his brother arrived. Marie was thirty-nine when her second son was born, and there were no more children. But the succession was safe, as Curtius would have wished. All his political manoeuvrings during the revolutionary years to keep the exhibition and the household safe had been justified.

Napoleon Bonaparte's star was still in the ascendant. When he returned to Paris, victorious after an Egyptian campaign, he posed a threat to the Directory. People felt that only General Bonaparte could give France the lasting, stable rule for which they yearned.

It was time for a new government. Bonaparte agreed. After a skilfully planned *coup d'état*, three Consuls were elected: Bonaparte, Sieyès, whose portrait figure, with its small head, had been in the exhibition, and out of it, since Curtius modelled it in 1789, and a less well-known politician called Ducos.

Bonaparte was chosen to be First Consul. In 1801 his wife Josephine commissioned Marie to model his portrait in wax. She still admired her own portrait, modelled soon after her marriage, and prominent in the *Salon de Cire*. She was determined to see her husband portrayed in wax beside her.

Marie was called to the Tuileries, where Bonaparte had his offices, at six o'clock in the morning. The General had little time to give and had only agreed to sit on Josephine pleading with him. She was at the Tuileries too, in spite of the early hour, and kept up a flow of talk during the session. Bonaparte said little and then his words were abrupt. When Marie told him, as she told all her sitters, not to be alarmed when his face was completely covered with the plaster, as the straws she would insert in his nostrils made breathing easy, the General was stirred to annoyance. 'Alarmed!' he exclaimed, 'I should not be alarmed if you were to surround my head with loaded pistols!'

He was, however, sufficiently pleased with the finished portrait figure to send along two of his generals to sit for their portraits also. They came to the studio. The prestige of the *Salon de Cire* was being maintained, as Curtius had intended it should be.

[186]

Madame Tussaud takes her Revolution to London

IN spite of important post-revolutionary patronage, like that of Madame Bonaparte and Talleyrand, Marie was still under financial stress. The prospect of clearing her mortgage and the loan she had been forced to raise seemed remote. The interest and Salomé Reiss's annuity were crippling her efforts. Though new attractions in the *Salon de Cire* brought in visitors, Marie had to recognise that in the new climate the wax exhibition no longer had the appeal to the public that it had once enjoyed. François Tussaud brought in little money and she had two children to provide for as well as her mother, who was nearing sixty years of age.

While harassed by these worries, Marie received an unexpected proposition. It came from the showman Philipstal who had earlier been saved from the guillotine by Curtius's intervention with Robespierre. Philipstal had continued with his magic-lantern-style entertainment, Phantasmagoria, when released from arrest, but he had found its popularity waning too.

Being of German birth Philipstal was able to cross the Channel, even though England was at war with his adopted country, France. In 1801 he took his Phantasmagoria to London and showed it with great success at the Lyceum Theatre. It was a novelty, and in February 1802, he was granted a Royal Patent for it.

Back in Paris for the summer, he decided to embark on a second winter season in London. He had kept in touch with Marie after Curtius's death, and now had an idea, a scheme that would be profitable to them both. There was room in the Lyceum Theatre for two presentations, and the wax portrait figures of the *Salon de Cire* were vastly superior to anything of the kind he had seen in England.

Philipstal suggested that Marie should join him in partnership with an exhibition of some thirty-five portrait figures, which she could display in the lower theatre, while he presented his Phantasmagoria again in the upper theatre. This double entertainment, he assured her, would do well for them both. Her artistry, her skill in grouping and lighting, and her portraits taken from life were superior to anything Londoners had yet experienced.

The future of the *Salon de Cire* was of paramount importance to Marie. To preserve it she must make more money. If money were to be made in London she would go there. The Treaty of Amiens, ending the war between France and England, had been signed in March 1802. It was now possible for a Frenchwoman to travel to London and work there. She needed only to obtain a passport.

For this document Marie had to apply to Fouché, the Commissioner of Police. She approached him with trepidation, for she feared a refusal. Fouché had been an ardent revolutionary, elected as a deputy to the National Assembly in 1792. There he had voted for the execution of Louis XVI. During the Terror Robespierre had sent Fouché to stamp out anti-revolutionary movements in Lyons. His bloodthirstiness had equalled that of many Commissioners who had been guillotined during the anti-Terror reaction. Fouché had merely been expelled from the Assembly.

By 1799 he had bounced back on to the political scene, been appointed Commissioner of Police, and supported Napoleon Bonaparte's *coup d'état*. Now a man of some power, he knew all about Curtius's and Marie's involvement in certain events of the Revolution. He knew about the severed heads the mob had carried to Marie after the fall of the Bastille, about the death-heads she had modelled by official command, and her orders to take the likeness of Marat, assassinated in his bath. He was also aware of the years she had spent in the service of Madame Elisabeth and the royal portraits she had made there, once so potent an attraction in the *Salon de Cire*.

Would a woman who knew, and had witnessed, so much be allowed to go to England? In spite of the Treaty of Amiens, relations between the two countries were still bad. Marie's apprehension was justified. At first Fouché refused to give her a passport. He said that so talented an artist could not be allowed to leave France.

She persisted, and finally persuaded Fouché to agree. After all, Curtius and Marie had served the revolutionary cause to the extent demanded of them, and more than eight years had passed since Marie had been involved in anything other than her normal work as a modeller in wax. She could go to England.

Now Marie was in a position to sign a contract with Philipstal. She would return to Paris, she told her husband, when she had a 'well-filled purse'. The contract gave Philipstal a lion's slice of the profits, and he proved reluctant to pay his share of the expenses. But it was an opportunity she could not afford to miss, and the whole venture depended on Philipstal's experience. He could dictate his terms.

The collection of wax portrait figures to be shown in London must have special impact. Philipstal's Phantasmagoria included depictions of the late King Louis XVI, depictions which had originally brought about his arrest and narrow escape from the guillotine. In London there was no such danger. Philipstal found the English public still intensely interested in the French Revolution. Although it was nine years since the unfortunate King's head had rolled, the shock was still strongly felt in England.

Marie determined that the figures she took with her would span the *ancien régime* and the events of the Revolution, and contain some historical items as well as contemporary portraits. Napoleon was now the bogyman for the English. Everyone would be interested in his lifelike effigy in wax, and that of his beautiful wife, both modelled from life and by request. All the death-heads she had moulded were packed, including those of the King and Queen, although the royal heads were not for display yet. Marie had no wish to cause distress and offence to members of the royal family and aristocrats still living in exile. The revolutionary heads and the tableau of the death of Marat were certain to attract attention. Marie had learned from Curtius's *Caverne des Grands Voleurs* how much people enjoyed a taste of horror.

She crossed the Channel in November 1802, taking her four-year-old son Joseph with her. Nothing must interrupt his training and he was a comfort, and even a help, in spite of his tender age. She presented her exhibition at the Lyceum Theatre under Curtius's celebrated name. Madame Tussaud was not yet well known, and she merely called herself 'the Artist'.

Her portrait figures were successful beyond her hopes and she herself was equally successful. French *emigrés* in London, and the public, were captivated by her vivacity and French manners. She was a link with the *ancien régime*, with the late royal family of France, had been forced to submit to revolutionary horrors, and barely escaped losing her own head.

Marie Tussaud never returned to France. In 1804, while touring Ireland with her exhibition, she bought out her partner Philipstal. She had learned that she could win success on her own, and took the hard decision to abandon her irresponsible husband. Only by her own hard work could she preserve what had once been Curtius's famous *Salon de Cire*, and in due course hand it on to her sons, Joseph and François. François was twenty-one before he joined his mother in England, but he had inherited her talent, like his older brother, and became a skilled and proficient artist in wax.

[189]

From her first appearance at the Lyceum Theatre in London, Madame Tussaud became identified in the public mind with the French royal Court of Versailles, and the horrors of the French Revolution in which she had, involuntarily, been so closely and personally involved. She never lost this identification, nor her French nationality, manners and vivacity during her long years of touring, and the establishment of her now famous exhibition as a London landmark.

The identification was sustained by four generations of her descendants who, like Curtius and Marie, made the exhibition their life work. Even today, when there are no descendants working in it, Versailles and the French Revolution are at the heart and core of 'Madame Tussaud's' worldwide celebrity.

Index

[191]